THE SPORTING SCOT

Edited by
Brian D. Osborne
and
Ronald Armstrong

Birlinn

First published in 2003 by
Birlinn Limited
West Newington House
10 Newington Road
Edinburgh
EH9 1QS

www.birlinn.co.uk

ISBN 1 84158 282 4

British Library Cataloguing-in-Publication Data
A catalogue record of this book is available from the
British Library

Typeset by Textype, Cambridge
Printed and bound by MPG Books Ltd, Bodmin

CONTENTS

★ ★ ★

ACKNOWLEDGEMENTS

★ ★ ★

The editors and publisher acknowledge the following for granting permission to reproduce extracts:*

B and W Publishers, for material from *The Shipbuilders* by George Blake

Hodder and Stoughton Publishers, for material from *Walking Wounded* and *The Big Man*, by William McIlvanney

Mainstream Publishing for material from *McIlvanney on Football* by Hugh McIlvanney

Methuen Publishing Limited, for material from *In Search of Scotland* by H.V. Morton (copyright © Marion Wadsell and Brian de Villiers)

The Neil Gunn Literary Estate, for material from *Highland Park*

Pan MacMillan, London, UK, for material from *Underworld* by Don DeLillo

Polygon, Edinburgh, for material from *The Thistle and the Grail* by Robin Jenkins

Time Warner Books, for material from *Crotal and White* by Finlay J. MacDonald

A.P. Watt, on behalf of The Lord Tweedsmuir and Jean, Lady Tweedsmuir, for material from the works of John Buchan

All introductory material is copyright © Brian D. Osborne and Ronald Armstrong

* Whilst every effort has been made to contact copyright holders, the editors and publisher have not been able to do so in every instance. In such cases we will be pleased to hear from copyright holders.

1

SCOTS AND THE WORLD OF SPORT

Introduction

★ ★ ★

The opening sequence of one of the best films ever made about sport, imprinted on the memories of a generation of film-goers around the world, has a clear Scottish connection. The Oscar-winning *Chariots of Fire* – with its memorable opening shots of the beach and town of St Andrews – focused on the 1920s Scottish athlete, Eric Liddell.

This ascetic figure, rather like a character in a novel of John Buchan, is the athlete who declined to run in the 1924 Paris Olympics 100-yard sprint on a Sunday. His subsequent career as a missionary and death in a Japanese prison camp contribute to his aura of doomed mysticism. Liddell is arguably the greatest, most iconic figure in Scottish and probably British sporting history, and a fine embodiment of the Greek or, more precisely, the 'Corinthian' spirit. This anthology of writing about Scots and the world of sport includes a memoir of Liddell by someone who knew him in the wake of Olympic glory.

The desire to 'play up and play the game', the British cult of the amateur in sport, was a striking feature of recreation in the nineteenth century and some of the twentieth, and probably reached its apogee in the late 1800s, when de Coubertin rekindled

1

the Olympic flame. Things have certainly changed in the 100 years since then. Instead of the old relaxed joyous sense of participation in sport, recent Scottish athletes such as world champion 10,000-metre runner Liz McColgan or Allan Wells, gold medal sprinter, exhibit a single-minded professionalism and a dedication and punishing training schedule that is more Spartan than Corinthian.

To return to *Chariots of Fire*, the opening sequence showed the athletes on the beach at St Andrews, alongside the Old Course, sacred site of that Scottish and now global sport, not to say commercial phenomenon, that is associated the world over with Scotland. Golf is one of the two sports that dominate our sporting scene, both from the point of view of the participant and the spectator. Accordingly, this book devotes a chapter to golf; and following that, a chapter is given over to the other dominant world sport and the acme of team spirit, football. Today, football, or soccer, couldn't really be described as Corinthian, always excepting the amateurs of Queen's Park (founded 1867 and still playing senior football in the Third Division); indeed some think it has become a rather unlovely game – scarcely the 'beautiful game' described by Pele. This chapter also covers the Rugby code.

The last chapter assembles pieces written about a mélange of sports, games and pastimes under the heading of 'Highland Games'. It contains distinctively Scottish sporting activities, some almost archaic, although one of them, curling, has recently cast off its rather quaint character and has stepped into the limelight – three million viewers for a midnight television broadcast of a ladies' Olympic final in Salt Lake City is proof of that. Shinty is one of three important sports given birth in Scotland – golf and curling being the others – a neglected but exciting sport that deserves to attain the same kind of status as the others.

This book is made up of selected writings from novels, short stories and light verse, and examples of journalism, reports and analysis about sport. In the first category, the context in which the piece was written is explained in a paragraph or two, along with some information about the author. There are also instances when journalism and literature overlap, when sports fiction is as immediate and exciting as reportage and great sports journalism attains the quality of literature.

★ ★ ★

This opening chapter looks at the Scottish connection with literature about various world sports and games. In the modern world such sports are important or in some cases essential parts of Western culture' and are rapidly being adopted by other cultures too. The modern Olympic Games, for example, are considered an integral part of the life of nations, for countries in North Africa as much as for the USA. In Scotland such sports include boxing, tennis and horse racing, even if not the more esoteric games like whippet racing, table curling and quoits still lingering in odd corners of the Central Belt. The international respectability won by players like Stephen Hendry in snooker is one that has come about only in the last two decades; when James Kelman wrote *Remember Young Cecil? – he used to be a very Big Stick indeed* the game was rather more dubious and Runyonesque:

> Young Cecil is medium sized and retired. For years he has been undisputed champion of our hall. Nowadays that is not saying much. This pitch has fallen from grace lately. John Moir who runs the place has started letting some of the punters rent a table Friday and Saturday nights to play Pontoons and as an old head pointed out the other day: that is it for any place, never mind Porter's.

Among the anthology items included in this chapter, two are about sports with an unlikely Scottish connection: real tennis from the European High Renaissance and the all-American game of baseball. Walter Scott's *Tales of a Grandfather* describes the Scottish King James I's assassination, as a tragic result of the king himself 'interfering with a hazard' at a real tennis court in the Blackfriars Monastery in Perth. James I, like other Stewart kings, had been keen to promote the (militarily important) sport of archery at the expense of the more frivolous football and golf. James is supposed to have done this in a comic poem, *Christ's Kirk on the Green,* and Scott comments on a scene in the poem that has an air of Falstaff and his followers, or an episode of Dad's Army:

> [James] particularly ridicules the Scots for want of acquaintance with archery. One man breaks his bow, another shoots his arrow wide of the mark, a third hits the man's body at whom he took aim, but with so little effect that he cannot pierce his leathern doublet.

The inclusion of baseball in this anthology in the shape of an extract from a modern American novel might seem surprising. However, Don DeLillo's *Underworld* begins with one of the greatest moments in the history of the USA's national game, and it so happens that the key figure in this famous 'play' is Bobby Thomson, born in Paisley. There is a more tenuous link in that the novel incorporates real historical characters, like Thomson or Frank Sinatra, into the otherwise fictional narrative in a fashion that is sometimes labelled 'faction'. This was of course a striking feature of much of Scottish fiction, from the inventor of the historical novel, Walter Scott, in dozens of works of fiction, through Stevenson (in books like *Kidnapped*) to other popular novelists like Neil Munro (in *John Splendid* and other novels).

The tremendous surge of interest, amounting almost to an obsession about sports, dates from the latter half of the nineteenth century and earlier part of the twentieth. In the Glasgow *Evening News* on 1 August 1908, in a story by Neil Munro called *The Age of Sport,* the Glasgow beadle and waiter Erchie MacPherson is listening to his wife Jinnet commenting on the craze for sport in the newspapers:

> Everywhere ye look it's naething but cricket, gowfin', soomin', rowin', shootin', yachtin', sodgers' camps, and Canadian boolers; ye wad think we had naething in the world to dae but play at games.

Included in Jinnet's list is cricket, the peculiar case of a game that has a world-wide following and a healthily growing Scottish Asian element, but that at times arouses unreasonable anti-English sentiments, even though there is a strong Scottish tradition.

> If the wild bowler thinks he bowls,
> Or if the batsman thinks he's bowled,
> They know not, poor misguided souls,
> They too shall perish unconsoled.
> I am the batsman and the bat,
> I am the bowler and the ball,
> The umpire and the pavilion cat
> The roller, wicket, stumps and all.

Items for this anthology have been selected partially for their literary merit. The cricketing pastiche of a poem of the American Ralph Waldo Emerson by Scottish man of letters Andrew Lang is a nicely surreal view of what some short-sightedly think of as an alien game. In the following Lang makes the point that cricket was a middle-class sport:

> Three things are prejudicial to Scottish cricket. First, there is the climate, about which mere words are superfluous. Next, boys leave school earlier than in England, for professions or for college. Lastly, the University session is in the winter months, and the University clubs are at a great disadvantage.

Regarding the climate – the Greenock Cricket Club is still one of the most enthusiastic in the land, and in one of the wettest spots. A song from the 1860s records a game rained off at a local landowner's estate:

> I know you'll all remember,
> Hurrah, the Greenock O!
> The nineteenth of September,
> Hurrah, the Greenock O!
> To Ardgowan we did go
> There to drub the sturdy foe

Instead, we drubbed the sherry O!
Hurrah, the Greenock O!

Cricket makes a surprising appearance in an important early nineteenth-century Scottish novel by James Hogg, and we include a humorous masterpiece written by a Scot about that quintessential English event, a village cricket match. Also finding a place is this account of the amazing 1985 victory by the real village of Freuchie, a team from the Howe of Fife in the Village Cricket Cup at Lord's.

FREUCHIE THE VICTORS

The Kingdom of Fife has many and varied claims to fame but cricket has not until now been among them. The village of Freuchie itself is hardly a household name either in the cricketing world or in any other, and the parish of Falkland, in which it lies, has perhaps been traditionally more associated with archery and real tennis. Still, it may be that Freuchie has long been secretly preparing for victory in St John's Wood, unknown to the unsuspecting innocents of Rowledge and elsewhere, for the 1952 Statistical Account comments that 'cricket is very popular in Freuchie.' Judging by the comments of the team the aim at Freuchie has been to play the game in the classic English village style. If so, it has overcome considerable handicaps – not just the east wind sweeping in from the Arctic but the lack of a village blacksmith, always a key figure in close encounters on English village greens. And any cricket club playing in the Howe of Fife presumably lacks the advantage of a steeply sloping ground. Cricket would seem, in fact, even more alien to Fife than to most of Scotland. It seems that we have the Jacobite rebellions to thank for cricket as well as for Wade's roads for it was imported by the occupying English regiments. In that case, there was a kind of revenge at St John's Wood, where Freuchie was cheered to victory by what is described as a tartan army. (Freuchie won by 2 wickets)

Glasgow Herald Leader, 2 September 1985

The game with the leather and willow has had some notable Scots players in the English game. Mike Denness from Ayr played twenty-eight tests for England, nineteen as captain; before him other Scottish captains of England numbered a clan chief, the redoubtable MacKinnon of MacKinnon, and Douglas Jardine, skipper in the infamous 'Bodyline' Ashes series in the 1920s. Incidentally, the greatest batsman of all time, Don Bradman of Australia, played his last innings in the Northern Hemisphere before a packed cricket ground in Aberdeen, and made 123 not out.

Bowls is here also, a game with its own interesting class structure – a sport that Scots gave its distinctive form, by writing down its 'laws', not 'rules', and so defined its code, rather like the English did with cricket. The game had been relatively shapeless until then, and Scotland far outstripped the other home countries in the move to give bowls an organised basis. This dates from 1848 when 200-odd Scottish clubs met in Glasgow to form the Scottish Bowling Association and draft the set of laws, a task that they delegated, appropriately enough, to a Glasgow solicitor, W.W. Mitchell. The game of bowls had earlier played a peculiar role in Scottish literary history, faintly reminiscent of Drake at Plymouth Ho. In 1759 the Scottish playwright and important literary figure John Home paid his annual visit to the fashionable spa of Moffat in Dumfriesshire and there met James 'Ossian' Macpherson, actually on the bowling green. Encouraged by this meeting and the support he received, Macpherson went on to tour the Highlands and produce *Fingal*, *Temora*, and other poetry, supposedly translated from third-century oral Gaelic tradition. The Ossianic poems took Europe by storm, until suspicion grew that they owed more to Macpherson, and the controversy that ensued was also Europe-wide. Modern opinion suggests that a core of ancient verse was arranged, supplemented and built on by Macpherson.

Scottish sport in general has recently been celebrated by the institution of the new Scottish Sports Hall of Fame, at the Royal Scottish Museum in Edinburgh. A view, diametrically opposed to the Corinthian spirit of the Hall of Fame, was voiced by the pessimistic George Orwell, an Englishman with close Scottish connections:

> Serious sport has nothing to do with fair play. It is bound up with hatred, jealousy, boastfulness, disregard of all rules and sadistic pleasure in witnessing violence: in other words it is war minus the shooting.
>
> 'The Sporting Spirit' from *Shooting an Elephant*

Neil Munro's Erchie, whom we met earlier, seems to share some of Orwell's views, but with rather more humour. Commenting on the place of sport in the year of the 1908 London Olympics, he opines:

> Thae Olympic Games in London were faur mair important than Jinnet thinks; it's on oor common interest in whit the papers ca' the realm of sport that the peace of the world depends; if ye live lang enough ye'll see that instead o' competin' in the buildin' o' big men-o'-war ships, the Great Powers'll put a' their money into trainin' likely chaps for hammer-throwin' and the hundred yards sprint.

As to that reference to the 'Great Powers' – a Scots member of the British athletics team, one Wyndham Halswelle, won Scotland's first ever track gold medal, for the 440 yards, at that very same Olympiad. And surely Baron de Coubertin would have approved of Erchie's grasp of the international significance of the Olympic spirit:

> If ye pay a shillin' to see a mixed lot o' champions o' the world daein' the hop-step-and-jump or heavin' javelins, ye're filled at yince wi' the deepest affection for a' yer fellow men, foreign as well as Christian.

Or, he might have added, 'daein' great deeds in the swimming pool'. Great Scottish names in aquatic circles have included Ian Black, Olympic silver medallist Bobby Macgregor, and, most famously, double gold medallist for Olympic and World Championship breaststroke, David Wilkie. Long distance swimming, too, has had its moments, and, as another character of Neil Munro's, Sunny Jim, explains jocularly, there are real opportunities for what would later be called commercialism and sponsorship, Sunny Jim promises to swim Loch Fyne from Skipness to Campbeltown:

> It's a' in the start. See? I'll jump in at the quay, and you'll collect the money from the Skipness folk, and pick me up whenever they're oot o' sicht. I'll dae the dive again afore we come into Campbeltown, and Dougie'll haud the watch and gie a guarantee I swam the hale length o' Kintyre in four oors and five-and-twenty minutes. Then bizz-bang – roon' the folk in Campbeltown wi' the bonny wee hat again!

The distinctive Scottish obsession about sport is not with sport for its own sake, as, to be fair, is true of the English, who are the great keepers of the modern Corinthian spirit. Scotland's obsession is of a more intense hue, with a smaller number of sports, each with its own distinctive social pattern of followers and participants. A democratic interest in sports and games is not exclusive to Scots – the USA's peculiar sports of baseball and football don't from this distance appear to be class specific – but there does appear to be a strong populist character to Scottish sport. Not that Scotland is totally absent from the recreations of the international jet-set, boasting racing drivers of the calibre of Jim Clark and Jackie Stewart. At an earlier period, Tommy Lipton and the Clark and Coats families of Paisley were also associated with conspicuous consumption in sport through their celebrated attempts at international fame in the yachting world. Para Handy empathises:

> If you're a Coats you lose a lot o' time makin' up your mind what boat you'll sail tomorrow; the whole o' the Clyde below the Tail o' the Bank is chock-a-block wi' steamboat-yats and cutters the Coats's canna hail a boat ashore from to get a sail, for they canna mind their names. Still-and-on, there's nothing wrong wi' them – tip top sportin' chentlemen!

So we see yet again the central role of 'chentlemen' in earlier days of

Scottish sport. A Scottish nobleman, John Sholto Douglas, Marquess of Queensberry, had of course a crucial part in the development of the sport of pugilism. In 1867 he supervised the formulation of the set of new rules to govern boxing. Professionalism was always associated with boxing – and great names like Benny Lynch and Jackie Paterson. Nevertheless, Dick McTaggart, an amateur lightweight from Dundee, was perhaps the most stylish boxer ever to represent Scotland. He won a gold medal and a special award at the 1960 Olympic Games. Truly a 'chentleman' of the ring, but not the same kind of ring as associated with the 'Bonny Earl o' Murray' in the old ballad:

> He was a true gallant
> And he played at the ring
> And the Bonny Earl o' Murray,
> He micht hae been a king.

I Remember Eric Liddell

DAVID J. MICHELL

★ ★ ★

Eric Liddell played rugby for Scotland as a wing three-quarter on seven occasions, while a student at university in Edinburgh, but it is as an athlete he is remembered. The Paris Olympics of 1924 formed a background to a sequence of events that has entered the realms of sporting legend. Although his strongest events were the short sprints and he won a bronze medal in the 220 yards, Liddell chose to run in the 440, since the longer distance's final was not to be held on a Sunday and, as anyone who saw Chariots of Fire *will remember, Liddell was adamant that a missionary son of missionary parents could not thereby break the Sabbath. Incidentally, Liddell managed to break the Olympic record in achieving his historic victory in the 440. In 1925 he returned to China and took up a missionary post with the Congregational Church, until World War II, when he was interned by the Japanese. Liddell died in the camp from a brain tumour. The title 'Chariots of Fire' comes from the verse in 2 Kings 2,11 'And it came to pass, as they still went on, and talked, that, behold, there appeared a chariot of fire, and horses of fire, and parted them both asunder; and Elijah went up by a whirlwind into heaven.' The film won Academy Awards for Best Picture, Best Original Screenplay, Best Score, and Best Costume Design.*

The following introduction to a theological work written by Liddell while working in China, Disciplines of the Christian Life, *is by a Canadian missionary colleague. In his book Liddell speaks of 'Victory over Fear' – and appropriately enough asks: 'Are you afraid in any situation? Stop a moment, surrender the feeling to God, make a decision which fully satisfies your conscience, and act quietly but firmly on it.'*

★ ★ ★

If you saw the Academy Award-winning film *Chariots of Fire*, you will recall the jolt you felt as you read at the close these words about one of the heroes of the film:

> Eric Liddell, missionary,
> died in occupied China
> at the end of World War II.
> All of Scotland mourned.

I remember seeing Eric Liddell just the day before he died. For more than two years of our wartime captivity our school was interned in the same camp he was. That day he was walking slowly under the trees near the camp hospital beside the open space where he had taught us children to play basketball and rounders. As usual, he had a smile for everyone, especially for us.

The athlete who had refused to run on a Sunday in the 1924 Olympic Games in Paris, but who later won the gold medal and created a world record in the 400 metres, was now – twenty-one years later at the age of forty-three – reaching the tape in his final race on earth. We knew nothing of the pain he was hiding, and he knew nothing of the brain tumour that was to take his life the next evening, February 21, 1945.

Eric Liddell's twenty years in China were eventful, to say the least. Within a year of his Olympic success, Eric had been farewelled from Edinburgh. More than a thousand people were unable to get in to the service. Deliberately walking away from the fame and glory that could have been his in Britain, he responded to God's call and went to China as a missionary with the London Missionary Society, following in his father's footsteps. For a number of years he taught science at the Anglo-Chinese College in Tientsin and then decided to tackle the more arduous task of rural evangelism, travelling many miles in rugged conditions by foot and bicycle.

On one occasion, as the hostilities between the Japanese and Chinese intensified in the late thirties, Eric Liddell heard about a wounded man who was dying in a derelict temple and whom none of the local people dared help for fear of reprisals from the Japanese. Despite natural fear of the consequences should they be caught, Eric persuaded a workman to accompany him with his cart to rescue the wounded man.

That night in a tumble-down Chinese inn, as the two men rested on their journey, God encouraged Eric through Luke 16,10: 'He that is faithful in that which is least is faithful also in much.'

When they reached the wounded man the next day, they lifted him on to the cart and began retracing their steps. Then, as they carefully led the swaying, creaking cart along the rough track, miraculously protected from encircling troops, they heard of another seriously injured man.

The second man had been one of six who were suspected of underground resistance and who had been lined up for beheading. 'Five knelt and were decapitated with the swift swish of the soldiers' swords. Because the sixth man refused to kneel, the sword missed its mark, inflicting, however, a deep gash from the back of the man's head to his mouth. He fell headlong and was left for dead. Villagers later came and helped him to a nearby shack. Though moving closer to danger, Eric and his companion reached the dying man, placed him in the shafts of the cart, and walked both desperately wounded men eighteen miles further to the mission hospital. Not only did this second man live, but he became a follower of Jesus Christ.

As conditions in China deteriorated in the weeks before the bombing of Pearl Harbour, Eric Liddell arranged for his wife and two children to leave China, planning himself to follow some months later. Safely in Canada, Florence Liddell gave birth to their third daughter, whom Eric never saw. Before he could get away, the Japanese armies had rounded up all 'enemy nationals' for internment in Weihsien, in the province of Shantung (Shandong), North China.

Sent to this same camp in Weihsien in August 1943 with many other missionaries' children, I will forever share with all the other hero-worshippers of my age that vivid memory of the man whom other prisoners described excitedly as the Olympic gold medalist who wouldn't run on a Sunday.

Eric Liddell stood out among the 1,800 people packed into our camp, which measured only 150 by 200 yards. He was in charge of the building where we younger children, who had already been away from our parents for four years because of the war, lived with our teachers. He lived in the very crowded men's dormitory near us (each man had a space of only three by six feet) and supervised our daily roll-call when the guards came to count us. One day a week 'Uncle Eric' would look after us, giving our teachers (all missionaries of the China Inland Mission and all women) a break. His gentle face and warm smile, even as he taught us games with the limited equipment available, showed us how much he loved children and how much he missed his own.

Eric Liddell helped organise athletic meets. Despite the weakening physical conditions of the people as the war dragged on, the spirit of competition and camaraderie in sports was very good for us. Young and old watched excitedly, basking in the aura of Olympic glory as Eric Liddell ran in the race for veterans, his head thrown back in his characteristic style, sailing through to victory.

Besides basketball, soccer and rounders, Eric Liddell taught us his favourite hymn:

> Be still, my soul: the Lord is on thy side;
> Bear patiently the cross of grief or pain;
> Leave to thy God to order and provide;
> In every change he faithful will remain.
> Be still, my soul: thy best, thy heavenly friend
> Through thorny ways leads to a joyful end.

These words were a great comfort to one of our missionaries who was not only separated from her husband throughout the war, but whose son was accidentally electrocuted by a bare wire running to one of the searchlight towers.

Eric Liddell often spoke to us on I Corinthians 13 and Matthew 5. These passages from the New Testament clearly portray the secret of his selfless and humble life. Only on rare occasions when requested would he speak of his refusal to run on Sunday and his Olympic record.

But once 'Uncle Eric' thrilled us with the story of the time he was persuaded to run in an extra race at an athletic meet in North China. The problem was that the race was scheduled just half an hour before his boat was due to leave to take him back to the college where he taught. He failed to have the boat's departure delayed but arranged for a taxi to take him from the track to the boat. Having won the race, Eric was just about to leap into the waiting taxi when the national anthem was played, followed straight off by the *Marseillaise*, forcing him to keep standing at attention as the minutes ticked by. The moment the music stopped he leaped into the taxi, and the vehicle sped off, reaching the wharf in under twenty minutes. By this time the boat was already moving out from the dock. But when a wave momentarily lifted the boat nearer, Eric threw his bags on board and then took a mighty gazelle-like leap, managing to land on the back of the moving boat!

Not only did Eric Liddell organise sports and recreation, but throughout his time in the internment camp he helped many people by teaching and tutoring. He gave special care to the older people, the weak, and the ill, for whom the conditions in camp were especially trying. He was always involved in the Christian meetings which were a part of camp life. Despite the squalor of the open cesspools, rats, flies, and disease in the crowded camp, life took on a normal routine, though without the faithful and cheerful support of Eric Liddell, many people would never have been able to manage. Particularly grateful for his visits and encouragement were the daughter of a widow and a Roman Catholic nun, both critically ill and quarantined in the camp morgue.

Eric was one of those responsible for keeping law and order in camp. Ours was a world in microcosm, with prisoners representing nearly twenty nationalities. When we boys were caught climbing the tall trees in the Japanese part of the compound, how glad we were that it was he and our teachers who dealt with us, and not the Japanese guards!

As the months of captivity turned into years, there were many reasons why discouragement came over the camp. But, like the rest of us, Eric was buoyed by news from the outside that made its way inside, and he faithfully passed it on to us. We were all mystified as to how the news came – even our informant didn't know. We found out after the war was over, but Eric Liddell didn't live to hear the story. And what a story it was!

Some fourteen months before the war ended, two men in the camp escaped with the help of a coolie who came in to empty the cesspools and who was in league with others on the outside. Manoeuvring past the electrified wire in black, tight-fitting Chinese clothes, and crawling through a Chinese cemetery in the pitch darkness, they fled, making their way to South China, living in caves amid terrible conditions. It took them months to get back to the region of the camp with a radio without being discovered.

From their hiding place they dispatched news into the camp, writing it in code on a tiny piece of silk, rolling it up tightly and encapsuling it in a bit of rubber film. The same coolie who had helped the men escape earlier would push the pellet up his nose and out of sight, let himself be searched at the gate, wait until he reached a certain place in the camp, then blow his nose in the old-fashioned Chinese manner, and out would come this little pellet. Once he and his guard were out of sight, a Catholic priest would retrieve the capsule and later that night decode the news to be circulated secretly in the camp. In this way the whole camp knew when Germany had surrendered and also when the war with Japan was finally over.

But for Eric Liddell death came just months before liberation. He was buried in the little cemetery in the Japanese part of the camp where others who had died during internment had been laid to rest. I remember being part of the honour guard made up of children from the Chefoo and Weihsien schools. None of us will ever forget this man who was totally committed to putting God first, a man whose humble life combined muscular Christianity with radiant godliness.

Wilson – Seeker of Champions

from The Wizard No. 1119
(21 Dec. 1946)

★ ★ ★

The comics produced by the Dundee firm of DC Thomson helped to shape the attitude to sport and adventure of several generations of boys. In particular, it could be argued, the Rover, Adventure *and* Wizard, *with their plain text format, encouraged a level of literacy comparable with that of novels like the Biggles series or, in our own day, Harry Potter.*

In the Wizard *of the 1940s and '50s 'Wilson' was the mysterious super-fit athlete who had an ascetic Spartan lifestyle akin to real dedicated contemporary sportsmen like Paavo Nurmi and Emil Zatopek, or even, a generation earlier, the great Eric Liddell himself. The Dundee publisher employed authors, many of them Scots, who showed a good deal of knowledge of the background appropriate to these and other stories like 'I Flew With Braddock' or 'Alf Tupper – the Tough of the Track', the latter telling of the exploits in middle-distance running of a more irreverent kind of working-class hero.*

★ ★ ★

WILSON TAKES THE FIELD

It was nearly a fortnight later that, on a Monday morning, Ducker lay in bed in his London flat, sipping a morning cup of tea and listening to the seven o'clock news on the radio before getting up. He was not paying a great deal of attention and was raising the cup to his lips when the announcer paused and then went on. 'Sports—' Ducker cocked up an ear. 'Wilson the British athlete, has arrived in Philadelphia to take part in the Decathlon starting tomorrow . . .'

Ducker's cup of tea splashed all over the bed. He flung the clothes aside and in his pyjamas, dashed to the phone. He dialed hastily and eventually got through. 'Is that the Trans-Atlantic Airways?' he roared. 'Listen, I want to go to America today. What's that? My only chance is to be at the airport in case anyone cancels a reservation at the last minute?' Ducker was fortunate. Two hours after hearing the radio announcement he was airborne. Twenty-four hours after leaving London, Ducker sat in a taxi-cab that was whirling him along a concrete highway towards the vast stadium at Philadelphia. A newspaper lay across his knees. His gaze scanned the big headline: 'Wilson Here As Gino Finn Challenger'. The article stated that the ten events in the Decathlon were, on the first day, the Hundred Metres Sprint, High Jump, Long Jump, Putting the Shot, and the Four Hundred Metres: on the second day, Throwing the Discus, Pole Jump, Throwing the Javelin, Hurdles, and Fifteen Hundred Metres. Points were awarded for each event as follows: First, one thousand; second, nine hundred; third, eight hundred; down to the sixth position. The writer, who struck Frank as knowing what he was talking about, held the opinion that the winner would total between five and six thousand points. He recalled that the winner of the 1944 Decathlon, the last held, won three events outright, was second in two events, and third in another. Gino Finn, the critic stated, would at least equal this record by his terrific running and jumping. The Kansas giant, Pete Purdo, was reckoned as unbeatable in putting the shot and throwing the discus. The pole vault was apparently a certainty for Joe Legunne, a Red Indian by ancestry, and Cal Lee, the Flying Yank, would take the thousand points for the hurdles. Wilson, the critic thought, would prove to be a back number against 'this shining constellation of American stars'. Frank put on a pair of sunglasses as he paid off the taxi and entered the stadium. His long journey had ended in the nick of time. The twenty athletes, who were competing for what was virtually the championship of America, were just marching out into the arena in single file to the blare of brass band music. The crowd were rooting for their favourites, but loudest of all was the cry of 'Gino! Gino!' In glistening white, except for the golden eagle on the front of his singlet, Gino Finn looked like a lord of the sun with his fair hair, piercing blue eyes and magnificent bronzed body. Pete Purdo, dark and grim, had a torso like the trunk of a tree. Joe Legume walked lightly with the inturned toes of his race. Cal Lee, the Flying Yank, moved with a long loping stride. Wilson, hardly heeded in the excitement, appeared last, shuffling along in his old black costume and canvas shoes, that he had not bothered to lace up. There were to be three heats for the hundred metres (one hundred and nine yards 1 foot 1 inch) sprint, the first two in each heat to run in the final. Wilson kicked off his shoes and walked bare-footed to the line when his name was called. The crowd first seemed to notice him for his bare feet – and then when he beat Joe Legume in first place in eleven seconds. The cheers thundered when Ginno Finn won the second heat in ten and three-tenth seconds, equaling the existing U.S. record. Cal Lee took the third heat in a tenth of a second slower time. The six finalists were called. Five crouched low on their marks, tensing themselves for the sprint into action. Wilson, despite a puzzled stare from the starter, just stood waiting with his arms hanging loosely. Ducker held his breath in excitement and anxiety. The gun cracked and Wilson flowed into movement. Before the crouchers had hit their fast stride he was in front of the lot of them. It was astonishing to see the heads of the spectators turning to follow his course. So tearaway was his speed, so big a lead did he gain that he could have finished walking, but he crossed the line like a flash and was carried on by his impetus for another ten yards. The voice that announced that Wilson had run one hundred metres in nine seconds was harsh with amazement. Gino Finn, in second place, had taken a second and a half longer, and one thousand points appeared against Wilson's name on the scoreboard.

Underworld

DON DELILLO

★ ★ ★

A website contains the following piece of baseball lore:

Fifty-two years ago, on October 3, 1951, in the third game of a three-game playoff against the Brooklyn Dodgers, New York Giant outfielder Robert Brown 'Bobby' Thomson blasted the dramatic 'shot heard round the world' when he hit a winning home run off Dodgers' pitcher Ralph Branca. After all these years, Thomson's clout remains among the most famous home runs in baseball history. 'The Giants win the pen-nant, the Giants win the pennant, the Giants win the pen-nant', repeated an ecstatic Russ Hodges, the Giants' broadcaster, to a radio audience numbering millions, as Thomson circled the bases and trotted into baseball immortality. On the mound, Ralph Branca, after watching the drive clear the nearly 17-foot high wall above the 315-foot marker, stood stunned. Dodger left fielder Andy Pafko, near the wall, looked up in disbelief. Giants fans everywhere were thrilled, while Dodger fans were, like the players, shocked. Born on October 25, 1923, in Paisley, Bobby went to America with his family at the age of three. A quiet, reserved, athletic youth with brown hair and brown eyes, he grew up and attended school on Staten Island, New York. Later, sportswriters often dubbed him the 'Staten Island Scot'.

This great sporting moment moved from the pages of sports papers and fan magazines and became the subject of a writer in the front rank of contemporary American novelists in 1997, when Don DeLillo published Underworld. *The novel was acclaimed as a 'masterwork' by critics such as Martin Amis and Salman Rushdie. The following extract from*

Underworld *weaves real events (and people like J. Edgar Hoover) and fictional narrative together with a description of sporting action on an epic scale. And at the centre of it is the Scots-born batter Bobby Thomson who strikes the mighty home-run that propels the ball into the crowd and sets off the chain of events of this 827-page novel.*

★ ★ ★

When in steps Thomson.

The tall fleet Scot. Reminding himself as he gets set in the box. See the ball. Wait for the ball.

Russ is clutching the mike. Warm water and salt. Gargle, said his mother.

Thomson's not sure he sees things clearly. His eyeballs are humming. There's a feeling in his body, he's digging in, settling into his stance, crowd noise packing the sky, and there's a feeling that he has lost the link to his surroundings. Alone in all this rowdy-dow. See the ball. Watch and wait. He is frankly a little fuddled is Bobby. It's like the first waking moment of the day and you don't know whose house you're in.

Russ says, 'Bobby Thomson up there swinging.'

Mays down on one knee in the on-deck circle half leaning on his cradled bat and watching Branca go into a full windup, push-pull click-click, thinking it's all on him if Thomson fails, the season riding on him, and the jingle plays in his head, it's the radio embrace of the air itself, the mosaic of the air, and it will turn itself off when it's ready.

There's an emergency station under the stands and what the stadium cop has to do is figure out a way to get the stricken man down there without being overrun by a rampant stomping crowd. The victim looks okay considering. He is sitting down, waiting for the attendant to arrive with the wheelchair. All right, maybe he doesn't look so good. He looks pale, sick, worried and infarcted. But he can make a fist and stick out his tongue and there's not much the cop can do until the wheelchair arrives, so he might as well stand in the aisle and watch the end of the game.

Thomson in his bent stance, chin tucked, waiting.

Russ says, 'One out, last of the ninth.'

He says, 'Branca pitches, Thomson takes a strike called on the inside corner.'

He lays a heavy decibel on the word, strike. He pauses to let the crowd reaction build. Do not talk against the crowd. Let the drama come from them.

Those big rich pages airing down from the upper deck.

Lockman stands near second and tries to wish a hit onto Thomson's bat. That may have been the pitch he wanted. Belt-high, a shade inside – won't see one that good again.

Russ says, 'Bobby hitting at two ninety-two He's had a single and a double and he drove in the Giants' first run with a long fly to center.'

Lockman looks across the diamond at home. The double he hit is still a presence in his chest, it's chugging away in there, a body-memory plays the moment over. He is peering into the deltoid opening between the catcher's knees. He sees the fingers dip, the blunt hand make a flapping action up and left. They'll give him the fastball high and tight and come back with the curve away. A pretty two-part scheme. Seems easy and sweet from here.

Russ says, 'Brooklyn leads it four to two.'

He says, 'Runner down the line at third. Not taking any chances.'

Thomson thinking, it's all happening too fast. Thinking quick hands, see the ball, give yourself a chance.

Russ says, 'Lockman without too big of a lead at second but he'll be running like the wind if Thomson hits one.'

In the box seats J. Edgar Hoover plucks a magazine page off his shoulder, where the thing has lighted and stuck. At first he's annoyed that the object has come in contact with his body. Then his eyes fall upon the page. It is a color reproduction of a painting crowded with medieval figures who are dying or dead – a landscape of visionary havoc and ruin. Edgar has never seen a painting quite like this. It covers the page completely and must surely dominate the magazine. Across the red-brown earth, skeleton armies on the march. Men impaled on lances, hung from gibbets, drawn on spoked wheels fixed to the tops of bare trees, bodies open to the crows. Legions of the dead forming up behind shields made of coffin lids. Death himself astride a slat-ribbed hack, he is peaked for blood, his scythe held ready as he presses people in haunted swarms toward the entrance of some helltrap, an oddly modern construction that could be a subway tunnel or office corridor. A background of ash skies and burning ships. It is clear to Edgar that the page is from Life and he tries to work up an anger, he asks himself why a magazine called Life would want to reproduce a painting of such lurid and dreadful dimensions. But he can't take his eyes off the page.

Russ Hodges says, 'Branca throws.'

Gleason makes a noise that is halfway between a sigh and a moan. It is probably a sough, as of rustling surf in some palmy place. Edgar recalls the earlier blowout, Jackie's minor choking fit. He sees a deeper engagement here. He goes out into the aisle and up two steps, separating himself from the imminent discharge of animal, vegetable and mineral matter.

Not a good pitch to hit, up and in, but Thomson swings and tomahawks the ball and everybody, everybody watches. Except for Gleason who is bent over in his seat, hands locked behind his neck, a creamy strand of slime swinging from his lips.

Russ says, 'There's a long drive.'

His voice has a burst in it, a charge of expectation.

He says, 'It's gonna be.'

There's a pause all around him. Pafko racing toward the left-field corner.

He says, 'I believe.'

Pafko at the wall. Then he's looking up. People thinking where's the ball. The scant delay, the stay in time that lasts a hairsbreadth. And Cotter standing in section 35 watching the ball come in his direction. He feels his body turn to smoke. He loses sight of the ball when it climbs above the overhang and he thinks it will land in the upper deck. But before he can smile or shout or bash his neighbor on the arm. Before the moment can overwhelm him, the ball appears again, stitches visibly spinning, that's how near it hits, banging at an angle off a pillar – hands flashing everywhere.

Russ feels the crowd around him, a shudder passing through the stands, and then he is shouting into the mike and there is a surge of color and motion, a crash that occurs upward, stadium-wide, hands and faces and shirts, bands of rippling men, and he is outright shouting, his voice has a power he'd thought long gone – it may lift the top of his head like a cartoon rocket.

He says, '*The Giants win the pennant.*'

A topspin line drive. He tomahawked the pitch and the ball had topspin and dipped into the lower deck and there is Pafko at the 315 sign looking straight up with his right arm braced at the wall and a spate of paper coming down.

He says, '*The Giants win the pennant.*'

Yes, the voice is excessive with a little tickle of hysteria in the upper register. But it is mainly wham and whomp. He sees Thomson capering around first. The hat of the first-base coach – the first-base coach has flung his hat straight up. He went for a chin-high pitch and cold-cocked it good. The ball started up high and then sank, missing the facade of the upper deck and dipping into the seats below – pulled in, swallowed up – and the Dodger players stand looking, already separated from the event, staring flat into the shadows between the decks.

He says, '*The Giants win the pennant.*'

The crew is whooping. They are answering the roof bangers by beating on the walls and ceiling of the booth. People climbing the dugout roofs and the crowd shaking in its own noise. Branca on the mound in his tormented slouch. He came with a fastball up, a pitch that's tailing in, and the guy's supposed to take it for a ball. Russ is shouting himself right out of his sore throat, out of every malady and pathology and complaint and all the pangs of growing up and every memory that is not tender.

He says, '*The Giants win the pennant.*'

Four times. Branca turns and picks up the rosin bag and throws it down, heading toward the clubhouse now, his shoulders aligned at a slant – he begins the long dead trudge. Paper falling everywhere. Russ knows he ought to settle down and let the mike pick up the sound of the swelling bedlam around him. But he can't stop shouting, there's nothing left of him but shout.

He says, 'Bobby Thomson hits into the lower deck of the left-field stands.'

He says, 'The Giants win the pennant and they're going crazy.'

He says, 'They're going crazy.'

Then he raises a pure shout, wordless, a holler from the old days – it is fiddlin' time, it is mountain music on WCKY at five-thirty in the morning. The thing comes jumping right out of him, a jubilation, it might be *heyyy-ho* or it might be *oh-boyyy* shouted backwards or it might be something else entirely – hard to tell when they don't use words. And Thompson's teammates gathering at home plate and Thomson circling the bases in gamesome leaps, buckjumping – he is forever Bobby now, a romping boy lost to time, and his breath comes so fast he doesn't know if he can handle all the air that's pouring in. He sees men in a helter-skelter line waiting at the plate to pummel him – his teammates, no better fellows in the world, and there's a look in their faces, they are stunned by a happiness that has collapsed on them, bright-eyed under their caps.

He tomahawked the pitch, he hit on top of it and now his ears are ringing and there's a numbing buzz in his hands and feet. And Robinson stands behind second, hands on hips, making sure Thomson touches every base. You can almost see brave Jack grow old.

Look at Durocher spinning. Russ pauses for the first time to catch the full impact of the noise around him. Leo spinning in the coach's box. The manager stands and spins, he is spinning with his arms spread wide – maybe it's an ascetic rapture, a thing they do in mosques in Anatolia.

People make it a point to register the time. . .

The clock atop the clubhouse reads 3:58.

25

Russ has got his face back into the mike. He shouts, 'I don't believe it.' He shouts, 'I don't believe it.' He shouts, 'I do *not* believe it.'

They are coming down to crowd the railings. They are coming from the far ends of the great rayed configuration and they are moving down the aisles and toward the rails.

Pafko is out of paper range by now, jogging toward the clubhouse. But the paper keeps falling. If the early paper waves were slightly hostile and mocking, and the middle waves a form of fan commonality, then this last demonstration has a softness, a selfness. It is coming down from all points, laundry tickets, envelopes swiped from the office, there are crushed cigarette packs and sticky wrap from ice-cream sandwiches, pages from memo pads and pocket calendars, they are throwing faded dollar bills, snapshots torn to pieces, ruffled paper swaddles for cupcakes, they are tearing up letters they've been carrying around for years pressed into their wallets, the residue of love affairs and college friendships, it is happy garbage now, the fans' intimate wish to be connected to the event, unendably, in the form of pocket litter, personal waste, a thing that carries a shadow identity – rolls of toilet tissue unbolting lyrically in streamers.

They are gathered at the netting behind home plate, gripping the tight mesh.

Russ is still shouting, he is not yet shouted out, he believes he has a thing that's worth repeating.

Saying, 'Bobby Thomson hit a line drive into the lower deck of the left-field stands and the place is going crazy.'

Death of James I
from Tales of a Grandfather

WALTER SCOTT

★ ★ ★

The charming Tales of a Grandfather *(written mainly for young folk) appeared late in Walter Scott's career, in the years from 1828–30. This particular story, an account of the death of King James I, is selected because of the involvement of what is probably 'real' or royal tennis in the narrative. James lived a very exciting life that makes him a fit subject for Scott's pen. As a twelve-year-old he was captured and held as a state prisoner and political pawn by Henry IV of England, acquired a reputation as a poet (writing the* Kingis Quair *or Book), and was used by Henry V as a hostage in battle against the French, including their Scots allies. Released after eighteen years in captivity, he tried to ensure order in his kingdom and to control the powerful Scottish nobles. However a plot brought his death in 1437.*

Scott's account follows legend in recording that James had 'played at ball in the courtyard', which we take to have been the game of real tennis, of French origin, and with considerable dramatic irony had ordered what might have been his escape route to be closed up.

★ ★ ★

The day had been spent by the King in sport and feasting, and by the conspirators in preparing for their enterprise. They had destroyed the locks of the doors of the apartment, so that the keys could not be turned; and they had taken away the bars with which the gates were secured, and had provided planks by way of bridges, on which to cross the ditch which surrounded the monastery. At

27

length, on the 20th February, 1437, all was prepared for carrying their treasonable purpose into execution, and Graham came from his hiding-place in the neighbouring mountains, with a party of nigh three hundred men, and entered the gardens of the convent.

The King was in his night-gown and slippers. He had passed the evening gaily with the nobles and ladies of his court, in reading romances, and in singing and music, or playing at chess and tables. The Earl of Athole, and his son Sir Robert Stewart, who expected to succeed James on the throne, were among the last courtiers who retired. At this time James remained standing before the fire, and conversing gaily with the Queen and her ladies before he went to rest. The Highland woman before mentioned again demanded permission to speak with the King, but was refused, on account of the untimeliness of the hour. All now were ordered to withdraw.

At this moment there was a noise and clashing heard, as of men in armour, and the torches in the garden cast up great flashes of light against the windows. The King then recollected his deadly enemy, Sir Robert Graham, and guessed that he was coming to murder him. He called to the ladies who were left in the chamber to keep the door as well as they could, in order to give him time to escape. He first tried to get out at the windows, but they were fast barred, and defied his strength. By help of the tongs, which were in the chimney, he raised, however, a plank of the flooring of the apartment, and let himself down into a narrow vault beneath, used as a common sewer. This vault had formerly had an opening into the court of the convent, by which he might have made his escape. But all things turned against the unfortunate James; for, two or three days before, he had caused the opening to be built up, because, when he played at ball in the court-yard, the ball used to roll into the vault through that hole.

While the King was in this place of concealment, the conspirators were seeking him from chamber to chamber throughout the convent, and, at length, came to the room where the ladies were. The Queen and her women endeavoured, as well as they might, to keep the door shut, and one of them, Catharine Douglas, boldly thrust her own arm across the door, instead of the bar, which had been taken away, as I told you. But the brave lady's arm was soon broken, and the traitors rushed into the room with swords and daggers drawn, hurting and throwing down such of the women as opposed them. The poor Queen stood half undressed, shrieking aloud; and one of the assassins would have slain her, had it not been for a son of Sir Robert Graham, who said to him, 'What would you do to the Queen? She is but a woman – Let us seek the King.'

They accordingly commenced a minute search, but without any success; so they left the apartment, and sought elsewhere about the monastery. In the meanwhile the King turned impatient, and desired the ladies to help him out of the inconvenient lurking place. At this unlucky moment the conspirators returned, one of them having recollected that there was such a vault, and that they had not searched it. And when they tore up the plank, and saw the King standing beneath in the vault, one of them called to the others, 'Sirs, I have found the bride for whom we have been seeking all night.' Then, first one, and then another of the villains, brethren of the name of Hall, descended into the vault, with daggers drawn, to dispatch the unfortunate King, who was standing there in his shirt, without weapons of any kind. But James, who was an active and strong man, threw them both down beneath his feet, and struggled to wrest a dagger from one or other of them, in which attempt his hands were severely cut and mangled. The murderers also were so severely handled that the marks of the King's gripe were visible on their throats for weeks afterwards. Then Sir Robert Graham himself sprung down on the King, who, finding no further defence possible, asked him for mercy, and for leisure to confess his sins to a priest. But Graham replied fiercely, 'Thou never hadst mercy on those of thine own blood, nor on anyone else, therefore thou shalt find no mercy here, and as for a confessor, thou shalt have none but the sword.' So speaking, he thrust the sword through the King's body. And yet it is said, that when he saw his Prince lying bleeding under his feet, he was desirous to have left the enterprise unfinished; but the other conspirators called on Graham to kill the King, otherwise he should himself die by their hands; upon which Graham, with the two men who had descended into the vault before him, fell on the unhappy Prince with their daggers, and slew him by many stabs. There were sixteen wounds in his breast alone.

By this time, but too late, news of this outrage had reached the town, and the household servants of the King, with the people inhabiting the town of Perth, were hastening to the rescue, with torches and weapons. The traitors accordingly caught the alarm, and retreated into the Highlands, losing in their flight only one or two, taken or slain by the pursuers. When they spoke about their enterprise among themselves, they greatly regretted that they had not killed the Queen along with her husband, fearing that she would be active and inexorable in her vengeance.

Indeed their apprehensions were justified by the event, for Queen Joanna made so strict search after the villainous assassins, that in the course of a month most of them were thrown into prison, and being tried and condemned, they were put to death with new and hideous tortures. The flesh of Robert Stewart, and of a private chamberlain of the King, was torn from their bodies with pincers; while, even in the midst of these horrible agonies, they confessed the justice of their sentence. The Earl of Athole was beheaded, denying at his death that he had consented to the conspiracy, though he admitted that his son had told him of it; to which he had replied, by enjoining him to have no concern in so great a crime. Sir Robert Graham, who was the person with whom the cruel scheme had origin, spoke in defence of it to the last. He had a right to slay the King, he said, for he had renounced his allegiance, and declared war against him; and he expressed his belief, that his memory would be honoured for putting to death so cruel a tyrant. He was tortured in the most dreadful manner before his final execution and whilst he was yet living, his son was slain before his eyes.

Sport and the Macabre
from The Private Memoirs and Confessions of a Justified Sinner

JAMES HOGG

★ ★ ★

This extract is taken from Hogg's masterpiece, The Private Memoirs and Confessions of a Justified Sinner, *an extraordinary and terrifying narrative that first appeared in 1824 and in the course of the twentieth century regained a reputation as a seminal Scottish novel about the divided self. The novel has accordingly made a striking contribution to a continuing theme of Scottish literature, one that anticipates other famous works like Stevenson's* Dr Jekyll and Mr Hyde. *To quote the book's 1824 editor: '[Edgar Allan] Poe never invented anything more horrible.' However, the appearance of an extract in an anthology of writing about sport is perhaps a little surprising, given that Hogg is best remembered (apart from this novel) for his poetry, such as 'Kilmeny'. Hogg described himself as the 'King of the Mountain and Fairy School' – but this macabre tale also includes a lengthy description of what he oddly calls a 'match at tennis', and another of 'a game at cricket', the latter called 'that violent and spirited game' – a surprising but strangely reassuring description for modern Scots cricket fans, well used to their beloved game being jeered at as a 'jessie' sort of sport.*

★ ★ ★

The very next time that George was engaged at tennis, he had not struck the ball above twice till the same intrusive being was again in his way. The party played for considerable stakes that day, namely, a dinner and wine at the Black Bull tavern; and George, as the hero and head of his party, was much interested in its honour;

consequently the sight of this moody and hellish-looking student affected him in no very pleasant manner. 'Pray, Sir, be so good as keep without the range of the ball,' said he.

'Is there any law or enactment that can compel me to do so?' said the other, biting his lip with scorn.

'If there is not, they are here that shall compel you,' returned George. 'So, friend, I rede you to be on your guard.'

As he said this, a flush of anger glowed in his handsome face and flashed from his sparkling blue eye; but it was a stranger to both, and momently took its departure. The black-coated youth set up his cap before, brought his heavy brows over his deep dark eyes, put his hands in the pockets of his black plush breeches, and stepped a little farther into the semicircle, immediately on his brother's right hand, than he had ever ventured to do before. There he set himself firm on his legs, and, with a face as demure as death, seemed determined to keep his ground. He pretended to be following the ball with his eyes; but every moment they were glancing aside at George. One of the competitors chanced to say rashly, in the moment of exultation, 'That's a d—d fine blow, George!' On which the intruder took up the word, as characteristic of the competitors, and repeated it every stroke that was given, making such a ludicrous use of it that several of the onlookers were compelled to laugh immoderately; but the players were terribly nettled at it, as he really contrived, by dint of sliding in some canonical terms, to render their game ridiculous.

But matters at length came to a crisis that put them beyond sport. George, in flying backward to gain the point at which the ball was going to light, came inadvertently so rudely in contact with this obstreperous interloper that he not only overthrew him, but also got a grievous fall over his legs; and, as he arose, the other made a spurn at him with his foot, which, if it had hit to its aim, would undoubtedly have finished the course of the young laird of Dalcastle and Balgrennan. George, being irritated beyond measure, as may well be conceived, especially at the deadly stroke aimed at him, struck the assailant with his racket, rather slightly, but so that his mouth and nose gushed out blood; and, at the same time he said, turning to his cronies: 'Does any of you know who the infernal puppy is?'

'Do you know, Sir?' said one of the onlookers, a stranger, 'the gentleman is your own brother, Sir – Mr. Robert Wringhim Colwan!'

'No, not Colwan, Sir,' said Robert, putting his hands in his pockets, and setting himself still farther forward than before, 'not a Colwan, Sir; henceforth I disclaim the name.'

'No, certainly not,' repeated George. 'My mother's son you may be – *but not a Colwan*! There you are right.' Then, turning around to his informer, he said: 'Mercy be about us, Sir! Is this the crazy minister's son from Glasgow?'

This question was put in the irritation of the moment, but it was too rude, and far too out of place, and no one deigned any answer to it. He felt the reproof, and felt it deeply, seeming anxious for some opportunity to make an acknowledgment, or some reparation.

In the meantime, young Wringhim was an object to all of the uttermost disgust. The blood flowing from his mouth and nose he took no pains to stem, neither did he so much as wipe it away; so that it spread over all his cheeks, and breast, even off at his toes. In that state did he take up his station in the middle of the competitors; and he did not now keep his place, but ran about, impeding everyone who attempted to make at the ball. They loaded him with execrations, but it availed nothing; he seemed courting persecution and buffetings, keeping steadfastly to his old joke of damnation, and marring the game so completely that, in spite of every effort on the part of the players, he forced them to stop their game and give it up. He was such a rueful-looking object, covered with blood, that none of them had the heart to kick him, although it appeared the only thing he wanted; and, as for George, he said not another word to him, either in anger or reproof.

When the game was fairly given up, and the party were washing their hands in the stone fount, some of them besought Robert Wringhim to wash himself; but he mocked at them, and said he was much better as he was. George, at length, came forward abashedly towards him, and said: 'I have been greatly to blame, Robert, and am very sorry for what I have done. But, in the first instance, I erred through ignorance, not knowing you were my brother, which you certainly are; and, in the second, through a momentary irritation, for which I am ashamed. I pray you, therefore, to pardon me, and give me your hand.'

As he said this, he held out his hand towards his polluted brother; but the froward predestinarian took not his from his pocket, but lifting his foot, he gave his brother's hand a kick. 'I'll give you what will suit such a hand better than mine,' said he, with a sneer. And then, turning lightly about, he added: 'Are there to be no more of these d—d fine blows, gentlemen? For shame, to give up such a profitable and edifying game!'

'This is too bad,' said George. 'But, since it is thus, I have the less to regret.' And, having made this general remark, he took no more note of the uncouth aggressor. But the persecution of the latter terminated not on the play-ground: he ranked up among them, bloody and disgusting as he was, and, keeping close by his brother's side, he marched along with the party all the way to the Black Bull. Before they got there, a great number of boys and idle people had surrounded them, hooting and incommoding them exceedingly, so that they were glad to get into the inn; and the unaccountable monster actually tried to get in amongst with them, to make one of the party at dinner. But the innkeeper and his men, getting the hint, by force prevented him from entering, although he attempted it again and again, both by telling lies and offering a bribe. Finding be could not prevail, he set to exciting the mob at the door to acts of violence; in which he had like to have succeeded. The landlord had no other shift, at last, but to send privately for two officers, and have him carried to the guard-house . . .

The next day George and his companions met as usual – all who were not seriously wounded of them. But, as they strolled about the city, the rancorous eye and the finger of scorn was pointed against them. None of them was at first aware of the reason; but it threw a damp over their spirits and enjoyments, which they could not master. They went to take a forenoon game at their old play of tennis, not on a match, but by way of improving themselves; but they had not well taken their places till young Wringhim appeared in his old station, at his brother's right hand, with looks more demure and determined than ever. His lips were primmed so close that his mouth was hardly discernible, and his dark deep eye flashed gleams of holy indignation on the godless set, but particularly on his brother. His presence acted as a mildew on all social intercourse or enjoyment; the game was marred, and ended ere ever it was well begun. There were whisperings apart – the party separated, and, in order to shake off the blighting influence of this dogged persecutor, they entered sundry houses of their acquaintances, with an understanding that they were to meet on the Links for a game at cricket.

They did so; and, stripping off part of their clothes, they began that violent and spirited game. They had not played five minutes till Wringhim was stalking in the midst of them, and totally impeding the play. A cry arose from all corners of: 'Oh, this will never do. Kick him out of the play-ground! Knock down the scoundrel; or bind him, and let him lie in peace.'

'By no means,' cried George. 'It is evident he wants nothing else. Pray do not humour him so much as to touch him with either foot or finger.' Then, turning to a friend, he said in a whisper: 'Speak to him, Gordon; he surely will not refuse to let us have the ground to ourselves, if you request it of him.'

Gordon went up to him, and requested of him, civilly, but ardently, 'to retire to a certain distance, else none of them could or would be answerable, however sore he might be hurt.'

He turned disdainfully on his heel, uttered a kind of pulpit hem! and then added, 'I will take my chance of that; hurt me, any of you, at your peril.'

The Village Cricket Match

from England, their England

A.G. MACDONELL

★ ★ ★

*This 1933 classic of humorous writing with a satirical edge is also a
classic of sports writing, appearing in virtually all of the cricketing
anthologies. It has been sadly neglected in recent years, but as we hope to
show, Macdonell's work (there are several other extracts in this book)
provides an unsurpassed view of the English at play written by a Scot.*

*Born in 1895 in Poona he was educated at Winchester and went through
the harrowing experience of the Great War as an officer in the artillery, an
experience clearly mirrored in the book's coolly ironic opening chapter.
Peacetime England is the setting of the following chapters and the
description of Donald Cameron's journey through its sports grounds and
courses becomes a blend of mild satire and affectionate farce. Donald is from
Aberdeen, like Macdonell himself, and he follows a well-worn literary trail
to the South as an innocent abroad, a sort of prototype Crocodile Dundee.
The extract describing the cricket match at the village of Fordenden is the
funniest comedy of sporting manners since its equivalent at another fictional
Kentish village, Dingley Dell in* The Pickwick Papers.

So good is England, their England *that we shall include further
extracts from the book in other chapters of this anthology.*

★ ★ ★

'Don't forget Saturday morning Charing Cross Underground
Station,' ran the telegram which arrived at Royal Avenue during the
week, 'at ten fifteen sharp whatever you do dont be late Hodge.'

Saturday morning was bright and sunny, and at ten minutes past

10 Donald arrived at the Embankment entrance of Charing Cross Underground Station, carrying a small suitcase full of clothes suitable for outdoor sports and pastimes. He was glad that he had arrived too early, for it would have been a dreadful thing for a stranger and a foreigner to have kept such a distinguished man, and his presumably distinguished colleagues, even for an instant from their national game. Laying his bag down on the pavement and putting one foot upon it carefully – for Donald had heard stories of the surpassing dexterity of metropolitan thieves – he waited eagerly for the hands of a neighbouring clock to mark the quarter-past. At twenty minutes to 11 an effeminate-looking young man, carrying a cricketing bag-wearing a pale-blue silk jumper up to his ears, sauntered up, remarked casually, 'You playing?' and, on receiving an answer in the affirmative, dumped his bag at Donald's feet and said, 'Keep an eye on that like a good fellow. I'm going to get a shave,' and sauntered off round the corner.

At five minutes to 11 there was a respectable muster, six of the team having assembled. But at five minutes past, a disintegrating element was introduced by the arrival of Mr. Harcourt with the news, which he announced with the air of a shipwrecked mariner who has, after twenty-five years of vigilance, seen a sail, that in the neighbourhood of Charing Cross the pubs opened at 11 a.m. So that when Mr. Hodge himself turned up at twenty-five minutes past 11, resplendent in flannels, a red-and-white football shirt with a lace-up collar, and a blazer of purple-and-yellow stripes, each stripe being at least two inches across, and surmounted by a purple-and-yellow cap that made him somehow reminiscent of one of the Michelin twins, if not both, he was justly indignant at the slackness of his team.

'They've no sense of time,' he told Donald repeatedly. 'We're late as it is. The match is due to begin at half-past 11, and it's fifty miles from here. I should have been here myself two hours ago but I had my Sunday article to do. It really is too bad.'

When the team, now numbering nine men, had been extricated from the tavern and had been marshalled on the pavement, counted, recounted, and the missing pair identified, it was pointed out by the casual youth who had returned, shining and pomaded from the barber, that the char-à-banc had not yet arrived.

Mr. Hodge's indignation became positively alarming and we covered the twenty yards to the public telephone box almost as quickly as Mr. Harcourt covered the forty yards back to the door of the pub. Donald remained on the pavement to guard the heap of suitcases, cricket-bags, and stray equipment – one player had arrived with a pair of flannels rolled in a tight ball under his arm and a left-hand batting glove, while another had contributed a cardboard box which he had bought at Hamley's on the way down, and which contained six composite cricket-balls, boys' size, and a pair of bails. It was just as well that Donald did remain on guard, partly because no one else seemed to care whether the luggage was stolen or not, partly because Mr. Hodge emerged in a perfect frenzy a minute or two later from the telephone box to borrow two pennies to put in the slot, and partly because by the time the telephone call was at last in full swing and Mr. Hodge's command over the byways of British invective was enjoying complete freedom of action, the char-à-banc rolled up beside the kerb.

At 12.30 it was decided not to wait for the missing pair, and the nine cricketers started off. At 2.30, after halts at Catford, the White Hart at Sevenoaks, the Angel at Tunbridge Wells, and three smaller inns at tiny villages, the char-à-banc drew up triumphantly beside the cricket ground of the Kentish village Fordenden.

Donald was enchanted at his first sight of rural England. And rural England is the real England, unspoilt by factories and financiers and tourists and hustle. He sprang out of the char-à-banc, in which he had been tightly wedged between a very stout publisher who had laughed all the way down and had quivered at each laugh like the needle of a seismograph during one of Japan's larger earthquakes, and a youngish and extremely learned professor of ballistics, and gazed eagerly round. The sight was worth an eager gaze or two. It was a hot summer's afternoon. There was no wind, and the smoke from the red-roofed cottages curled slowly up into the golden haze. The clock on the flint tower of the church struck the half-hour, and the vibrations spread slowly across the shimmering hedgerows, spangled with white blossom of the convolvulus, and lost themselves tremulously among the gardens. Bees lazily drifted. White butterflies flapped their aimless way among the orchards. Delphiniums, larkspur, tiger-lilies, evening-primrose, monk's-hood, sweet-peas, swaggered brilliantly above the box hedges, the wooden palings, and the rickety gates. The cricket field itself was a mass of daisies and buttercups and dandelions, tall grasses and purple vetches and thistle-down, and great clumps of dark-red sorrel, except, of course, for the oblong patch in the centre – mown, rolled, watered – a smooth shining emerald of grass, the Pride of Fordenden, the Wicket.

The entire scene was perfect to the last detail. It was as if Mr. Cochran had, with his spectacular genius, brought Ye Olde Englyshe Village straight down by special train from the London Pavilion, complete with synthetic cobwebs (from the Wigan factory), hand-made smocks for ye gaffers (called in the cabaret scenes and the North-West Mounted Police scenes, the Gentlemen of the Singing Ensemble), and aluminium Eezi-Milk stools for the dairymaids (or Ladies of the Dancing Ensemble). For there stood the Vicar, beaming absent-mindedly at everyone. There was the forge, with the black-smith, his hammer discarded, tightening his snake-buckled belt for the fray and loosening his braces to enable his terrific bowling-arm to swing freely in its socket. There on a long bench outside the Three Horseshoes sat a row of elderly men, facing a row of pint tankards, and wearing either long beards or clean-shaven chins and long whiskers. Near them, holding pint tankards in their hands, was another group of men, clustered together and talking with intense animation. Donald thought that one or two of them seemed familiar, but it was not until he turned back to the char-à-banc to ask if he could help with the luggage that he realized that they were Mr. Hodge and his team already sampling the proprietor's wares. (A notice above the door of the inn stated that the proprietor's name was A. Bason and that he was licensed to sell wines, spirits, beers, and tobacco.)

All round the cricket field small parties of villagers were patiently waiting for the great match to begin – a match against gentlemen from London is an event in a village – and some of them looked as if they had been waiting for a good long time. But they were not impatient. Village folk are very seldom impatient. Those whose lives are occupied in combating the eccentricities of God regard as very small beer the eccentricities of Man.

Blue-and-green dragonflies played at hide-and-seek among the thistle-down and a pair of swans flew overhead. An ancient man leaned upon a scythe, his sharpening-stone sticking out of a pocket in his velveteen waistcoat. A magpie flapped lazily across the meadows. The parson shook hands with the squire. Doves cooed. The haze flickered. The world stood still.

At twenty minutes to 3, Mr. Hodge had completed his rather tricky negotiations with the Fordenden captain, and had arranged that two substitutes should be lent by Fordenden in order that the visitors should field eleven men, and that nine men on each side should bat. But just as the two men on the Fordenden side, who had been detailed for the unpleasant duty of fielding for both sides and batting for neither, had gone off home in high dudgeon, a motor-car arrived containing not only Mr. Hodge's two defaulters but a third gentleman in flannels as well, who swore stoutly that he had been invited by Mr. Hodge to play and affirmed that he was jolly well going to play. Whoever stood down, it wasn't going to be him. Negotiations therefore had to be reopened, the pair of local Achilles had to be recalled, and at ten minutes to 3 the match began upon a twelve-a-side basis.

Mr. Hodge, having won the toss by a system of his own founded upon the differential calculus and the Copernican theory, sent in his opening pair to bat. One was James Livingstone, a very sound club cricketer, and the other one was called, simply, Boone. Boone was a huge, awe-inspiring colossus of a man, weighing at least eighteen stone and wearing all the majestic trappings of a Cambridge Blue.

Donald felt that it was hardly fair to loose such cracks upon a humble English village until he fortunately remembered that he, of all people, a foreigner admitted by courtesy to the National Game, ought not to set himself up to be a judge of what is, and what is not, cricket.

The Fordenden team ranged themselves at the bidding of their captain, the Fordenden baker, in various spots of vantage amid the daisies, buttercups, dandelions, vetches, thistle-down, and clumps of dark-red sorrel; and the blacksmith having taken in, just for luck as it were, yet another reef in his snake-buckle belt, prepared to open the attack. It so happened that, at the end at which he was to bowl, the ground behind the wicket was level for a few yards and then sloped away rather abruptly, so that it was only during the last three or four intensive, galvanic yards of his run that the blacksmith, who took a long run, was visible to the batsman or indeed to anyone on the field of play except the man stationed in the deep field behind him. This man saw nothing of the game except the blacksmith walking back dourly and the blacksmith running up ferociously, and occasionally a ball driven smartly over the brow of the hill in his direction.

The sound club player having taken guard, having twiddled his bat round several times in a nonchalant manner, and having stared arrogantly at each fieldsman in turn, was somewhat surprised to find that, although the field was ready, no bowler was visible. His doubts, however, were resolved a second or two later, when the blacksmith came up, breasting the slope superbly like a mettlesome combination of Vulcan and Venus Anadyomene. The first ball which he delivered was a high full-pitch to leg, of appalling velocity. It must have lighted upon a bare patch in the long grass near long-leg, for it rocketed, first bounce, into the hedge and four byes were reluctantly signalled by the village umpire. The row of gaffers on the rustic bench shook their heads, agreed that it was many years since four byes had been signalled on that ground, and called for more pints of bitter. The other members of Mr. Hodge's team blanched visibly and called for more pints of bitter. The youngish professor of ballistics, who was in next, muttered something about muzzle velocities and started to do a sum on the back of an envelope.

The second ball went full-pitch into the wicket-keeper's stomach and there was a delay while the deputy wicket-keeper was invested with the pads and gloves of office. The third ball, making a noise like a partridge, would have hummed past Mr. Livingstone's left ear had he not dexterously struck it out of the ground for six, and the fourth took his leg bail with a bullet-like full-pitch. Ten runs for one wicket, last man six. The professor got the fifth ball on the left ear and went back to the Three Horseshoes, while Mr. Harcourt had the singular misfortune to hit his wicket before the sixth ball was even delivered. Ten runs for two wickets and one man retired hurt. A slow left-hand bowler was on at the other end, the local rate-collector, a man whose whole life was one of infinite patience and guile. Off his first ball the massive Cambridge Blue was easily stumped, having executed a movement that aroused the professional admiration of the Ancient who was leaning upon his scythe. Donald was puzzled that so famous a player should play so execrable a stroke until it transpired, later on, that a wrong impression had been created and that the portentous Boone had gained his Blue at Cambridge for rowing and not for cricket. Ten runs for three wickets and one man hurt.

The next player was a singular young man. He was small and quiet, and he wore perfectly creased white flannels, white silk socks, a pale-pink silk shirt, and a white cap. On the way down in the char-à-banc he had taken little part in the conversation and even less in the beer-drinking. There was a retiring modesty about him that made him conspicuous in that cricket eleven, and there was a gentleness, an almost finicky gentleness about his movements which hardly seemed virile and athletic. He looked as if a fast ball would knock the bat out of his hands. Donald asked someone what his name was, and was astonished to learn that he was the famous novelist, Robert Southcott himself.

Just as this celebrity, holding his bat as delicately as if it was as if it was a flute or a fan, was picking his way through the daisies and thistle-down towards the wicket, Mr. Hodge rushed anxiously, tankard in hand, from the Three Horseshoes and bellowed in a most unpoetical voice: 'Play carefully, Bobby. Keep your end up. Runs don't matter.'

'Very well, Bill,' replied Mr. Southcott sedately. Donald was interested by this little exchange. It was the Team Spirit at work – the captain instructing his man to play a type of game that was demanded by the state of the team's fortunes, and the loyally individual suppressing his instincts to play a different type of game.

Mr. Southcott took guard modestly, glanced furtively round the field as if it was an impertinence to suggest that he would survive long enough to make a study of the fieldsmen's positions worth while, and hit the rate-collector's first ball over the Three Horseshoes into a hay-field. The ball was retrieved by a mob of screaming urchins, handed back to the rate-collector, who scratched his head and then bowled his fast yorker, which Mr. Southcott hit into the saloon bar of the Shoes, giving Mr. Harcourt such a fright that he required several pints before he fully recovered his nerve. The next ball was very slow and crafty, endowed as it was with every iota of fingerspin and brain-power which a long-service rate-collector could muster. In addition, it was delivered at the extreme end of the crease so as to secure a back ground of dark laurels instead of a dazzling white screen, and it swung a little in the air; a few moments later the urchins, by this time delirious with ecstasy, were fishing it out of the squire's trout stream with a bamboo pole and an old bucket.

The rate-collector was bewildered. He had never known such a travesty of the game. It was not cricket. It was slogging; it was wild, unscientific bashing; and furthermore, his reputation was in grave danger. The instalments would be harder than ever to collect, and Heaven knew they were hard enough to collect as it was, what with bad times and all. His three famous deliveries had been treated with contempt – the leg-break, the fast yorker, and the slow, swinging off-break out of the laurel bushes. What on earth was he to try now? Another six and he would be laughed out of the parish. Fortunately the village umpire came out of a trance of consternation to the rescue. Thirty-eight years of umpiring for the Fordenden Cricket Club had taught him a thing or two and he called 'Over' firmly and marched off to square-leg. The rate-collector was glad to give way to a Free Forester, who had been specially imported for this match. He was only a moderate bowler, but it was felt that it was worth while giving him a trial, if only for the sake of the scarf round his waist and his cap. At the other end the fast bowler pounded away grimly until an unfortunate accident occurred. Mr. Southcott had been treating with apologetic contempt those of his deliveries which came within reach, and the blacksmith's temper had been rising for some time. An urchin had shouted, 'Take him orf!' and the other urchins, for whom Mr. Southcott was by now a firmly established deity, had screamed with delight. The captain had held one or two ominous consultations with the wicket-keeper and other advisers, and the blacksmith knew that his dismissal was at hand unless he produced a supreme effort.

It was the last ball of the over. He halted at the wicket before going back for his run, glared at Mr. Harcourt, who had been driven out to umpire by his colleagues – greatly to the regret of Mr. Bason, the landlord of the Shoes – glared at Mr. Southcott, took another reef in his belt, shook out another inch in his braces, spat on his hand, swung his arm three or four times in a meditative sort of way, grasped the ball tightly in his colossal palm, and then turned smartly about and marched off like a Pomeranian grenadier and vanished over the brow of the hill. Mr. Southcott, during these proceedings, leant elegantly upon his bat and admired the view. At last, after a long stillness, the ground shook, the grasses waved violently, small birds arose with shrill clamours, a loud puffing sound alarmed the butterflies, and the blacksmith, looking more like Venus Anadyomene than ever, came thundering over the crest. The world held its breath. Among the spectators conversation was suddenly hushed. Even the urchins, understanding somehow that they were assisting at a crisis in affairs, were silent for a moment as the mighty figure swept up to the crease. It was the charge of Von

Bredow's Dragoons at Gravelotte over again.

But alas for human ambitions! Mr. Harcourt, swaying slightly from leg to leg, had understood the menacing glare of the bowler, had marked the preparation for a titanic effort, and – for he was not a poet for nothing – knew exactly what was going on. Mr. Harcourt sober had a very pleasant sense of humour, but Mr. Harcourt rather drunk was a perfect demon of impishness. Sober, he occasionally resisted a temptation to try to be funny. Rather drunk, never. As the giant whirlwind of vulcanic energy rushed past him to the crease, Mr. Harcourt, quivering with excitement and internal laughter, and wobbling uncertainly upon his pins, took a deep breath and bellowed, 'No ball!'

It was too late for the unfortunate bowler to stop himself. The ball flew out of his hand like a bullet and hit third-slip, who was not looking, full pitch on the knee-cap. With a yell of agony third-slip began hopping about like a stork until he tripped over a tussock of grass and fell on his face in a bed of nettles, from which he sprang up again with another drum-splitting yell. The blacksmith himself was flung forward by his own irresistible momentum, startled out of his wits by Mr. Harcourt's bellow in his ear, and thrown off his balance by his desperate effort to prevent himself from delivering the ball, and the result was that his gigantic feet got mixed up among each other and he fell heavily in the centre of the wicket, knocking up a cloud of dust and dandelion-seed and twisting his ankle. Rooks by hundreds arose in protest from the vicarage cedars. The urchins howled like intoxicated banshees. The gaffers gaped. Mr. Southcott gazed modestly at the ground. Mr. Harcourt gazed at the heavens. Mr. Harcourt did not think the world had ever been, or could ever be again, quite such a capital place, even though he had laughed internally so much that he had got hiccups.

Mr. Hodge, emerging at that moment from the Three Horseshoes, surveyed the scene and then the scoreboard with an imperial air. Then he roared in the same rustic voice as before:

'You needn't play safe any more, Bob. Play your own game.'

'Thank you, Bill,' replied Mr. Southcott as sedately as ever, and, on the resumption of the game, he fell into a kind of cricketing trance, defending his wicket skilfully from straight balls, ignoring crooked ones and scoring one more run in a quarter of an hour before he inadvertently allowed, for the first time during his innings, a ball to strike his person.

'Out!' shrieked the venerable umpire before anyone had time to appeal.

The score at this point was sixty-nine for six, last man fifty-two.

The only other incident in the innings was provided by an American journalist, by name Shakespeare Pollock – an intensely active, alert, on-the-spot young man. Mr. Pollock had been roped in at the last moment to make up the eleven, and Mr. Hodge and Mr. Harcourt had spent quite a lot of time on the way down trying to teach him the fundamental principles of the game. Donald had listened attentively and had been surprised that they made no reference to the Team Spirit. He decided in the end that the reason must have been simply that everyone knows all about it already, and that it is therefore taken for granted.

Mr. Pollock stepped up to the wicket in the lively manner of his native mustang, refused to take guard, on the ground that he wouldn't know what to do with it when he had got it, and, striking the first ball he received towards square leg, threw down his bat, and himself set off at a great rate in the direction of cover-point. There was a paralysed silence. The rustics on the bench rubbed their eyes. On the field no one moved. Mr. Pollock stopped suddenly, looked round, and broke into a genial laugh.

'Darn me –' he began, and then he pulled himself up and went on in refined English, 'Well, well! I thought I was playing baseball.' He smiled disarmingly round.

'Baseball is a kind of rounders, isn't it, sir?' said cover-point sympathetically.

Donald thought he had never seen an expression change so suddenly as Mr. Pollock's did at this harmless, and true, statement. A look of concentrated, ferocious venom obliterated the disarming smile. Cover-point, simple soul, noticed nothing, however, and Mr.

Pollock walked back to the wicket in silence and was out next ball. The next two batsmen, Major Hawker, the team's fast bowler, and Mr. Hodge himself, did not score, and the innings closed at sixty-nine, Donald not-out nought. Opinion on the gaffers' bench, which corresponded in years and connoisseurship very closely with the Pavilion at Lord's, was sharply divided on the question of whether sixty-nine was, or was not, a winning score.

After a suitable interval for refreshment, Mr. Hodge led his men, except Mr. Harcourt who was missing, out into the field and placed them at suitable positions in the hay.

The batsmen came in. The redoubtable Major Hawker, the fast bowler, thrust out his chin and prepared to bowl. In a quarter of an hour he had terrified seven batsmen, clean bowled six of them, and broken a stump. Eleven runs, six wickets, last man two.

After the fall of the sixth wicket there was a slight delay. The new batsman, the local rate-collector, had arrived at the crease and was ready. But nothing happened. Suddenly the large publisher, who was acting as wicket-keeper, called out, 'Hi! Where's Hawker?'

The words galvanized Mr. Hodge into portentous activity.

'Quick!' he shouted. 'Hurry, run, for God's sake! Bob, George, Percy, to the Shoes!' and he set off at a sort of gallop towards the inn, followed at intervals by the rest of the side except the pretty youth in the blue jumper, who lay down; the wicket-keeper, who did not move; and Mr. Shakespeare Pollock, who had shot off the mark and was well ahead of the field.

But they were all too late, even Mr. Pollock. The gallant Major, admitted by Mr. Bason through the back door, had already lowered a quart and a half of mild-and-bitter, and his subsequent bowling was perfectly innocuous, consisting, as it did, mainly of slow, gentle full-pitches to leg which the village baker and even, occasionally, the rate-collector hit hard and high into the long grass. The score mounted steadily.

Disaster followed disaster. Mr. Pollock, presented with an easy chance of a run-out, instead of lobbing the ball back to the wicket-keeper, had another reversion to his college days and flung it with appalling velocity at the unfortunate rate-collector and hit him in the small of the back, shouting triumphantly as he did so, 'Rah, rah, rah!' Mr. Livingstone, good club player, missed two easy catches off successive balls. Mr. Hodge allowed another easy catch to fall at his feet without attempting to catch it, and explained afterwards that he had been all the time admiring a particularly fine specimen of oak in the squire's garden. He seemed to think that this was a complete justification of his failure to attempt, let alone bring off, the catch. A black spot happened to cross the eye of the ancient umpire just as the baker put all his feet and legs and pads in front of a perfectly straight ball, and, as he plaintively remarked over and over again, he had to give the batsman the benefit of the doubt, hadn't he? It wasn't as if it was his fault that a black spot had crossed his eye just at that moment. And the stout publisher seemed to be suffering from the delusion that the way to make a catch at the wicket was to raise both hands high in the air, utter a piercing yell, and trust to an immense pair of pads to secure the ball. Repeated experiments proved that he was wrong.

The baker lashed away vigorously and the rate-collector dabbed the ball hither and thither until the score – having once been eleven runs for six wickets – was marked up on the board at fifty runs for six wickets. Things were desperate. Twenty to win and five wickets – assuming that the blacksmith's ankle and third-slip's knee-cap would stand the strain – to fall. If the lines on Mr. Hodge's face were deep, the lines on the faces of his team when he put himself on to bowl were like plasticine models of the Colorado Canyon. Mr. Southcott, without any orders from his captain, discarded his silk sweater from the Rue de la Paix, and went away into the deep field, about a hundred and twenty yards from the wicket. His beautifully brushed head was hardly visible above the daisies. The professor of ballistics sighed deeply. Major Hawker grinned a colossal grin, right across his jolly red face, and edged off in the direction of the Shoes. Livingstone, loyal to his captain, crouched alertly. Mr. Shakespeare Pollock rushed about enthusiastically. The remainder of the team drooped.

But the remainder of the team was wrong. For a wicket, a crucial wicket, was secured off Mr. Hodge's very first ball. It happened like this. Mr. Hodge was a poet, and therefore a theorist, and an idealist. If he was to win a victory at anything, he preferred to win by brains and not by muscle. He would far sooner have his best leg-spinner miss the wicket by an eighth of an inch than dismiss a batsman with a fast, clumsy full-toss. Every ball that he bowled had brain behind it, if not exactness of pitch. And it so happened that he had recently watched a county cricket match between Lancashire, a county that he detested in theory, and Worcestershire, a county that he adored in fact. On the one side were factories and the late Mr. Jimmy White; on the other, English apples and Mr. Stanley Baldwin. And at this particular match, a Worcestershire bowler, by name Root, a deliciously agricultural name, had outed the tough nuts of the County Palatine by placing all his fieldsmen on the leg-side and bowling what are technically known as 'in-swingers'.

Mr. Hodge, at heart an agrarian, for all his book-learning and his cadences, was determined to do the same. The first part of the performance was easy. He placed all his men upon the leg-side. The second part – the bowling of the 'in-swingers' – was more complicated, and Mr. Hodge's first ball was a slow long-hop on the off-side. The rate-collector, metaphorically rubbing his eyes, felt that this was too good to be true, and he struck the ball sharply into the untenanted off-side and ambled down the wicket with as near an approach to gaiety as a man can achieve who is cut off by the very nature of his profession from the companionship and goodwill of his fellows. He had hardly gone a yard or two when he was paralysed by a hideous yell from the long grass into which the ball had vanished, and still more by the sight of Mr. Harcourt, who, aroused from a deep slumber amid a comfortable couch of grasses and daisies, sprang to his feet and, pulling himself together with miraculous rapidity after a lightning if somewhat bleary glance round the field, seized the ball and unerringly threw down the wicket. Fifty for seven, last man twenty-two. Twenty to win: four wickets to fall.

Mr. Hodge's next ball was his top-spinner, and it would have, or might have, come very quickly off the ground had it ever hit the ground; as it was, one of the short-legs caught it dexterously and threw it back while the umpire signalled a wide. Mr. Hodge then tried some more of Mr. Root's stuff and was promptly hit for two sixes and a single. This brought the redoubtable baker to the batting end. Six runs to win and four wickets to fall.

Mr. Hodge's fifth ball was not a good one, due mainly to the fact that it slipped out of his hand before he was ready, and it went up and came down in a slow, lazy parabola, about seven feet wide of the wicket on the leg-side. The baker had plenty of time to make up his mind. He could either leave it alone and let it count one run as a wide; or he could spring upon it like a panther and, with a terrific six, finish the match sensationally. He could play the part either of a Quintus Fabius Maximus Cunctator, or of a sort of Tarzan. The baker concealed beneath a modest and floury exterior a mounting ambition. Here was his chance to show the village. He chose the sort of Tarzan, sprang like a panther, whirled his bat cyclonically, and missed the ball by about a foot and a half. The wicket-keeping publisher had also had time in which to think and to move, and he also had covered the seven feet. True, his movements were less like the spring of a panther than the sideways waddle of an aldermanic penguin. But nevertheless he got there, and when the ball had passed the flashing blade of the baker, he launched a mighty kick at it – stooping to grab it was out of the question – and by an amazing fluke kicked it on to the wicket. Even the ancient umpire had to give the baker out, for the baker was still lying flat on his face outside the crease.

'I was bowling for that,' observed Mr. Hodge modestly, strolling up the pitch.

'I had plenty of time to use my hands,' remarked the wicket-keeper to the world at large, 'but I preferred to kick it.'

Donald was impressed by the extraordinary subtlety of the game. Six to win and three wickets to fall.

The next batsman was a schoolboy of about sixteen, an

ingenuous youth with pink cheeks and a nervous smile, who quickly fell a victim to Mr. Harcourt, now wideawake and beaming upon everyone. For Mr. Harcourt, poet that he was, understood exactly what the poor, pink child was feeling, and he knew that if he played the ancient dodge and pretended to lose the ball in the long grass, it was a hundred to one that the lad would lose his head. The batsman at the other end played the fourth ball of Mr. Livingstone's next over hard in the direction of Mr. Harcourt. Mr. Harcourt rushed towards the spot where it had vanished in the jungle. He groped wildly for it, shouting as he did so, 'Come and help. It's lost.' The pink child scuttered nimbly down the pitch. Six runs to win and two wickets to fall. Mr. Harcourt smiled demoniacally.

The crisis was now desperate. The fieldsmen drew nearer and nearer to the batsmen, excepting the youth in the blue jumper. Livingstone balanced himself on his toes. Mr. Shakespeare Pollock hopped about almost on top of the batsmen, and breathed excitedly and audibly. Even the imperturbable Mr. Southcott discarded the piece of grass which he had been chewing so steadily. Mr. Hodge took himself off and put on the Major, who had by now somewhat lived down the quart and a half.

The batsmen crouched down upon their bats and defended stubbornly. A snick through the slips brought a single. A ball which eluded the publisher's gigantic pads brought a bye. A desperate sweep at a straight half-volley sent the ball off the edge of the bat over third-man's head and in normal circumstances would have certainly scored one, and possibly two. But Mr. Harcourt was on guard at third-man, and the batsmen, by nature cautious men, one being old and the sexton, the other the postman and therefore a Government official, were taking no risks. Then came another single off a mis-hit, and then an interminable period in which no wicket fell and no run was scored. It was broken at last disastrously, for the postman struck the ball sharply at Mr. Pollock, and Mr. Pollock picked it up and, in an ecstasy of zeal, flung it madly at the wicket. Two overthrows resulted.

The scores were level and there were two wickets to fall. Silence fell. The gaffers, victims simultaneously of excitement and senility, could hardly raise their pint pots – for it was past 6 o'clock, and the front door of the Three Horseshoes was now as wide open officially as the back door had been unofficially all afternoon.

The Major, his red face redder than ever and his chin sticking out almost as far as the Napoleonic Mr. Ogilvy's, bowled a fast half-volley on the leg-stump. The sexton, a man of iron muscle from much digging, hit it fair and square in the middle of the bat, and it flashed like a thunderbolt, waist-high, straight at the youth in the blue jumper. With a shrill scream the youth sprang backwards out of its way and fell over on his back. Immediately behind him, so close were the fieldsmen clustered, stood the mighty Boone. There was no chance of escape for him. Even if he had possessed the figure and the agility to perform back-somersaults, he would have lacked the time. He had been unsighted by the youth in the jumper. The thunderbolt struck him in the midriff like a red-hot cannonball upon a Spanish galleon, and with the sound of a drumstick upon an insufficiently stretched drum. With a fearful oath, Boone clapped his hands to his outraged stomach and found that the ball was in the way. He looked at it for a moment in astonishment and then threw it down angrily and started to massage the injured spot while the field rang with applause at the brilliance of the catch.

Donald walked up and shyly added his congratulations. Boone scowled at him.

'I didn't want to catch the bloody thing,' he said sourly, massaging away like mad.

'But it may save the side,' ventured Donald.

'Blast the bloody side,' said Boone.

Donald went back to his place.

The scores were level and there was one wicket to fall. The last man in was the blacksmith, leaning heavily upon the shoulder of the baker, who was going to run for him, and limping as if in great pain. He took guard and looked round savagely. He was clearly still in a great rage.

The first ball he received he lashed at wildly and hit straight up in the air to an enormous height. It went up and up and up, until it became difficult to focus it properly against the deep, cloudless blue of the sky, and it carried with it the hopes and fears of an English village. Up and up it went and then at the top it seemed to hang motionless in the air, poised like a hawk, fighting, as it were, a heroic but forlorn battle against the chief invention of Sir Isaac Newton, and then it began its slow descent.

In the meanwhile things were happening below, on the terrestrial sphere. Indeed, the situation was becoming what the French call *mouvementé*. In the first place, the blacksmith forgot his sprained ankle and set out at a capital rate for the other end, roaring in a great voice as he went, 'Come on, Joe!' The baker, who was running on behalf of the invalid, also set out, and he also roared 'Come on, Joe!' and side by side, like a pair of high-stepping hackneys, the pair cantered along. From the other end Joe set out on his mission, and he roared 'Come on, Bill!' So all three came on. And everything would have been all right, so far as the running was concerned, had it not been for the fact that Joe, very naturally, ran with his head thrown back and his eyes goggling at the hawk-like cricket-ball. And this in itself would not have mattered if it had not been for the fact that the blacksmith and the baker, also very naturally, ran with their heads turned not only upwards but also backwards as well, so that they too gazed at the ball, with an alarming sort of squint and a truly terrific kink in their necks. Half-way down the pitch the three met with a magnificent clang, reminiscent of early, happy days in the tournament-ring at Ashby-de-la-Zouche, and the hopes of the village fell with the resounding fall of their three champions.

But what of the fielding side? Things were not so well with them. If there was doubt and confusion among the warriors of Fordenden, there was also uncertainty and disorganisation among the ranks of the invaders. Their main trouble was the excessive concentration of their forces in the neighbourhood of the wicket. Napoleon laid it down that it was impossible to have too many men upon a battlefield, and he used to do everything in his power to call up every available man for a battle. Mr. Hodge, after a swift glance at the ascending ball and a swift glance at the disposition of his troops, disagreed profoundly with the Emperor's dictum. He had too many men, far too many. And all except the youth in the blue silk jumper, and the mighty Boone, were moving towards strategical positions underneath the ball, and not one of them appeared to be aware that any of the others existed. Boone had not moved because he was more or less in the right place, but then Boone was not likely to bring off the catch, especially after the episode of the last ball. Major Hawker, shouting 'Mine, mine!' in a magnificently self-confident voice, was coming up from the bowler's end like a battle-cruiser. Mr. Harcourt had obviously lost sight of the ball altogether, if indeed he had ever seen it, for he was running round and round Boone and giggling foolishly. Livingstone and Southcott, the two cracks, were approaching competently. Either of them would catch it easily. Mr. Hodge had only to choose between them and, coming to a swift decision, he yelled above the din, 'Yours, Livingstone!' Southcott, disciplined cricketer, stopped dead. Then Mr. Hodge made a fatal mistake. He remembered Livingstone's two missed sitters, and he reversed his decision and roared 'Yours, Bobby!' Mr. Southcott obediently started again, while Livingstone, who had not heard the second order, went straight on. Captain Hodge had restored the *status quo*.

In the meantime the professor of ballistics had made a lightning calculation of angles, velocities, density of the air, barometer-readings and temperatures, and had arrived at the conclusion that the critical point, the spot which ought to be marked in the photographs with an X, was one yard to the north-east of Boone, and he proceeded to take up station there, colliding on the way with Donald and knocking him over. A moment later Bobby Southcott came racing up and tripped over the recumbent Donald and was shot head first into the Abraham-like bosom of Boone. Boone stepped back a yard under the impact and came down with his spiked boot, surmounted by a good eighteen stone of flesh and blood, upon the professor's toe. Almost simultaneously the portly wicket-keeper, whose movements were a positive triumph of the spirit over the body, bumped the professor from behind. The learned man was thus neatly sandwiched between Tweedledum and Tweedledee, and the sandwich was instantly converted into a ragout by Livingstone, who made up for his lack of extra weight – for he was always in perfect training – by his extra momentum. And all the time Mr. Shakespeare Pollock hovered alertly upon the outskirts like a Rugby scrum-half, screaming American University cries in a piercingly high tenor voice.

At last the ball came down. To Mr. Hodge it seemed a long time before the invention of Sir Isaac Newton finally triumphed. And it was a striking testimony to the mathematical and ballistical skill of the professor that the ball landed with a sharp report upon the top of his head. Thence it leapt up into air a foot or so, cannoned on to Boone's head, and then trickled slowly down the colossal expanse of wicket-keeper's back, bouncing slightly as it reached the massive lower portions. It was only a foot from the ground when Mr. Shakespeare Pollock sprang into the vortex with a last ear-splitting howl of victory and grabbed it off the seat of the wicket-keeper's trousers. The match was a tie. And hardly anyone on the field knew it except Mr. Hodge, the youth in the blue jumper, and Mr. Pollock himself. For the two batsmen and the runner, undaunted the last, had picked themselves up and were bent on completing the single that was to give Fordenden the crown of victory. Unfortunately, dazed with their falls, with excitement, and with the noise, they all three ran for the same wicket, simultaneously realised their error, and all three turned and ran for the other – the blacksmith, ankle and all, in the centre and leading by a yard, so that they looked like pictures of the Russian *troika*. But their effort was in vain, for Mr. Pollock had grabbed the ball and the match was a tie.

And both teams spent the evening at the Three Horseshoes, and Mr. Harcourt made a speech in Italian about the glories of England and afterwards fell asleep in a corner, and Donald got home to Royal Avenue at 1 o'clock in the morning, feeling that he had not learnt very much about the English from his experience of their national game.

A Ballade of Cricket

ANDREW LANG

★ ★ ★

Andrew Lang was a man of letters, born in Selkirk in the Borders in 1844. In a distinguished academic career he became a fellow of Merton College, Oxford, specialising in ritual, myth and totemism. Turning to full-time writing he produced several important works on mythology and folklore. More famously, Lang also wrote the enormously popular Red (and other colours) Fairy Book. *This interest probably influenced his verse on countryside and sporting matters, including several poems on country sports and this amusing mock-heroic one on cricket. Lang evidently played the game with much enjoyment – it is interesting to note how many examples of cricket jargon, like 'skyer' and 'yorker', have remained the same for about 100 years, although a 'bailer' is not a phrase heard much these days.*

★ ★ ★

The burden of hard hitting: slog away!
Here shalt thou make a 'five' and there a 'four',
And then upon thy bat shalt lean, and say,
That thou art in for an uncommon score.
Yea, the loud ring applauding thee shall roar,
And thou to rival THORNTON shalt aspire,
When lo, the Umpire gives thee 'leg before', –
'This is the end of every man's desire!'

The burden of much bowling, when the stay
Of all thy team is 'collared', swift or slower,

When 'bailers' break not in their wonted way,
And 'yorkers' come not off as here-to-fore,
When length balls shoot no more, ah never more,
When all deliveries lose their former fire,
When bats seem broader than the broad barn-door, –
'This is the end of every man's desire!'

The burden of long fielding, when the clay
Clings to thy shoon in sudden shower's downpour,
And running still thou stumblest, or the ray
Of blazing suns doth bite and burn thee sore,
And blind thee till, forgetful of thy lore,
Thou dost most mournfully misjudge a 'skyer',
And lose a match the Fates cannot restore, –
'This is the end of every man's desire!'

ENVOY

Alas, yet liefer on Youth's hither shore
Would I be some poor Player on scant hire,
Than King among the old, who play no more, –
'*This* is the end of every man's desire!'

Benny Lynch –
Scenes from a Short Life

BILL BRYDEN

★ ★ ★

Many of Scotland's sporting icons have feet of clay. Make your own list, beginning with a whole squad of footballers, but never forget the wee men with the big gloves and their capacity for self-destruction.

Bill Bryden, best-known in Scotland for his play Willie Rough, *has chosen as his subject the archetypal figure of flyweight boxer Benny Lynch, world champion and, some would say, born loser. He was the first Scot to hold a world title, in 1935, and he held it again undisputed, from 1937 to 1938. Glasgow-born Lynch won 82 out of 110 bouts during his professional career, but it was marred by weight problems, together with drink to a greater or lesser extent. Adored by the Scottish public, the Lynch story ended in a series of anticlimactic disappointments. Post-war boxers such as Ken Buchanan and Jim Watt were also to hold world titles in happier circumstances. This is a scene from Bryden's gritty 1974 drama about the doomed fighter.*

★ ★ ★

5. BELLE VUE STADIUM,
MANCHESTER: 9 SEPTEMBER 1935

Overhead lights bounce harshly down on to the boxing-ring, make it shine in a dazzle surrounded by blackout. The sound of bagpipes is heard as BENNY *comes through the audience and ducks under the ropes into the ring. With him,* PUGGY MORGAN, *wearing his white polo-neck sweater with 'BENNY LYNCH' written on the front,* JOHNNY KELLY, *similarly dressed, and* NICK CAVALLI, *Italian, dark, in his thirties, with a similar sweater. They have towels, basins, and all the usual props. Cheering accompanies the bagpipes as* BENNY *moves to his corner, where he begins to dance and throw punches as he loosens up.*

The Champion, JACKIE BROWN, *enters, with a similar entourage. He quickly comes through the ropes to his corner opposite* BENNY. *Both boxers prepare. A fanfare of trumpets is given on the Tannoy.*

The MASTER OF CEREMONIES, *in evening dress, with patent-leather shoes and a carnation, comes to the centre of the ring. He pulls a suspended microphone down to his mouth. The microphone is almost big enough to hide his face.*

M.C. Gentlemen. Gentlemen, please! My lords, ladies, and gentle*men*. The main event of the evening. A flyweight contest of fifteen three-minute rounds for the British, European, and World Flyweight Championships! [*Cheering*] . . . Between . . . on my right . . . the challenger from Glasgow . . . the Scottish Flyweight Champion . . . BENNY LYNCH! [*Pandemonium. The crowd is heard singing and chanting:* 'Scotland! *Scot*land aye sae braw!' STOORIE *runs up and places a tartan Tammy on* BENNY'S *head.*] . . . And on my left . . . the British, British Empire, European, and World Flyweight Champion . . . the Manchester Express . . . JACKIE BROWN! [*More cheers*] . . . At the weigh-in today . . . Lynch weighed seven stone thirteen pounds four ounces . . . Brown weighed seven stone twelve pounds ten ounces . . . Your referee is Mr Moss Deyong . . . time-keeper Mr Arthur Timmons . . .

The M.C. *leaves the ring.*
The REFEREE *has entered the ring as his name was called, to the accompaniment of boos from the crowd. He signs for the two boxers to come to the centre. Through the microphone we hear him give them their instructions. The handlers are with the fighters, massaging them, listening.*

REFEREE I want a good clean fight. Break when I say 'Break'. I'll have no hesitation in disqualifying a boxer for a low punch. In the event of a knockdown I want the man on his feet to retire to a neutral corner. You both know the rules. Now shake hands, return to your corners, and when the bell rings, come out fighting . . . and may the best man win! . . .

The boxers touch gloves and return to their corners. PUGGY *takes off* BENNY'S *dressing-gown. He points a finger at* BENNY, *but we cannot hear his instructions.* JOHNNY KELLY *jumps out of the ring.*

TIME-KEEPER Seconds away! Time!
> *The bell rings. Both boxers face each other, dancing.* BENNY *delivers a terrific left hook to the body.* BROWN *steps aside giving a smart right to* BENNY'S *jaw.* BENNY *hangs on.*

REFEREE Break! [*They break . . .* BROWN *attempts another right hook.* BENNY *side-steps and delivers a surprising left hook to* BROWN'S *chin.* BROWN *falls to the canvas.*] One . . . two . . . three . . . [BROWN *gets to his feet. A barrage of blows, lefts and rights, from* BENNY. BROWN *crashes to the canvas again.*] One. . . two. . . three. . . four. . . five . . . six . . . seven . . . eight . . . [BROWN *gets to his feet again. He dances round* BENNY. BENNY *chases him. . . . A left hook to the liver from* BENNY. BROWN *retaliates weakly.* BENNY *scores with a left to the stomach.* BROWN *doubles up like a jack-knife and falls once more to the canvas.*] One . . . two . . . three . . . four . . . five . . . six . . . . [BROWN *is miraculously on his feet again. He scores with a right to* BENNY'S *jaw, but there is no power behind the punch.* BENNY *shakes his head, then wades in two-handed to the body. Pandemonium from the crowd. The bell rings for the end of Round One.* BROWN *staggers to his corner.* BENNY *dances to his.*]

PUGGY *and* JOHNNY *jump into the ring with water, stool, and sponge.* JOHNNY *takes* BENNY'S *gumshield and washes it.*

JOHNNY Miraculous, Benny, miraculous, son! We're goin hame wi the title the-night.
BENNY We'll see.
PUGGY Listen, Benny. He's got a lot o experience. Just don't get big-heided. Right? Take it easy, an' ye'll chin 'im.
JOHNNY Ye've sickent him, Benny. Gie 'im a tuppeny wan, an' we'll be on time for the last train hame.

PUGGY Shut it, Johnny. Remember, he's still the world's champion. . . .

BENNY We'll see. Don't worry.

PUGGY I'll always worry.

TIME-KEEPER Seconds away! Time!

The bell rings. The boxers dance towards each other again.

BROWN *drives* BENNY *back to the ropes with a hail of blows. On the ropes.* BROWN *scores with a beautiful short right to* BENNY'S *jaw.* BENNY *scores with a jabee to the pit of* BROWN'S *stomach.* BROWN *falls back.* BENNY *scores with an overhead chop to the chin.* BROWN *falls to the canvas.*

REFEREE One . . . two . . . three . . . [BROWN *drags himself to his feet.* BENNY *hits out with a vicious left to* BROWN'S *head.* BROWN *falls on to his backside and stares up at the* REFEREE, *bewildered.*] One . . . two . . . three . . . four . . . five . . . six . . . . [BROWN *is on his feet again.* BENNY *is on the attack. Lefts and rights go pounding into* BROWN'S *body. Finally, a right hand, seeming to come all the way from the ground, scores on* BROWN'S *jaw. The* REFEREE *jumps between the boxers to stop the fight just as* BROWN *hits the canvas.* BENNY *jumps up and down in the air in triumph. He runs to his corner and is embraced by* PUGGY MORGAN.]

BENNY I've done it! I've done it! Are ye proud o me, Puggy?

PUGGY I am, Benny. I am! . . .

Pandemonium and singing from the crowd. Above this is heard the M.C.

M.C. The winner . . . and new . . . British, European, and World Flyweight Champion . . . BENNY LYNCH!

BENNY *is borne shoulder-high by* PUGGY *and* JOHNNY KELLY, *as* FATHER FLETCHER, DINGLEY, TIM, STOORIB, HARRY, *and* DR MILLER *and others rush into the ring.* BENNY *waves his gloved hand from above the tumult. There is a towel draped from his shoulder. The scene is punctuated by the photographers' flash-bulbs.* BENNY *waves in triumph.*

Bagpipes. The crowd sings 'He belongs to Glasgow!'. . .

Curtain.

The Bout

from The Big Man

WILLIAM McILVANNEY

★ ★ ★

Hugh McIlvanney, the 'non-pareil' of sports journalism, has an unsurpassed literary facility of making sporting activity come alive. Something of this is shared with his brother William, the novelist, when he gives a fictional dimension to sport, as in The Big Man *(1985), an account of the illegal fight game, set in McIlvanney's familiar Ayrshire landscape. The novel, which was filmed in 1990, shows the hero Dan Scoular caught up in the unsavoury circumstances surrounding a bare-knuckle fight that brings a crisis in his life. This savage scrap provides a wonderful central set-piece to the novel and takes the sport back to its raw and brutal origins.*

★ ★ ★

'Ah'll thank all of yese to hold your positions. Don't crowd in. We have people present who will deal with troublemakers. Trouble is *any* form of interference. Unless ye want to have an unofficial fight yerself – an' ye'll be starting at very long odds – do not, I repeat *not*, either hinder or help any of the two fighters. If ye so much as put yer hand on one of their elbows, that's a serious infringement of the rules. Punishable by punishment. The only people allowed to collect bodies are the corner-men. All right! Remember what ye've been told.'

He held his stop-watch high in the air.

'Ah'm now beginning the countdown to the contest.'

He made an expansive gesture of pressing the button.

'Beginning in thirty seconds from . . . Now!'

'Move a lot,' Matt Mason said.

The advice seemed preposterous to Dan at the time, like 'Try to win'. But it glanced off his mind without effect. He was hearing and seeing with an odd, aberrant clarity. He seemed to be aware of almost everything, of many fragments of the scene around him, and yet somewhere in him choices of what mattered were being made.

'Ten seconds!'

There was a woman with a marvellous face. Her cheeks were gently hollowed as if she were inhaling life with quiet intensity.

'Twenty seconds!'

He would rather have talked to her for half an hour than be doing what he was going to do.

'Twenty-five seconds!'

Yet presumably she wanted him to do this. Hands were pushing him forward. He walked towards the rope. Cutty Dawson was there already, smiling his shield of a smile. They stood within touching distance, awkwardly.

'Prepare! Time!'

Dan was aware of the handkerchief fluttering to the ground. Voices came at them as they circled each other, half-formed incantations that were meant to influence the outcome. Cutty rushed him suddenly, his arms pumping venom at him. Dan moved easily aside and threw a left that, meeting shoulder-bone, fused his own arm solid for a second. Cutty swung on to him at once, tested his stomach with a right, knuckled his head above the temple with a left.

From that first core of contact was spawned a complicated series of movements, a wild progression of punches and counter-punches, blocks, sidesteps and lunges, where chance and purpose fought each other in them. They had entered a labyrinth of possibilities down which they pursued each other, a place where the crowd's understanding couldn't follow them. The onlookers might catch fragments and force them into a shape but only the two men knew how lost they were, caught the sudden swerves of fortune, heard triumph in a grunt, panic in a whimper, convulsed in secret pain, saw fear down the tunnel of an iris.

Part of Dan still felt outside of the event. He was aware of the bystanders around them like a frieze, a clash of colours significantly brighter than he had noticed them to be before the fight. A face would suddenly detach itself in his vision with an etched clarity. Cutty's pale body was blotched where the first punches had hit him, faint, ugly roses. It was as if the tension in which he functioned was the generator that lit up everything around him, putting it under bright lights.

Even the tactical conclusions he was coming to were coldly clear, came to him like ways of approaching an abstract problem. He was struck by how much room there was. This was unlike any fight he had ever been in before, where it had all been about immediacy and speed and tightness of movement and where first advantage was usually final. This was less a battle than a war. It was like the difference he had felt between playing indoor football and playing on a full-sized pitch, where your skills needed to be harnessed to energy and fitness because big distances always stood between them and their realisation.

He was glad of the training he had done, even of Tommy Brogan's fanaticism. Cutty was heavier and slower and the covering of a lot of ground should cost him more than it would cost Dan. But his mind had barely assimilated that idea when a contradictory perception called it in question.

The ground was uneven, catching the foot every so often in a trap, so that fluidity of movement would freeze without warning and you were left for a second longer in a place your reflexes had already abandoned. Twice within a minute, because of the ground, Cutty had found him, once on the head, once on the body, with big punches he had already foreseen and arranged to avoid. The punches were less powerful than they might have been because Cutty, noticing Dan's evasion, had been redirecting them towards where their target should have been. Their glancing impact gave enough hurt to serve as a warning. This place was mined with risks for a fast mover.

But the first one the ground significantly helped was Dan. Trying to turn quickly in pursuit, Cutty found an unevenness that jarred his foot and left him standing square-on. Dan had hit him four times on the head before he went down.

The suddenness of it, the ease with which Cutty collapsed, drew an awed sound from the crowd, one of those reactions by which people create what has happened in preference to observing it. For a second of dazzled elation, Dan admitted the crowd's sense of what was taking place into his own. But it was like introducing a shaft of light into a cave. It hadn't clarified his vision, it had blinded him. Within a moment, Dan knew it was the imbalance that had put Cutty down more than the punches and that the very ease with which he fell had neutralised Dan's impact. Cutty was rising again at once. All that had happened was a chance for a rest.

Dan didn't sit down because he was surprised at how near to being tired he felt, and afraid to give in to the feeling. Matt Mason was saying something about 'a walkover' and Dan ignored him, since they didn't seem to be present at the same event.

In those desperately inhaled seconds, Dan took in knowledge with each breath. How trivial our skills are, he understood. We choose where we deploy our skills and project from that our own sense of ourselves. Then we believe it. How often did the professor dare to live outside his special subject, the politician live in the streets, the poet forgo words? Dan, outside of that confrontation with his father, had never lost a fight in his life. Gifted with literally stunning reflexes, he had fabricated a fake sense of himself. A few minutes of different experience had disproved it. He wasn't who he was supposed to be. He'd better find out who he was.

He was glad he hadn't sat down because there would hardly have been time. The shortness of the rest time made him almost plead for more. He hadn't had long enough to settle his breathing before the referee was shouting, 'Prepare!' He decided he had better not get knocked unconscious or he would never make it back to the line where he now stood with Cutty smiling at him.

'Time!'

He heard someone shouting for him to finish it off and instead of encouraging him the shout angered him because its empty confidence diminished the reality of what was going on. They were still introducing themselves, finding their way past the surface gestures towards a real meeting between force and force at the centre of each. Cutty's strength seemed undiminished and he twice broke past Dan's attempts to parry him. Those were bad moments when Dan found himself struggling not to be overwhelmed. All he could do was try to keep moving and chip at Cutty's strength with a persistence that was already beginning to lose confidence in itself. It was like trying to chop down a tree without being able to hit it twice in the same place.

Cutty had started to talk in the wrestling clinches. 'Ye've no chance, son,' he was saying. 'No chance.' 'Make it easy for yerself.' 'Go down, stay down.' 'Now or later, same thing.'

A troubling realisation had entered Dan's understanding of the fight. Basic talent wasn't going to settle this. He had already brought to bear the skills that had always been enough for him before, the great natural reflexes that could take an opening almost before it was there or leave a thrown blow expended half an inch from his face, the instinctive correctness of punch that fed power every time up from the legs through the body's leverage. He had found out already that he was simply better at this than Cutty was now. But that wasn't going to be enough.

An accident might be enough, coupled with exhaustion. Whichever of them lost his legs first would probably lose everything because the rough ground was full of bad places for tiredness, and fatigue would kill the ability to make fast readjustments and it would be like trying to dance in quicksand. Even as he struggled to hold Cutty's body, greased with sweat, and, failing to throw Cutty off, threw himself off and staggered back, Dan was thinking that this fight would prove nothing that he believed in. They were both caught in it now, heading each other off into a happening it seemed to him they couldn't significantly settle, both obliged to wait till accident or unearned circumstance swatted one or the other down, while the shouts of the crowd refined the meaningless raw material of their contest into the meaning they chose. He sensed the people undulate around the progress of their conflict like protoplasm.

In a despondent panic, Dan poured himself on to Cutty. While his left hand buzzed distractingly around Cutty's head, he hit him three times on the left biceps and, as the arm wilted, chopped down on Cutty's jaw and deposited him on one knee. Cutty threw himself back up but the referee declared the end of a round.

Dan felt like walking on past Mason and Tommy Brogan but they fussed round him with the towel. Mason was complimenting him and Dan's head rejected the praise like counterfeit money. He was angry at everything, the way Tommy Brogan roughed his abraded cheek with the towel, the noise of the crowd like an appetite he was being forced to feed, the remorselessness of the referee's voice. He felt nobody could give him anything that he could take back in there. Mason and Tommy Brogan didn't know what was going on. He despised the crowd that needed their blood like a plasma-bank. He felt anger against Cutty for taking part in this.

He had hit Cutty the moment after the word 'Time!' was heard, and unloaded his banked rage in a cumulative fury of punches. Cutty stumbled back and fell.

Matt Mason interpreted the shouts for him. 'That was the turning-point, big man.' Dan was afraid he was right. Cutty had been on his feet again before his handlers could get to him. Dan felt more exhausted by his attack than Cutty seemed to be. He didn't know where he was supposed to go from here. That line was somewhere he never wanted to go back to. He had done as much as he could do. Wasn't that enough? He wanted to stay on this canvas seat for ever.

'Time!' was a command to go to a place he had never been before but Cutty seemed familiar with it.

Dan was listening for the voices of the crowd to lead him. They suggested, he imagined, that he was winning but he couldn't believe that from the inside. He wondered if they were still seeing the previous round.

Pain had found its way past the anaesthesia of tension and every punch seemed to bring the aches from all the earlier punches out in chorus. He felt as if he was discovering for the first time the reality of violence. He seemed pitted against a force that was just naturally greater than his. There are no fair fights, it occurred to him. He heard the voices draw on his spilled blood. As he began to founder, he knew something with certainty and yet knew that his knowledge was discredited because of where it came from, because it would be seen as the excuse of a loser. And he was losing, he was certain. He knew he was giving as much as Cutty, the same in his own terms, that what was being demonstrated here wasn't the superiority of one but the similarity of both, that they were expressing something jointly, not individually. The voices lied. What was there was as much as anybody could offer, was the same gift whoever made it. The voices lied, but he had accepted them and he was caught in them now.

He had to move back and he could find no further to go, in the field or in himself. He knew nothing but hurt coming at him. He thought every noise, every shout, the crowd, the whole day was attacking and the world was just vendettas against him. He hated them all. He hated them all and found there in the sheerness of his hate a hardness that defiantly didn't want to yield, clenched fist of his rage, marrow of his will. He found some small, last seed of himself still needing to flower. He must let it be fulfilled but he was stunned and stumbling. His feet groped along a maze of edges, trying to find footholds in air, until he stepped off suddenly into blackness.

Weights pressed against him at various parts and he felt himself tilt and plane awkwardly, find different angles in air. He couldn't tell himself upright or not, what position he held. The darkness was spiral. There was sound.

'Twenty seconds.'

'Twenty-five seconds.'

His mind held the voice like a rope to pull him out of the pit.

'Prepare.'

And he burst into dizzying light. The day was in pieces. Pressure was pushing his body out of shape towards somewhere. His knees couldn't hold. Ground bobbled, trees spun, the sky slowly turning.

'Time!'

He was moving. But he had surfaced again into pain, volleyed forces.

'Bedtime, son,' Cutty was saying.

'Only a matter of time.'

'No chance.'

The voice helped him. It was an assumption about what he was and he was determined not to allow that. Its glibness located the last of his anger. The anger came because he felt Cutty betraying both of them, aligning himself with the lie that was the crowd's sense of what had been happening. However this ended, Dan had fought honestly to the limits of himself. Nobody was going to take that from him. This fight wasn't over yet because he felt as if he had just discovered what he was fighting. He knew that stony certainty, had heard it since childhood from so many other voices. It came from the same place as Cutty's smile, it was an echo of all those corner-standers who had peopled his boyhood. It was the voice that had spoken inside himself for years. And he knew now that he didn't agree with it. It spoke as if it knew the truth and it was hiding the truth. It overruled those who couldn't meet the terms it demanded. In declaring its own strength it trampled on the weakness of others.

Trying to focus on the fragmentary images of Cutty that felt as if they were coming at him from every angle, Dan seemed to himself to be fighting all those working-class hardmen who had formed the pantheon of his youth, men who in thinking they defied the injustice of their lives had been acquiescing in it because they compounded the injustice by unloading their weakness on to someone else, making him carry it. Dan's past self was among them. So was his father on the back green. Like an argument Dan was still involved in, his father's voice came from somewhere: 'Whit is it you believe in, boay?' As he stumbled about the field, being flayed of his arrogance, he was looking for an answer.

He tried to rally against Cutty. He couldn't, but as he felt himself stagger and fall again, even as he pitched sickeningly on to the ground with a jolt that threatened to bring his bones out through the skin, a part of his mind hung on to consciousness like a cliff-edge bush it wasn't sure would hold, and he was already struggling to rise when Matt Mason and Tommy Brogan forced him and half-carried him to the canvas seat.

Their voices were talking to themselves. Dan sat staring at Cutty while the referee counted off the time and the sounds of the crowd were like translations of what was happening into different languages. Dan felt a terrible coldness spreading through his mind, an ice killing off everything but the most basic thought, the crudest life-forms. He was waiting to see what survived to take with him when he rose. Suddenly his own voice came to him from the past, something he had once said, he couldn't remember where. 'Living's the only game in town and it's fucking crooked.' Thinking that now, he felt the prodigious strength of despair. The whole thing was unbearable. To bear it he wanted his wife and his family. He must have them. To have them, he must win.

'Time!'

As Cutty crowded him again at once, Dan's bleak decision that he must win stayed with him and the fixity of his will revealed to him at last the way he might do it. He heard, as if in a time-lock, Tommy Brogan saying something that mattered, as he sat on the canvas seat. His mind, while Cutty buffeted his body, was crouched patiently, waiting for the remark to come back. It was something Tommy Brogan had been saying since the beginning and Dan had been too tense to register it.

'His right eye. It's dead. That's what finished him wi' boxing.'

Dan understood suddenly what he had noticed throughout the fight. He hadn't missed Cutty with a left hand. Working on that, he began slowly to reassert himself and he knew what was going to happen. His will envisioned his victory and moved his body towards it.

He would do nothing but try to keep moving and hit Cutty there. Purpose gave him energy. He would make that dismissive voice stop talking, admit its weakness in silence. He would punch the bastard blind. He was galvanised with venom. He swung weight remorselessly from both shoulders into Cutty's eyes, drawing renewed strength from the juddering impact of his blows. He felt him go back and let himself be towed by the staggering bulk and, when the arms dropped, battered his face till he shuddered on to the ground.

Dan moved back and stood at the line, having held up his hand to warn off Matt Mason and Tommy Brogan. He wanted to waste no energy. He fed on the voices now. The line he stood at was some final marker of himself. He watched as they worked frantically on Cutty, throwing water on his face and standing him up and getting him to the line as time was called.

Dan stood and watched the handkerchief fall.

Cutty raised his hands by instinct. His beaten body sagged softly, looked unnatural, hardly like human flesh, more like a mollusc with its shell ripped off. His head moved, blind as a worm.

Dan felt only a rush of instinct, had tapped a force in himself that roared to fill his body, a dark greed of triumph that took him and Cutty to it like a chameleon's tongue. Dan looked down the maw of another man's exhaustion, saw a future. Cutty's weakness was a feast he wanted. His fists fed on it as if enough wasn't possible, wouldn't be satisfied till Cutty could give him no more, and he fell as hollow as rind, discarded waste of Dan Scoular's need.

The moment held its awe. Something was seen that held its watchers still, a black truth they had shared, a presence come that couldn't be denied, and seconds passed in utter silence while they endured its passing out of them. And in those seconds, just in seconds, banality came back to cover their naked awareness in the decency of facts.

A man was lying unconscious, the wind making a waving frond of his hair. His body lay in mud. The mud was all that was left of their intricacy and energy of movement, the infinite patterns that their feet had made, the courage of their efforts. Another one stood alone on the line. His face was cut and bleeding. He was leaning into the wind, eating chunks of the air.

Cutty was carried back to his canvas seat. Dan Scoular was alone at the line, crouched over the void his desperation had brought him to. The crowd was almost silent. Nobody approached him. He hung there wasted with effort, as dead to the meaning of what might have happened as Cutty Dawson was. Bleak emptiness was in his mind. The referee's voice was meaningless. A white handkerchief drifted to the ground aimlessly.

The cheering tugged him slowly erect, pulled him away from an unbearable place. His eyes, blind from the pit of where he had been, reached determinedly towards focus. People were waving and moving towards him. Faces bobbed like lights through the darkness, showing him the human ordinariness of the place where he was. The wind was the wind, the grass was the grass, Cutty Dawson was beaten. But glancing down at himself, Dan saw his own body blotched bizarrely as if he wore the map of a strange place.

And in seconds – it only took seconds – he was standing solidly inside himself again, letting the voices and faces tell him what had happened. This had been a hard fight but he was the winner. This hadn't been so bad. His smile answered the shouts of the crowd, so strongly, so clearly, it seemed as if no great distance had lain between them. He raised his right hand in the air, made a whinny of triumph.

The crowd broke towards him. He was their man, meant something they wanted to believe in. As he turned, Matt Mason was with them. He embraced Dan like a brother and they danced, tugging as if a lost member of the family had at last come home.

Erchie Suffers a Sea Change

from Erchie My Droll Friend

NEIL MUNRO

★ ★ ★

This story is taken from 'Erchie My Droll Friend', a new collection of the famous Glasgow stories about the kirk beadle and waiter, and regular 'character'. The stories originally appeared in Munro's regular column in the Glasgow Evening News *and they have a tremendous immediacy because they relate to contemporary events – this one appeared on 1 June 1903. So Erchie is invariably well up with the news – here he tackles what we would call now the celebrity sport of yachting. Munro wrote this at a time when Sir Thomas Lipton was the centre of 'media' attention and at the same time was generating a considerable amount of self-publicity.*

Thomas Johnstone Lipton (1850–1931), born in humble circumstances in Crown Street, Glasgow, established a chain of food stores through an original and dynamic approach to food retailing – he made his first million by the age of thirty. He spent a fortune on ultimately unsuccessful attempts to win back the America's Cup from the United States with a series of yachts called, in tribute to his Irish origins, Shamrock. *He was knighted in 1898 and in 1902 made a baronet by King Edward VII, another keen yachtsman.*

★ ★ ★

'I'm feelin' fine,' said Erchie to me on Saturday night. He came up the street with a peculiar travesty of a sailor's walk, rolling as men do after a protracted exercise of their 'sea legs'. He laughed slyly, and made a comical attempt to imitate the stage jack-tar's manner

73

of 'hitching up his slacks'. 'Dae ye see that?' he asked. 'Erchie MacPherson, A.B. the good ship Jinnet Grant, A1 at Lloyd's; no smokin' abaft the brig; all passengers on the efter deck pay cabin fare!' And he chuckled again.

'What's in the wind, Erchie?' I asked.

'Man! need ye ask?' said he. 'Shairly ye never read the papers. There's been naething in them a' this week past but Lipton's yats. Naebody needs to gang to the coast this summer; a' they need to dae's to bide at hame in bonny wee Gleska and spend their bawbees on newspapers. Deevil the hate else is in them but Sir Tummas and his yats. I get fair sun-burned readin' them; if I had a neif-fu' o' wulks and my feet in a byne o' saut watter, I wad think I was at Rothesay a' the time. Naethin' in the papers but yats – 'The challenger in Gourock Bay'; '*Shamrock* dirty bate on a run to windward'; 'the Lipton fleet preparin' to start'; 'Sir Tummas mak's three speeches and says he'll bring back the cup or never smile again.' Naethin' in the papers but yats; I havena seen a guid wife-beatin' case since *Shamrock III* was lenched. Whit Erchie MacPherson disna ken noo aboot yattin' and ships and sails and port-the-helms and things is no' worth kennin'. The first half-croon I ha'e to spare I'm gaun to buy a cheese-cutter kep.

'It's terrible the dangers o' the deep! When I read aboot the gallant fellows strugglin' oot yonder aff the Gantocks in a twa-knot breeze, and the puir sowls as dry's onything, and the accidents that happened to them, I get fair sea-sick. They hadna their new mainsail a day till it was bent, and naething they could dae tae't wad straighten't oot again. Every noo and then they were breakin' oot their jib top-sail or daein' somethin' o' that sort; it must ha'e been awfu' chawin'. But Sir Tummas never lost he'rt. "It's a' richt, boys," says he; "I'm wan o' yersel's, I'm jist the same as I used to be afore I made my money. If we bend a' the sails ever was sewed, or break the backs o' them, we'll bring back the cup." A wunnerfu' man Sir Tummas! I ken him fine; him and oor Rubbert's aboot an age. I was waitin'' at a dinner he got the ither day in Greenock, and I took the chance when haundin' him the ceegaurs to wish him luck. "Thank ye, Erchie," says he, "I'm prood to see ye. Hoo's Jinnet?"

"Oh, she's no' complainin, Sir Tummas," says I. "She aye gets her tea in your shop; the rale Ceylon – nane o' their foreign trash." "Ah! ye're weel aff to be the wye ye are," says he. "I never had better health than when I had my brattie on and was busy workin'. This sport's an awfu' harassin' thing; the eyes o' the warld's on me, and, forbye, I ha'e to keep mind o' the names o' the sails and ropes and things; ye ha'e nae idea whit a job it is. Never you tak' to the yattin', Erchie." "Nae fears o' that," says I; "My feet's ower flet, forbye, it taks a lot o' siller to keep it up." "It does that, Erchie," says he, and he slips a shillin' and an aluminium rivet aff the *Shamrock* in my haund.

'A yat a year is Lipton's motto. He's fair hotchin' wi' yats; they're stickin' to his feet. When he's lyin' aff Gourock yonder the *Columba* and the *Lord o' the Isles* canna get awa' frae the quay till they pick a dizzen or twa o' Lipton's yats aff their paiddle-wheels or propellers. Sir Tummas canna mind the names o' half o' them; he buys yats by the gross, the wye oor Jinnet buys her claes-pins, or the wye he used to buy the Irish eggs afore he was a company. If yats could win the America Cup it wad ha'e been here lang syne. "Whit sort o' a cup will it be dae ye ken?" Jinnet asks me. "It maun be awfu' fancy when there's sae much fracaw aboot it. Dae ye think it'll be a wally yin?" "It's mair nor I can tell," I said to her. "It's maybe pewther, and hauds an awfu' lot. It's cost a bonny penny to Sir Tummas, onywye." "I think," says Jinnet, "he wad be better for to gi'e the money to the puir." "And whit wad the puir ha'e to hurrah at then, wumman?" I asks her. "It's easy seen ye havena studied human nature. Lipton's keepin' the Americans in mind that there's a place ca'd Britain on the map o' Europe; they're that throng ower yonder makin' boots and nocks, and tinnin' salmon and corned beef, that they wad clean forget a aboot us if it wasna for the *Shamrocks*. "Lord! here's yon chap again," they say when they see him sailing ower. "Whaur in the warld does he come frae?" Then they scoor up yin o' their auld yats, or tack thegither a new yin, and hide the cup up the lum in case he gets a haud o't. The friendly rivalry o' nations – that's whit it leads to," says I; "at least, that's whit they ca' it in the papers." "Dod! dae ye tell me?" says Jinnet.

'Her and me gaed doon on Thursday to see the yats gang aff. It was a grand day; the only thing that vexed me was that I hadna a doo-lichter bunnet. Every man ye saw at Gourock Quay had bell-moothed troosers and an awfu' smell o' tar. The bay was jammed wi' Lipton's boats. The *Erin* lay among them as big as a man-o'war, and a brass baun' frae Greenock did the best it could at blawin' on the quay when the polis wasna lookin'. 'Whatna steam yat's that?' asked Jinnet. "That's the *Erin*," I telt her, "Sir Tummass's floatin' palace home." She got an awfu' start, puir body. "Gae awa' wi' ye, Erchie!" she tells me, "it has only ae lum, and the *Galatea* has twa." "Believe't or no'," I assured her, "that's the *Erin*; she has a silver keel, and the common sailors in her get their tea in their beds afore they rise in the mornin'." "She's awfu' white," says Jinnet. "Of coorse!" says I; "white's a' the go for yats noo." "Dod! it maun tak' a lot o' pipe-clye to gang ower them a'," says Jinnet. Noo and then Sir Tummas he wad come on deck and gi'e a keek to see if naebody was lookin', for he wanted to slip awa' as quate as possible, and every time the Greenock baund saw him it played anither Irish tune as nice as onything. He was sair vexed to see croods and croods come poorin' aff the Gleska trains, and says "Tut! tut! it's an awfu' thing a man canny dae onything withoot folk glowerin' at him; I wish I had gaun awa' through the nicht; I'll ha'e to mind and dae that next time." A grand day! A' the wee boys plunked the schule, and a' the yats frae Rothesay and Hunter's Quay, as weel as frae Mudhook and Corinthia and them places that's no' in the maps, came puffin' up and got nearly run ower by the skoosh steamer, the *King Edward*. "He maun be a prood man this day," says Jinnet. "He is that," says I.

'When the quay was crooded that thick the folk were hingin' on by their tae nails, and Sir Tummas saw there was no chance o' their gaun awa', he threw aff a' disguise and ordered the yats to start. Cannons begood to bang, and every boat that had a steam whistle put a trained musician to the playin' o't till they nearly burst yer lugs. The twa *Shamrocks* were dragged past the quays that close that even the folk wi' the third-class tickets could get a fine view o' Sir Tummas and his gallant men. He stood on the deck o' *Shamrock III*, tryin' hard no' to greet at the sicht o' his country's devotion. His kep was in his haund, and he was lookin' as spruce as onything. "Ye're no' a bad sort," says I to mysel'; "I mind fine o' ye in Stockwell." It was an occasion for a speech as the yat slipped past the quay and anither special train from Gleska came in; Sir Tummas raised his haund and I daursay he micht ha'e found something new to say aboot the cup, but the Greenock baund thocht it was a signal, and begood to play, 'Will ye no' come back again?' while the sailors on the *Shamrock III* started to gie their patent a'thegither-yin-twa-three yell. Wan by wan the Lipton fleet poored oot o' the bay, and though it wisna near the 'oor for't, the tide begood to turn As faur as the eye could see there was naethin' but Lipton's yats. Flags wagged frae every hoose to let furnished, wi' attendance in Gourock, every auld retired captain wi' a pension in the place let aff a cannon and the coastgaird let aff twa, no' ha'ein' to pay for the poother themsel's.

'At aboot Lamlash Sir Tummas, on the *Erin*, her wi' the silver keel, got a' his fleet aboot him and bade his challenger God-speed. It was a movin' spectacle. "Boys!" he says, and his voice jist clean choked wi' emotion. "Boys! the 'oor has come when ye ha'e to set oot across the heavin' billow in quest o' the cup. Afore ye go I wad like to mention whit I never tauld anither leevin' sowl afore – that we ha'e a fine boat in oor new yat, that Mister Fyfe did the best he could, that I did the best I could, that Wringe did the best he could, and that I'm confident we'll bring back the cup. Whither we dae or no', my motto is to please; mind and be good lads, and no' gie back-chat to the Yankees. Mind the eyes o' the world's on ye. They're on mysel' too, but I'm used to't, and it disna put me aboot. My last word to ye is – Bring Back the Cup!" Havin' said that, he ordered every man a special tot o' rum, and then broke doon, so that he had to be taken back to Gourock on a tug steamer.'

The Tam o' Shanter Jug

from Rhyme in Fun

JAMES HEMPSTEAD

★ ★ ★

James Hempstead is a Burnsian of some note, having published three books about the poet. He is well known in many parts of Scotland for this and for his comic verses (his collection Rhyme for Fun*), from which this humorous tale about the game of bowls is taken. The characters are for the most part Dumbarton worthies, but surely would be recognisable to people from other airts. The verse is in rhyming couplets, like Burns's wonderful 'Tam o' Shanter' itself, and this drives on the narrative with great vim and vigour.*

★ ★ ★

A booler ye can always tell,
Wi' badges pinned doon each lapel,
Like campaign medals they proclaim
The competitions he's won at hame.
And others on some foreign green,
Twixt Garelochhead and Aberdeen;
While special badges represent
Life member and ex-president.

John Dow is of this happy breed,
And a' his cronies are agreed
That few could match or e'er compare,
Wi' this booler extraordinaire.
He's played the bools for forty years,

On many a cup his name appears,
Collected badges by the score –
Big Ernie Johnson's not got more!
Even Liz invited him along
To her but an' ben to get a gong;
His front room mantelpiece at hame
Is decked wi' trophies o' the game,
Which gudewife Pat dusts ower wi' care
And polishes a' his silverware.

There's a rumour and nae doubt it's true
(I heard it in the Post Office queue);
To put his badges a' on show,
John bought two blazers oot the Co,
Baith ready made wi' broad lapels –
A style in which the Co excels;
Sae monie badges have ne'er been seen
Even on the breast o' Idi Amin!

There was ae trophy John had won,
Nae ither like it neath the sun;
No' made o' silver, bronze or gold,
But fashioned in some potter's mould
It is the Tam o' Shanter Jug,
A sort of large haun-painted mug,
A souvenir o' Burns's tale,
Bought at a Boy Scout jumble sale,
Depicting Tam wi' nose cerise –
No' meant for onie mantelpiece!

Each year this wally jug's the prize,
In a game the Burns Club organise,
Played on one o' thae twa Big Greens,
'Mang rookies, hopefuls an' auld has-beens,
And I'm sure it comes as nae surprise

To learn that John has won this prize,
Nae less than four times on the trot,
And seven times since the jug was bought.
But to tell the truth and shame the Deil,
A fact that naething can conceal,
This annual Burns Club competition
Provides nae serious opposition –
Nae boolers wi' lang pedigree
Amang the Burns Club Committee.

Successful moments in our life
Are often dampened by the wife,
Just when we're feeling o'er the moon,
They leave us like a burst balloon –
And so it was wi' John and Pat,
His triumph on the green fell flat.
When Pat first saw the Shanter Jug,
She put a flea in Johnnie's lug;
She couldnae quite believe her eyes
That this jug was a boolin' prize,
'Oh John', she cried, 'For pity's sake,
I'd rather hae a sirloin steak!
But on one thing my mind is clear,
That ugly thing's no' stayin' here,
It reminds me o' that poor wife Kate,
Wed to that drunken reprobate.'
Wee wifie Pat, the lass frae Wales,
Fair took the wind oot Johnnie's sails;
John, aye a man to keep the peace,
Took Tam doon aff the mantelpiece!

Each year he won he had to shut
The jug inside the garden hut,
Completely hidden there it lay
And never saw the light o' day,

Except upon a night in June,
When a' the members gathered roon,
To see if John retained the jug,
Or lost it to some ither mug.

For the competition in ninety-three,
The Burns Committee did agree,
If Dow again the board should sweep,
He'd get the bluidy thing to keep;
Moir Nelson felt the Club had hit
On the best way to get rid of it!
But Hutton said the Club should seek
Someone to stop Dow's winning streak,
Bill Hendry was the one he thought
Could match John Dow and stop the rot,
Apart from spouting' Rabbie's rhymes,
He'd been champion of the Rock four times
And though his skill's not now the same,
He'd maybe chaff John aff his game.

So Bill agreed to meet John Dow,
And there and then he made a vow,
'This "Big Green" booler I will tame,
Or William Hendry's not my name.'
Mad keen to gie the Dow a fright,
He was seen oot trainin' ev'ry night –
Twice roon the Common wi' the wife,
And a dram to bring him back to life!
Like the Renton team of eighty three,
She fed him up on chicken bree,
But her preparations met a hitch,
She found her diet was too rich –
Bill's pulse went up to ninety-five,
And his hormones were in overdrive.

At length the contest date cam' roon,
It fell upon a night in June –
Dumbartonians of every rank
Were lined three deep roon every bank;
The scene was like an annual fair,
The press and VIPs were there –
Wee Pat O'Neill wi' his Provost's chain,
Led a District Cooncil train . . .

'Fore Bill took up his boolin' station,
They rubbed him doon wi' embrocation,
And fortified wi' a good stiff hauf,
To loosen up his smoker's cough.
He shed his heavy Damart drawers
And went like sodger to the wars.

When the players cam oot the Clubhouse door
The crowd let oot a mighty roar;
John Cairns, who heard it in Church Lane,
Thought the ceilin' had come doon again!
Bill wore a McLaren tartan bunnet,
Wi' a muckle scarlet toorie on it,
But Dow was far more circumspeck,
Wi' the Big Green tie aroon his neck,
Whites as white as they could be
Befitting for an M.B.E.

Bill won the toss and set the jack,
And right away went on the attack
Nae aches or pains or feelin' tired,
He was playin' like a man inspired.
By the time the twelfth end came in sight,
John knew that he would have to fight,
For Bill was playin' oot his skin.

Determined he was gaun to win –
His weight was perfect and his grass,
Even David Bryant could not surpass.
But Johnnie Dow was naebody's fool,
He kept the heid and played it cool,
And gradually his craft and skill
Could match the very best o' Bill.

Oh had Rabbie Burns been there that night,
What matchless verses he could write,
To tell what brilliant shots were played,
What boolin' history there was made,
To pour oot his poetic skill,
Immortalising John and Bill;
For sic a match has ne'er been seen
Upon Dumbarton's Boolin' Green!

At length the scoreboard on the wall,
Showed that the game was twenty all –
One end to play, it would decide
If the Shanter Jug was gaun to hide
Another year in a garden shed
Or sit by 'Rabbie' Hendry's bed.

The crowd was hushed, the air was tense
Would Bill break through John's dour defence?,
Wi' his last bool he trailed the jack
To where his bools lay at the back;
John didnae need to ask the score –
He kent that Bill was lyin' four!
But he had still one bool to play,
Could he draw the shot and save the day?

Or should he now the game concede –
It was decision time indeed!

Pat's words kept ringing in his ear –
'Don't bring that ugly jug back here!'

He stood a long time on the mat,
Still haunted by those words of Pat.
But Johnnie's pride withstood the test,
He couldnae grant wee Pat's request,
At twenty all it wasnae right,
He should gie up without a fight;
He played the bool – it came up wide,
Glanced aff another and went inside,
Got another wick then found the track
And finished up against the jack.
As Johnnie gied two victory hops,
Bill's eyes stood oot like organ stops,
He muttered as he gazed in wonder,
'Ye cannae fart against sic thunder'.

The sequel to this brilliant game
Unfolded soon as John got hame;
What passed that night 'tween John and Pat,
I think we'll draw a veil o'er that;
Suffice to say, to end this tale –
The Tam o'Shanter Jug's for sale.
All offers should be sent in now,
Addressed to booler Johnnie Dow!

Home Thoughts from Abroad

JOHN BUCHAN

★ ★ ★

When simmer brings the lang bricht e'en,
I'll daunder doun to the bowling-green.

John Buchan's interest in writing about sport and games is explored more
fully elsewhere in this anthology, but on this occasion a poem has been
selected which is more subtle and has to do with gentler recreation and the
contentment it brings. The sporting reference, a brief but pleasant one to a
bowling-green, comes late in the poem, and perfectly captures the
sedentary ease traditionally associated with the game of bowls (although
Scots like Richard Corsie from the bowling heartland of Ayrshire have
done much to give the game a more thrusting and professional image in
recent years).

★ ★ ★

Aifter the war, says the papers, they'll no be content at hame,
The lads that hae feucht wi' death two 'ear i' the mud and the
rain and the snaw;
For aifter a sodger's life the shop will be unco tame;
They'll ettle at fortune and freedom in the new lands far awa'.

No me!
By God! No me!
Aince we hae lickit oor faes
And aince I get oot o' this hell,
For the rest o' my leevin days

I'll mak a pet o' mysel'.
I'll haste me back wi' an eident fit   eager
And settle again in the same auld bit.
And oh! the comfort to snowk again   snuff
The reek o' my mither's but-and-ben,
The wee box-bed and the ingle neuk
And the kail-pot hung frae the chimley-neuk!
I'll gang back to the shop like a laddie to play,
Tak doun the shutters at skreigh o' day, break
And weigh oot floor wi' a carefu' pride,
And hear the clash o' the countraside. gossip
I'll wear for ordinar' a roond hard hat,
A collar and dicky and black cravat.
If the weather's wat I'll no stir ootbye
Wi'oot an umbrella to keep me dry.
I think I'd better no tak a wife –
I've had a' the adventure I want in life. –
But at nicht, when the doors are steeked, I'll sit,
While the bleeze loups high frae the aiken ruit,
And smoke my pipe aside the crook,   pot-hook
And read in some douce auld-farrant book; old-fashioned
Or crack wi' Davie and mix a rummer,
While the auld wife's pow nid-nods in slum'er;
And hark to the winds gaun tearin' bye
And thank the Lord I'm sae warm and dry.
When simmer brings the lang bricht e'en,
I'll daunder doun to the bowling-green,
Or delve my yaird and my roses tend
For the big floo'er-show in the next back-end. autumn
Whiles, when the sun blinks aifter rain,
I'll tak my rod and gang up the glen;
Me and Davie, we ken the püles
Whaur the troot grow great in the howes o' the hills;
And, wanderin' back when the gloamin' fa's
And the midges dance in the hazel shaws,

We'll stop at the yett ayont the hicht
And drink great wauchts o' the scented nicht,
While the hoose lamps kin'le raw by raw
And a yellow star hings ower the law.
Davie will lauch like a wean at a fair
And nip my airm to mak certain shüre
That we're back frae yon place o' dule and dreid,
To oor ain kind warld –

> *But Davie's deid!*
> *Nae mair gude nor ill can betide him.*
> *We happit him doun by Beaumont toun,*
> *And the half o' my hert's in the mools aside him.*   mould

The Bonnie Earl of Murray

ANONYMOUS

★ ★ ★

Whole books have been written about this popular ballad, and much effort expended in an attempt to identify the exact circumstances of the affair involving 'the Earl' and 'the Queen' that is hinted at. There are echoes perhaps of Lancelot and Guinevere and the playboy earl or 'braw gallant' undoubtedly has a tremendous air of romanticism. There seem to be three references to sports or games: riding 'at the ring' is probably practice at jousting or tilting; playing 'at the glove' is clearly falconry; on the other hand, playing 'at the ba' could be real tennis, golf, football or just about any ball game.

★ ★ ★

Ye Highlands, and ye Lawlands,
O where have you been?
They have slain the Earl of Murray,
And layd him on the green.

'Now wae be to thee, Huntly!
And wherefore did you sae?
I bade you bring him wi' you,
But forbade you him to slay.'

He was a braw gallant,
And he rid at the ring;
And the bonny Earl of Murray,
O he might have been a king!

He was a braw gallant,
And he play'd at the ba;
And the bonny Earl of Murray
Was the flower amang them a'.

He was a braw gallant,
And he play'd at the glove;
And the bonny Earl of Murray,
O he was the Queen's true-love!

O lang will his Lady
Look o'er the Castle Doune,
Ere she see the Earl of Murray
Come sounding thro' the toon!

2

THE ROYAL AND ANCIENT GAME

Introduction

★ ★ ★

Golf is arguably Scotland's greatest sporting gift to the world. The fact that the game may have actually originated in the Netherlands and probably came to Scotland along with pantiles and law degrees is a mere quibble. Scotland is the home of golf. The advertisements say so, and advertisers never lie.

Certainly the game was well established here by 1458 when a statute against it and that other unprofitable sport of football was introduced in the rather vain hope of diverting the nation's energies into archery. Nevertheless, the game survived such attacks and has flourished. It has, notably, been played by all classes in this country, in curious contrast to the symbol of wealth and privilege which it has become in every other country to which it has been transported. Robert Burns, the ploughman poet, isn't known as a golfer, nor indeed a sportsman of any sort, but in *Epistle to Davie* he seems to make reference to the common view of the game as subject to fickle fortune, almost in the manner of a clubhouse raconteur:

> The honest heart that's free frae a'
> Intended fraud or guile,
> However Fortune kick the ba',
> Has aye some cause to smile

Some years before, the Renton-born father of the English novel, Tobias Smollett, had also described the exceptionally democratic reputation of golf, in *Humphry Clinker:*

> Hard by, in the fields called the Links, the citizens of Edinburgh divert themselves at a game called golf, in which they use a curious kind of bat, tipt with horn, and small elastic balls of leather, stuffed with feathers, rather less than tennis balls, but of a much harder consistence – this they strike with such force and dexterity from one hole to another, that they will fly to an incredible distance. Of this diversion the Scots are so fond, that when the weather will permit, you may see a multitude of all ranks, from the senator of justice to the lowest tradesman, mingled together in their shirts, and following the balls with the utmost eagerness.

Despite this long history not every Scot has an unalloyed delight in the game – 'a good walk spoiled' represents one common view, and the novelist Eric Linklater observed of the game that 'All I've got against it is that it takes you so far from the clubhouse.' Linklater did appear to welcome the company of golfers, at least at the nineteenth hole. Not every Scottish writer has been so tolerant. John Buchan, in *The Three Hostages,* opens the novel with his Scots-South African hero Richard Hannay in a suburban train listening to golf talk:

> The talk in the compartment was now of golf. Matches were being fixed up for the following Sunday. My *vis-à-vis* had evidently some repute as a golfer, and was describing how he had managed to lower his handicap. Golf 'shop' is to me the most dismal thing on earth, and I shut my ears to it. 'So I took my mashie, you know, my *little* mashie' – the words seemed to have all the stuffiness of which Lombard had complained.

Dr John Strang, in his *Glasgow and its clubs* records that:

> The game of golf is one of the oldest amusements in Scotland,

and is still in great favour in Edinburgh and St Andrews. In Glasgow it was long a favourite pastime, and continued to be so till the improvements on the Public Green took away all the hazards, without which there is no play.

It is interesting to note that Strang, writing at the beginning of the nineteenth century, clearly viewed golf as an old amusement but one then largely confined to Edinburgh and St Andrews.

Of course Strang was wrong to talk of golf as an amusement. Whatever it is, the word 'amusement' seems inadequate. The Victorian essayist, poet and critic, Andrew Lang (some of whose delightful verse about golf appears in this chapter), had no doubt about the centrality of golf to Scotland: 'Golf is a thoroughly national game; it is as Scotch as haggis, cockie-leekie, high cheekbones or rowanberry jam.' The Scotch-American steel magnate and philanthropist Andrew Carnegie, who had taken up the game at the age of sixty-three, left $200,000 to Yale to enable that university to build a golf-course, observing that 'Golf is an indispensable adjunct to high civilisation.' Carnegie even wrote an article, 'Dr Golf', praising the game as the best physical therapy in the world.

Carnegie's view was in line with much learned opinion – the Rev. James Wemyss, Minister of Burntisland in Carnegie's native Fife, writing in the *Old Statistical Account* in the 1790s observed:

> To those who are fond of the healthful and manly diversion of the golf, there is adjoining, one of the finest pieces of links, of its size, in Scotland. A great part of it is like velvet, with all the variety of hazards, necessary to employ the different clubs, used by the nicest players. A golfing club was instituted lately, by the gentlemen of the town and neighbourhood.

A more open-minded view of the 'healthful' properties of the game of golf is given by Jerry Melford in Smollett's *Humphry Clinker*. He writes to a friend in England from Edinburgh, indicating that the 'nineteenth hole' could involve the very best of wines:

Among others, I was shewn one particular set of golfers, the youngest of whom was turned of fourscore – they were all gentlemen of independent fortunes, who had amused them- selves with this pastime for the best part of a century, without having ever felt the least alarm from sickness or disgust; and they never went to bed, without having each the best part of a gallon of claret in his belly.

There has always been a strong clerical interest in 'the golf' and that leading eighteenth-century Scottish minister, Alexander 'Jupiter' Carlyle of Inveresk, waxed eloquent on the game when he came to write of his parish for the *Statistical Account*.

The golf, so long a favourite and peculiar exercise of the Scots, is much in use here. Children are trained to it in their early days, being enticed by the beauty of the links, (which lie on each side of the river between the two towns and the sea), and excited by the example of their parents. To preserve the taste for this ancient diversion, a company of gentlemen, about 18 years ago, purchased a silver cup, which is played for annually in the month of April, and is for a year in the possession of the victor, who is obliged to append a medal to it, when he restores it to the company. The inhabitants of Musselburgh had need to watch over this precious field for health and exercise, lest in some unlucky period the magistrates and council should be induced to feu it out, on pretence of increasing the revenue of the town.

If Robert Marshall, the author of the classic golf novella *The Haunted Major*, is to be believed, no less a cleric than Cardinal David Beaton (disguised as 'Cardinal Smeaton') was a devotee of the game, and intervenes to assist the Major in his needle-match on the sacred links of St Magnus (St Andrews). All this religious involvement in the game perhaps does account for the sacerdotal atmosphere of the game and such sacred sites as St Andrews, Turnberry, Gleneagles, Carnoustie and the pilgrim trail of the Lothian coast.

H.V. Morton recognises both the obsessive quality of golf and the quasi-religious atmosphere of its shrines in his 1929 travel book *In Search of Scotland*, from which we take a description of the holy of holies, St Andrews. However the modern game of golf, like some virulent disease, has penetrated to all parts of Scotland and Angus MacVicar's description of the horrors of putting, in *The Black Yips*, has something of the air of his homeland, Southend, near the Mull of Kintyre. Scotland so dominated the game through nineteenth-century professionals like 'Old' Tom Morris, four times Open Champion, and through course designers and clubmakers, that even such a quintessentially English writer as P.G. Wodehouse manages to impart a strongly Scottish flavour to some of his inimitable golfing stories. Even if in this connection Wodehouse is mostly remembered for his acerbic (and accurate?) remark in *Blandings Castle and Elsewhere*:

> It is never difficult to distinguish between a Scotsman with a grievance and a ray of sunshine, and Lord Emsworth, gazing upon the dour man, was able to see at once into which category Angus MacAllister fell.

Yet another clerical figure of importance was a St Andrews minister, the Reverend Dr Paterson, who was credited with the invention of the 'guttie' or ball made from gutta percha, one of several technological innovations that transformed the game, in the way that carbon fibre is doing currently.

Such improvements were transforming the skill and accuracy of golfers at a time when the first professional players were emerging; and among these professionals none was more remembered than 'Young' Tom Morris, son of 'Old' Tom and another native of St Andrews. However, Morris won his first two Open Championships at Prestwick as a professional there, but it was the decision of the St Andrews club to invite him back as their first professional which set the pattern for the game's future development. He won his third Open there in 1864 and his fourth in 1866.

The early professionals were expected to carry out a range of, some quite menial, tasks but men like Morris gradually imposed a greater degree of single-mindedness. Other professionals like Willie Dunn were involved in a seismic shift of the game when they crossed the Atlantic to the rich pickings of the emergent golf scene. Golf was on course to become the global sporting and commercial phenomenon that it is today, but only in Scotland, its cradle, was it a game for all.

Golf at St Andrews

from In Search of Scotland

H.V. MORTON

Read this extract from Morton's In Search of Scotland *(1929) and you might wonder how much of our perception of the 'Home of Golf' has been shaped by this English author. Morton was one of the most successful travel writers in the period before and immediately after the Second World War. His popular and easy style made his books extremely successful commercially:* In Search of Scotland, *for example, passed through six impressions in six months. This extract shows some of the best features of Morton's style – he manages to combine a quantity of information with a relaxed approach to storytelling, interspersed with flashes of eye-catching phraseology ('In the early morning St Andrews, having dreamt of getting over the burn in two, awakens to thoughts of golf'), and vivid characterisation of the people he meets on his journeys.*

★ ★ ★

Never shall I forget my first night in St. Andrews. A dangerous small boy was swinging a new driver at an invisible ball on the hotel mat. Three men, leaning on the visitors' book, were arguing about a certain mashie. A girl in the lounge was shrilly defending her conduct on the home green. At the next table to me in the dining-room sat a man in plus fours who cheered his solitude by practising approach shots with his soup-spoon. When the spoon, fresh from a bunker of oxtail, was no longer playable, he did a little gentle putting with a bread pill and a fork.

I sat there thinking of Newmarket. Both these towns are lost to the world in a magnificent obsession. All Newmarket runs to the windows at the click of bloodstock on the road; all Newmarket lives with prints of Diomed winning the Derby in 1780; as far as Newmarket is concerned Shakespeare and Dante lived in vain; but let any man challenge Mr. Ruff or appear to scorn Nat Gould!

To a St. Andrews' man the sight of the stars at night is a hint that the time has come to uproot daisies from a green. When he sees a shooting star I am sure he cries, 'What a drive!'

In Newmarket and in its golfing parallel a man feels as he felt the first time he stayed in a monastery. He is back in the age of faith! His load of worldly knowledge lies heavy on his shoulders, and all he can do is helplessly to watch other people performing their offices. There is something almost religious in this single-mindedness. After a life spent in planting tea in Ceylon or commanding cavalry in India, how sweet to take an enlarged liver to a mental monastery where faith burns with an almost savage heat, and each day brings a new point to argue.

There has been nothing quite like Newmarket and St. Andrews since the Dissolution!

The town is a delight; an old grey town of ancient houses and monastic ruins; full of men in plus fours and women with golf bags on their tweed shoulders; of undergraduates in splendid scarlet gowns; of happy meetings in cakeshops; of wayside gossip, of fine windows full of silk nightdresses, Fair Isle jumpers, brogues, golf clubs, golf bags, and, strange to say, one or two bookshops, presumably for the use of the Oxford of Scotland.

All the time the North Sea unwraps itself restlessly on the curve of the lovely bay, beyond which lies that sacred strand, the golf links, backed by the stern bulk of the M.C.C. of golf – the 'Royal and Ancient'.

In the early morning St. Andrews, having dreamt of getting over the burn in two, awakens to thoughts of golf. Men go to factories behind small shops and turn out clubs destined to react to various handicaps all over the world; but specially in America. St. Andrews affects the American golfer much as Stratford-on-Avon affects the American college girl. It also attracts many a reckless 'birthplace fan' who has never in his life swung a club. Such men – a well-known type – go quickly round the world collecting useless experiences, apparently as an aid to after-dinner conversation. They arrive breathless in St. Andrews, but smiling all over their faces.

'Guess I cain't go home,' they declare winningly, 'without saying I've hit a ball over this course of yours! Now, see here, can a guy hire a club in this town for half an hour? Gee, that's fine ! Say, now – what kinder club do I want?'

I would much like to see this sacrilege in progress. One of the most Batemanesque sights of the year must be that of St. Andrews weakly ministering to the ambition of such phenomena.

I was invited to the 'Royal and Ancient'. Its atmosphere is as solemn and masculine as that of the M.C.C. Its air of supreme authority is equalled only by the Jockey Club – and the Law Courts in the Strand!

There is a 'silence' room. (I suppose no club is in greater need of this retreat.) In this room an enormous safe is let into the wall. Inside, in an illuminated glass case which suggests the Crown Jewels in the Tower, lies the Regalia of Golf.

Foremost among the treasures is the silver club given in 1754, by certain 'noblemen and gentlemen being admirers of the ancient and healthfull exercise of the Golf', who each contributed five shillings to the first St. Andrews trophy. Then comes the gold medal given in 1837 by William IV, who endowed the club with the title of 'Royal and Ancient'. Golf is spelt on this medal 'golph', the error, presumably, of some uncivilized London goldsmith!

Members may be observed gazing reverently at the Crown Jewels of Golf, tiptoeing up in silence and sighing a little. There is also a museum containing clubs of antique shape and golf balls made of leather stuffed with feathers.

The windows of the club provide an unsurpassed view of players setting out over the Old Course – how critically we watch them take their first drive – and of the fine, green sweep of the links, bounded by sand-dunes and the white horses of St. Andrews Bay.

This 'setting out' is among the most solemn events of the day. The caddies sit cynically in, and around, a glass pavilion in which the result of the daily ballot is set up for all men to see at what time 'the B. of London' – for such is Dr. Ingram at St. Andrews – will go forth with 'Wilkins', who may be a lord or only major.

The balloted sit waiting in the club telling one another stories about the 'Elysian Fields', smoking, watching, waiting until the time comes for them to rise like men called on to prove themselves. Then as they go out there is a stir among the corralled caddies, a whisper of interest among spectators who hang round the links all day, then soft turf under their feet and the tee under the ball.

But I am told the best golf at St. Andrews is often played by the ratepayers, who are the hereditary owners of the links. They have been practising their strokes since the sixteenth century. Every ratepayer in St. Andrews has the freedom of the links, and at certain times in the day and year the chimney-sweep takes precedence over the most urgent visiting millionaire. Golf in St. Andrews is a sport in its most democratic form. The famous links faithfully reproduce the spirit of a game whose first championship match was played by a king and a tradesman in partnership against two nobles.

I am sure that the man who snored in the next bedroom was the man in plus fours who played golf with his soup-spoon. His snore sounded exactly like: 'Fore!'

I bought a book called *St. Andrews Ghost Stories*, published locally and written by Mr. W.T. Linskill, Dean of Guild. I read it in bed by the friendly light of an electric table lamp.

I had no idea that St. Andrews was so fearful a spot. There is a phantom coach which runs locally on certain nights. The horses make a queer ticking sound on the road, and no one has ever seen the face of the shrouded figure of the driver. There is 'The Screaming Skull of Greyfriars', 'The Smothered Piper of the West Cliffs', 'The Beautiful White Lady of the Haunted Tower', and many another perfect bedside story.

What interested me as much as the ghosts was the rich aroma between the lines. The author's convivial cheerfulness, like that of the would-be philosopher, insisted on 'breaking through' the gloom.

The real ghosts in these stories, to me at least, were undergraduate days in Cambridge, days in London when peers were interested in the Gaiety chorus, and days in those Continental spas frequented by Edward VII. This is a typical opening to one of Mr. Linskill's blood-curdlers:

'We were sitting over a cosy fire after dinner. It was snowing hard outside, and very cold. Our pipes were alight, and our grog on the table, when Allan Beauchamp suddenly remarked:

'"It's a deuced curious thing for a man to be always followed about the place by a confounded grinning skull."

'"Eh? What?" I said. "Who the deuce is being followed about by a skull? It's rubbish, and quite impossible."'

I like the word 'grog'.

In one story he mentions a 'cheery golfing Johnny'; in another a military friend of the author says, 'Zounds, sir,' in a moment of emotion.

This author, I thought, is no anæmic, psychic investigator. There is nothing clammy about him. In the morning a St. Andrews man said:

'You don't know old Linskill? Go and meet him at once. He founded the Cambridge University Golf Club. He is seventy-four and looks fifty. He knows more about St. Andrews than the rest of us put together . . .'

I found the ghost-hunter looking remarkably like a possibly violent retired major-general. My first feeling was one of pity for the ghost who attempts to haunt him. An enormous voice, a baggy suit of plus fours, a pipe, a drooping grey moustache, a pair of eyes which have not altered since he was thirty. Here were seventy-four years carried with the gallantry of fifty. He looked as though his life had agreed with him like a good dinner. He talked exactly like the 'military friends' in his ghost stories:

'Well, sir, and what the deuce can I do for you?'

'I hoped that you might talk, sir.'

'Be seated, sir. Cigar ? Well – smoke what the deuce you like!'

Meeting Mr. Linskill is rather like exchanging salutes before coming on guard in a fencing school.

'Yes; I took golf to Cambridge when I was an undergraduate. Founded the Cambridge University Golf Club. Initiated the inter-'Varsity match! Played in two of 'em! Dashed long time ago! Deuced difficult game to start in Cambridge; in fact, the most deuced difficult thing I ever did in my life! When undergraduates appeared in public carrying golf clubs the whole town turned out to laugh. It took some pluck to play golf in those days. *However . . .*'

Mr. Linskill has a trick of clearing his voice and booming the word 'however', which has the effect of a wet rag wiped over a blackboard, clearing it for the next topic.

'Golf to-day,' he said, 'is a ladies' game compared with the golf I remember at St. Andrews half a century ago. I remember playing with hand-hammered gutta-percha balls. Damned annoying things when they broke! The rule in those days was that you put the new ball on the place where the largest fragment of the old one fell!

'I was taught by "Young Tom" Morris. By gad, sir, in those days the daisies were so thick at St. Andrews that we never played a white ball! I remember how the caddie used to say: "Red or yellow ball, sir!" And, by Jove – the moonlight games ! How dashed well I remember playing when the moon was full, with 'fore caddies to tell us where the ball had gone, and a fellow following behind with a wheelbarrow full of refreshments!'

I Begin to Golf

from The Haunted Major

ROBERT MARSHALL

★ ★ ★

This extract is taken from the very popular novella written in 1902 by the Scottish playwright Robert Marshall. The far-from-modest eponymous Major is one Jacky Gore, who relates the tale of what happens when he takes up golf. In the opening section Gore parades before the reader the multifarious sports and games at which he excels and which entitle him to his own description of 'the finest sportsman living'. The absence of golf from this list he puts down to the fact that it, unlike most other sports, does not possess 'an element, however slight, of physical danger to the player'. When he finally decides to take it up after all, the complicated plot that is subsequently unravelled leads him into a whole series of dangerous situations, in the surroundings of the 'gray and bleak-looking city' of St Magnus – obviously based on St Andrews. These adventures include an encounter with the ghost of the fearsome Cardinal Smeaton, as well as the phlegmatic caddy Kirkintulloch, who share a wonderful mastery of the broad Scots tongue. This extract takes us through the agony of his first lesson.

★ ★ ★

The morning of the 8th dawned with a warm flush of saffron, rose, and gold, behind which the faint purple of the night that was gone died into the mists of early morning. The pure, sweet air was delicious as the sparkling vapour that rises from a newly opened bottle of invigorating wine. The incoming tide plashed on the beach with lazy and musical kisses, and a soft, melodious wind was stirring the bending grasses that crowned the sand dunes on the outskirts of the links.

I inhaled the glorious air with the rapture of the warrior who sniffs the battle from afar . . .

Kirkintulloch was waiting for me at the first putting green.

I may say at once that during my entire stay in St Magnus I never quite mastered this man's name. It became confused in my mind with other curious-sounding names of Scotch towns, and I addressed him promiscuously as Tullochgorum, Tillicoutry, Auchtermuchty, and the like. To his credit, be it said that after one or two attempts to put me right, he suppressed any claim to nominal individuality and adapted himself philosophically to my weakness; answering cheerfully to any name that greeted his surprised but resigned ears.

He was the brawny son of honest fisher folk. Of middle height, he was sturdily yet flexibly built. His hands were large and horny; his feet, I have no doubt, the same. At all events his boots were of ample proportions. He had blue eyes, with that alert, steady, and farseeing gaze that is the birthright of folk born to look out over the sea; sandy hair and moustache, and a ruddy colour that suggested equally sunshine, salt winds, and whisky. His natural expression was inclined to be sour, but on occasion this was dissipated by a quite genial smile. His manner and address had the odd deferential familiarity that belongs exclusively to the old-fashioned Scotch peasantry. His face I soon found to be a sort of barometer of my progress, for every time I struck a ball I could see exactly the value of the stroke recorded in the grim lines of his weather-beaten features. In movement he was clumsy, except, indeed, when golfing, for then his body and limbs became possessed of that faultless grace which only proficiency in a given line can impart.

'It's a fine moarn fur goalf,' was his greeting.

'So I suppose,' said I. 'Where do we go?'

'We'll gang ower here,' he replied, as, tucking my clubs under his arm, he led me in the direction of a comparatively remote part of the links.

As we went I thought it advisable to let him know that, although not yet a golfer, I could more than hold my own in far higher branches of sport. I told him that I was one of the best-known polo players of the day.

There was a considerable pause, but we tramped steadily on.

'Whaat's polo?' said he, at length.

I gave him a brief description of the game.

'Aweel, ye'll no hae a hoarse to help ye at goalf.'

'But, don't you see, Tullochgorum –'

'Kirkintulloch, sir.'

'Kirkintulloch, that the fact of playing a game on ponies makes it much more difficult?'

'Then whaat fur d'ye hae them?'

'Well, it's the game, that's all.'

'M'hm' was his sphinxlike response.

I felt that I had not convinced him.

I next hinted that I was a prominent cricketer, and, as a rule, went in first wicket down when playing for my regiment.

'Ay, it's a fine ploy fur laddies.'

'It's a game that can only properly be played by men,' I replied with indignant warmth.

'Is't?'

'Yes, is't – I mean it is.' He had certain phrases that I often unconsciously and involuntarily repeated, generally with ludicrous effect.

The reader, of course, understands that I was not in any sense guilty of such gross taste as to imitate the man to his own ears. I simply could not help pronouncing certain words as he did.

'Aweel, in goalf ye'll no hae a man to birstle the ba' to yer bat; ye'll just hae to play it as it lies.'

'But, man alive,' I cried, 'don't you see that to hit a moving object must be infinitely more difficult than to strike a ball that is stationary?'

'Ye've no bunkers at cricket,' he replied, with irrelevant but disconcerting conviction, adding, with an indescribable and pro-phetic relish, 'No, nor yet whins.'

I could make no impression on this man, and it worried me.

'I take it,' I resumed presently, 'that what is mainly of importance at golf is a good eye.'

'That's ae thing.'

'What's ae thing?'

'Yer e'e. The thing is, can ye keep it on the ba'?'

'Of course I can keep it on the ba' – ball.'

'We'll see in a meenit,' he answered, and stopped. We had reached a large field enclosed by a wall, and here Kirkintulloch dropped the clubs and proceeded to arrange a little heap of damp sand, on which he eventually poised a golf ball.

'Noo, tak' yer driver. Here,' and he handed me a beautifully varnished implement decorated with sunk lead, inlaid bone, and resined cord. 'Try a swing' (he said 'swung') 'like this,' and, standing in position before the ball, he proceeded to wave a club of his own in semicircular sweeps as if defying the world in general and myself in particular, till suddenly and rapidly descending on the ball, he struck it with such force and accuracy that it shot out into the faint morning mist and disappeared. It was really a remarkably fine shot. I began to feel quite keen.

'Noo it's your turn,' said he, as he teed a second ball, 'but hae a wheen practice at the swung first.'

So I began 'addressing' an imaginary ball.

We wrestled with the peculiar flourishes that are technically known as 'addressing the ball' for some minutes, at the end of which my movements resembled those of a man who, having been given a club, was undecided in his mind as to whether he should keep hold of it or throw it away. I wiggled first in one direction, then in another. I described eights and threes, double circles, triangles, and parallelograms in the air, only to be assailed with –

'Na, na!' from Kirkintulloch.

'See here, dae it like this,' he cried; and again he flourished his driver with the easy grace of a lifetime's practice.

'I'll tell you what, Kirkcudbright –'

'Kirkintulloch, sir.'

'Kirkintulloch, just you let me have a smack at the ball.'

'Gang on then, sir. Hae a smack.'

I took up position. I got my eye on the ball. I wiggled for all I was worth, I swung a mighty swing, I swooped with terrific force down on the ball, and behold, when all was over, there it was still poised on the tee, insolently unmoved, and Kirkintulloch sniffing in the direction of the sea.

'Ye've missed the globe,' was his comment. 'An' it's a black disgrace to a gowfer.'

I settled to the ball again – and with a running accompaniment from Kirkintulloch of 'Keep yer eye on the ba'; up wi' yer richt fut; tak' plenty time; dinna swee ower fast' – I let drive a second time, with the result that the ball took a series of trifling hops and skips like a startled hare, and deposited itself in rough ground some thirty yards off, at an angle of forty-five degrees from the line I had anxiously hoped to take.

'Ye topped it, sir,' was Kirkintulloch's view of the performance.

'I moved it, anyhow,' I muttered moodily.

'Ay, ye did that,' was the response; 'and ye'll never move that ba' again, fur it's doon a rabbit hole and oot o' sicht.'

Nevertheless, I went steadily on, ball after ball. They took many and devious routes, and entirely different methods of reaching their destinations. Some leaped into the air with halfhearted and affrighted purpose; others shot along the ground with strange irregularity of direction and distance; a number went off at right or left angles with the pleasing uncertainty that only a beginner can command; whilst not a few merely trickled off the tee in sickly obedience to my misdirected energy. At length I struck one magnificent shot. The ball soared straight and sure from the club just as Kirkintulloch's had, and I felt for the first time the delicious thrill that tingles through the arms right to the very brain, as the clean-struck ball leaves the driver's head. I looked at Kirkintulloch with a proud and gleaming eye.

'No bad,' said he, 'but ye'll no do that again in a hurry. It was gey like an accident.'

'Look here, Kirkincoutry,' I said, nettled at last, 'it's your business to encourage me, not to throw cold water; and you ought to know it.'

'Ma name's Kirkintulloch,' he answered phlegmatically; 'but it doesna' maitter.' (And this was the last time he corrected my errors as to his name.) 'An' I can tell ye this, that cauld watter keeps the heed cool at goalf, and praise is a snare and a deloosion.' Then with the ghost of a smile he added, 'Gang on, ye're daein' fine.'

The field was now dotted with some fifteen balls at such alarmingly varied distances and angles from the tee that they formed an irregular semicircle in front of us (one ball had even succeeded in traveling backward); and as I reflected that my original and sustained purpose had been to strike them all in one particular line, I began to perceive undreamed-of difficulties in this royal and ancient game.

But I struggled on, and Kirkintulloch himself admitted that I showed signs of distinct, if spasmodic, improvement. At seven o'clock the driver was temporarily laid aside, and I was introduced in turn to the brassie, the iron, the cleek, the putter, and the niblick, the latter a curious implement not unlike a dentist's reflector of magnified proportions. The brassie much resembled the driver, but the iron opened out quite a new field of practice; and my first attempts with it were rather in the nature of sod-cutting with a spade, varied at intervals by deadly strokes that left deep incisions on the ball.

As the clock of the parish church tolled the hour of 8:30, I returned to the hotel with an enormous appetite and a thoughtful mind.

The Black Yips

from Golf in my Gallowses: Confessions of a Fairway Fanatic

ANGUS MACVICAR

★ ★ ★

Golf is a game that attracts scientific and pseudo-scientific analysis and Angus MacVicar's description of his fear and dread of his ability or inability to putt – what Conrad might have called 'The Horrors' – is rather like an anatomy of putting. You don't have to be a golfer to recognise the humour (or is it 'schadenfreude'?) that arises when we see a victim in the grip of an obsession. The book from which this chapter is taken is aptly named Golf in my Gallowses: Confessions of a Fairway Fanatic. *In it, Angus MacVicar, prolific author and former famous resident of Southend on the Mull of Kintyre, really lays his soul bare. This piece was written quite a few years ago now, and the technology or hardware of putting has become even more complex and expensive, but the psychology remains as elusive as ever.*

★ ★ ★

As Jock implies, my putting has for some time been a matter for levity among fellow members at Dunaverty. I can neither 'drive for show' (principally on account of waning suppleness) nor 'putt for dough', though with a 4-iron down to a pitching-wedge I believe I can still hold my own with anybody over the age of seventy. That is not to say, however, that I have failed to study the art of putting. In fact, even as this is being written a corner of my brain is busy analysing a new method which may lead me to perform astonishing deeds when I have mastered it. (Later in the chapter I will describe it, in shy detail.)

My father (the Padre) never believed in the old adage, 'Practise what you preach.' His advice to his parishioners was more sophisticated: 'Don't do as I do, do as I say!' If I had a drink problem (which, fortunately, I do not have, due to no personal merit but entirely to my chemical make-up) I would rather look for guidance from an alcoholic than from an innocent teetotaller. Arguing along such lines, I believe that what I have to say about putting may be found useful by fellow sufferers. On the other hand, if you are a good putter, then perhaps you ought to take Jock's implied advice and read no farther, in case of infection. 'Out, damned spot!' said Lady Macbeth. 'Hell is murky!'

In my young days I was a competent putter; at times, indeed, inspired. I remember winning a monthly medal by sinking a 30-foot putt across the 18th green, in full view of the crowded clubhouse windows. This is as fragrant and valuable a memory to me as his long putt to win the Open at Troon in 1962 is to Palmer, all happiness being relative to an individual's life-style or golfing ability. But I can scarcely bear to describe what would happen to me now, some thirty years later, in the unlikely event of my having the same length of putt to win a medal, especially with the faces of my 'friends' leering from vantage places in the clubhouse.

Whereas, on that distant day, I stood firm and straight and steady, nerves well under control, now I might crouch over the ball with contorted limbs, nerves twitching like the tappets in an engine. Whereas, on that distant day, I took the putter-head smoothly back and followed through with insouciant grace, now, after long travail of spirit, I might utter a soundless scream of agony, jerk and stab at the ball and, probably after hitting it twice, send it scuttering in a direction bearing no relation to the hole. No medal. No handshakes. No smug and falsely modest reference to a 'flukey one' as I enter the clubhouse. Only semi-hysterical laughter to camouflage pain and a repetition of Tommy Armour's ghastly joke: 'Once you've had 'em, boys, you've got 'em.'

My partner might try to comfort me by re-telling Bobby Jones's story about 'Wild Bill' Mellhorn, one of America's foremost professionals between the wars, who, finding his approach only three feet from the hole, lunged at the ball so desperately that it shot across the green into a bunker. But there would be no comfort in the story. I am only too well aware that after his traumatic experience 'Wild Bill' never played competitive golf again. And I have no desire at all to give up competitive golf. Indeed, I approach every game with the hope that my Creator will suddenly smile and whisper in my ear: 'You have suffered enough, my son. Today the yips will entirely vanish and you will be a good putter again.' (How long, O Lord, how long?)

In the 'corridors of the ages', when I could putt, it never occurred to me to consult books on the subject. I simply held the club comfortably and naturally and swung its head easily through the ball. If the ball went into the hole, well and good. If it did not, then it was because of a hidden slope on the green or a worm that had cast up earth in the wrong place. It was never my fault that I missed. I had full confidence in the rectitude of my 'method'. Indeed, I was unaware that I did have a 'method'.

The years passed. During a spell when I was missing putts more often than usual – an inevitable spell in every golfer's experience – I began to study what the top professionals had to say on the subject. It was a mistake. From then on my confidence was eroded, deteriorating like a rusty car to a stage of almost complete collapse.

My decline and fall began with the realization that every 'master' who has written about putting has a method which is strictly his (or her) own.

For example, Roger and Joyce Wethered advised: 'Do not think of following through.' Bobby Locke wrote: 'Concentrate on following through as far as the putter goes back in the backswing.'

Bobby Jones said: 'Take plenty of time to get your breathing and heart tranquilized.' 'Miss 'em quick,' growled George Duncan, an exhortation that was to be repeated, years later, by Babe Zaharias.

'Never hit a putt with the heel of the club,' insisted Locke, 'because that puts check on the ball, and it will not run as far as you expect.' Seve Ballesteros declares that he strikes the ball near the heel of his putter 'to see that it stays square'. 'Keep your weight mostly on your left foot,' writes Don Herold. Mark Harris, an American golfer for whom, curiously, Herold says he has a deep admiration, takes the view that 'your weight should be evenly distributed'.

Claude Harmon, the American professional, once said that 'a good putter can be made'. Peter Dobereiner believes that 'putting is such an individual matter that it is impossible to lay down dogmatic rules'. I am now inclined to agree with Dobereiner. But such a negative statement was of no great assistance in my search for truth.

Perhaps the most positive and helpful hint about putting that I have come across in a book was offered not by a champion golfer but by a champion golfer's wife. One evening in their hotel, during an important tournament, Ben Hogan was complaining to his wife about his putting.

'Would you like to know how to sink those putts?' she asked

'You know how?' Hogan said.

'Yes, I do.'

'Then why the hell haven't you told me? How?'

'Just hit the ball a little nearer the hole,' said Valerie.

The logic of it is breathtaking. It affected me like a flare of sunshine in the midst of a rainstorm, and for a time I putted better. But soon, as I continued to read instructional books and watch professionals at work on the greens, confusion returned.

Bobby Locke putted off the left foot, with a closed stance. So did Eric Brown. Roberto de Vicenzo putted off the right foot, with an open stance. So, at times, did John Panton. Arnold Palmer putted from dead centre, with a square stance. So does Seve Ballesteros. Jack Nicklaus crouches over the ball. Tom Weiskopf stands straight. Isao Aoki, from Japan, perhaps the most successful putter of them all, addresses the ball with the toe of his putter pointing heavenwards, apparently in defiance of the laws of nature.

Doggedly I tried all those methods, one by one. I rapped the ball with firm wrists and did not think about following through. I stroked the ball with supple wrists and determinedly followed through. I putted off my left foot. I putted off my right. I struck the ball near the heel of the club. I struck it off the toe. I crouched. I stood straight. I leant forward on my left leg. I leant back on my right. I bent forward with straight arms until the toe of the putter pointed to the sky, like Isao Aoki's. But I still could not putt. Rather did I begin to suspect that all the physical stress involved in such experiments might be the cause of the rheumatic twinges now occurring in my elbows and right hip.

In the end it dawned upon my woolly and unscientific mind that since all those 'masters' were – and are – good putters, their varied styles and apparently contradictory advice must surely contain some common denominator. After long study I found it. 'Keep your eye on the back of the ball, your head and body perfectly still at impact.' It was like a revelation from on high.

Jean, my wife, has always been a good putter. At one stage, before the slipped disc put an end to her competitive days, she won several putting prizes in a row and I made the suggestion that she ought to turn professional and put up a notice at Achnamara front gate: 'Putting Taught Here.' She was not amused. Nor was she particularly impressed when I told her about my 'revelation'.

'Keep your eye on the ball and remain still at impact?' she said. 'Everybody knows that!'

'Well, I haven't been doing it,' I said.

'That's why you can't putt.'

Valerie Hogan and Jean MacVicar: sisters under the skin. I knew then how Ben must have felt when faced with his wife's simple logic. Like murder.

But I put aside inhuman emotions. I went out on to the course and began to practise putting with new hope. And as I held my putter in a way that felt natural – albeit with the 'over forty' forefinger of my right hand pointed down the shaft – and swung it naturally at the ball, without moving head or body, I was amazed – and made instantly euphoric – by the results.

I remembered an obscure pamphlet I had once read, prepared by William B. Langford, an American golf-course consultant, which indicated the quality of putting required from champions. I went home, rummaged like a frenzied mole in my disorganised filing system, found the pamphlet and consulted the simple table it contained.

With putts of from 1 to 3 feet a champion ought to sink 9 out of 10; from 3 to 5 feet, 8 out of 10; from 5 to 7 feet, 7 out of 10; from 7 to 9 feet, 6 out of 10; from 9 to 11 feet, 5 out of 10; from 11 to 13 feet, 4 out of 10; from 13 to 15 feet, 3 out of 10; from 15 to 17 feet, 2 out of 10; and from 17 to 24 feet, 1 out of 10.

From a distance of 1 to 3 feet I had indeed been sinking 9 putts out of 10 and from 3 to 5 feet, 8 out of 10. I gave thanks to my Creator: I had the quality of a champion. During the following days and weeks – as I remembered to keep head and body still – my confidence built up like red-hot lava within a volcano. I won two monthly medals in a row. (Sceptics seeking verification of this statement are invited to consult the Dunaverty records for January and February 1981.)

'Who's the one to give putting lessons now?' I said to Jean.

She merely smiled. Was there a trace of pity in that smile?

Then one day it happened. The occasion was a hard-fought four-ball with Jim McPhee against Boskers and Big Allan. I had a four-foot putt to win the game on the 18th green. In my eagerness to get the ball into the hole I forgot, for the fraction of a second, the great truth about stillness. I swayed forward on the putt, realized the mistake immediately and jerked my head back and the club-head forward in an effort to counteract it. In a blur of mental pain I saw the ball shoot six feet past the hole.

I felt as an ancestor of mine at the Mull of Kintyre must have felt in the plague year of 1648 when he saw the first blotch on his body and realized that he had contracted the Black Death. I had contracted the Black Yips. The bubbling lava of confidence burst out of the volcano and flowed away, to become a grey, congealing mass of hopelessness.

In an effort to follow the advice that had helped me in my spell of putting health – 'keep the head and body still' – and, at the same time, to prevent the sway forward which is the genesis of the yip, I tried various stances. Upright like a pillar of salt, feet together, arms swinging pendulum-wise. Bent almost double, feet splayed wide (like Michael Bonallack), hands half-way down the shaft. Left toe almost touching the ball (like Neil Coles). Right toe almost touching the ball and stance so wide that it threatened trouble to the spine. All in vain. I still yipped.

The disease progressed. Ultimately it took so bizarre a turn that my companions were in the habit, as I prepared to putt, of moving away and contemplating the distant hills. The symptoms occurred only on putts of about a yard down to six inches. With steely resolution I would gaze down at the ball. 'Head still, body still,' I would tell myself. 'Slow back, slow forward and – ' At this point, with the putter-head approaching the ball, a spasm of terror would pass through my body like an electric shock. I would jump several inches in the air. Darkness would cover my eyes. When my sight cleared the ball would be far beyond the hole and I would be shaking, almost sweating. The day Jock let loose a howl of laughter, as he watched, I understood why the others turned away.

Non-golfers – and, indeed, golfers not affected by the yips – may look upon the above as a humorous exaggeration. They can be assured it is as coldly factual as any case-history published in *The Lancet*.

But how to find a cure? I loved my golf. On contracting the yips Henry Longhurst put his clubs away in an attic and gave up the game. I refused to take so defeatist an attitude.

I had a word with a friend who is a psychiatrist. Having listened to the tale of my symptoms he smiled with tolerance. 'A common trauma in my line of business,' he said. 'You are simply afraid of being afraid.'

'That's a diagnosis,' I said. 'It's a cure I'm after.'

'Well' – he hesitated – 'that's entirely up to yourself.'

'I'll do anything,' I said.

'Rid yourself of fear.'

'But how?'

'What about prayer?' He was laughing.

I have always suspected that psychiatrists are no earthly good to anybody. This one was certainly no good to me. Like everybody else he just laughed. He knew nothing about golf. But I took to heart one thing he had said. The cure, it seemed, was up to myself.

I began by experimenting with putters. For years I had played with a 'Wee Benny', a Sayers product with an orthodox blade and without too much rake on the steel shaft. Now I laid it aside and flirted with other models. I had no idea so many were available.

In spite of his superior attitude to my putting, Jock does not seem to have any greater confidence in his own, if the number of putters he uses is any guide. At one stage he had thirteen, of various shapes and sizes. Being a golf writer, he has the duty of keeping up to date with every new development in club design, and I suppose he is open to temptation while listening to smart salesmen describing the magic quality in each of their new products. His present favourite is a Japanese creation, which looks like something I might have made from Meccano in a bygone age. It operates well for him.

From Jock – and from other sympathizers – I borrowed a selection of weird instruments. Things like branding-irons. Things twisted and curved like discards from the old bowmaker's shop in Perth which had a king for a customer. Things which went *ping*, and things which went *pong*. Things with tiny blades, and things with blades so large that they could have been used to drive in fencing-posts. Things with hickory shafts, steel shafts, carbon shafts, wooden heads and brass heads. Things with the shaft rising straight from the centre of the blade, and wry-necked models which made you stand so far away from the ball that you felt like a fisherman with a rod and line.

Fortunately, at the time, Gene Littler's new putter had not yet come upon the market. This has to be seen to be believed. A 'wrong-way-round' model, the blade points back from the shaft towards the player's body. The makers claim that such an arrangement keeps the face of the club flush with the ball at impact. I have a notion that if someone had offered me the Littler club at the height of my trouble, my mind, already boggled, might have fused altogether, like an electric plug with positive and negative wires transposed.

None of the putters I tried made any difference. By the exercise of immense willpower I was able to keep the yips at bay during 'friendly' four-balls. But when it came to scoring in a medal round the dreadful paroxysms would return whenever I was faced with a put of anything under five feet.

'It's all in the mind,' said Jock one day. 'Try to realize that even if you miss a putt it's not the end of the world.'

I took a deep breath and faced the truth. Salvation was not to be found in putters. I went back to my 'Wee Benny'.

Are the yips infectious? I put the question seriously, because before they took hold of me they had been torturing Big Allan, and for long periods I was exposed to the sight of his agonies. It must be admitted, however, that I watched those agonies with an amusement which I now acknowledge was shameless. Perhaps the simple answer is that my Creator decided to punish me for lack of proper sympathy with a fellow human being.

In any case, a time came when Big Allan and I suffered together. But then, after a holiday with his elder son at a distant course, he returned to Dunaverty with a glow of joy on his face. While away, he had practised Sam Snead's 'sidewinder' method and it had cured his yips. (Strangely enough, from that day to this, no trace of the disease has been apparent in his golf – except perhaps in the matter of short chips.)

Inspired by a spirit of envy, I began working on my own 'method', chiefly from a psychological angle. After making a few experiments I decided that the 'sidewinder' was not for me.

But one day, by chance, I took up a fairly wide crouching stance, with my left foot well towards the hole to prevent sway and with most of my weight on it. The ball was mid-way between my feet and immediately below my head. Suddenly I felt comfortable and relaxed. I remembered what Jock had said about a missed putt not being the end of the world. I remembered that the day was fine and that I was striking my irons with authority and grace. My partner and opponents were all nice people; the salt of the earth, in fact. High in the blue a lark was singing, and I could actually feel the scent of the wild thyme. I had written a thousand words that morning which were not all bad. Jean had promised me a tasty curry on my return home. All in all, the world was fair and bright.

'A putt?' I said to myself. 'What the hell!'

I moved the blade back, paused, then moved it forward with careless ease, but with Harry Vardon's advice to Tommy Armour still clear in my mind: 'If you don't move your head, you won't move your body off balance and you've got to hit with your hands.'

The ball clunked as it struck the back of the hole and stayed in.

Life is meant to be happy, and a missed putt is but a tiny wrinkle on the graph of time, irrelevant to the fate of your immortal soul. Such a philosophy, I submit, is a prescription which may well be a cure for the Black Yips. For some time I have been free of them.

At any rate, the violent, jumping symptoms of the disease have not recurred, thanks, I believe, in part to that firmly planted weighted left foot and in part to a more positively cheerful attitude. But I know only too well that the virus still lurks in my blood, like the virus of the stammer I used to have as a boy, ready at any sign of irresolution to leap out, gibbering.

Those of you who do not play golf – and even some of you who do – may wonder why I love the game so much when it causes me a deal of pain in both mind and body. The question is complex and would require the combined skills of Burns, Shakespeare and P.G. Wodehouse to provide a comprehensive answer. Such an answer would treat of fresh air, exercise, beautiful scenery, good companionship, pride in achievement and the sublimation of aggression. It would deal with the vicissitudes of life and the love of a man for a maid. Life can be cruel, but in the widest sense it is exciting and ours to enjoy. A maid can be fickle and hurtful, but if she is your girl then nothing can change your love for her.

And putting, remember, is only a part of golf: an important part but not the be-all and end-all of the game. It has to be understood that if sometimes you miss a putt it does not necessarily mean you are a weakling or a coward or a failure in your business or profession. It simply means that you have missed a putt, and every golfer misses a putt, sooner or later. Cotton did it. So do Nicklaus and Watson and Greg Norman. And so – to the anguish of all who watch – does Bernhard Langer.

Bernhard was afflicted by the Black Yips at a surprisingly early age. But in this gallant golfer from Germany we have an example of a man who has come to terms with the disease and continues to play wonderful golf. He misses many short putts, but, to outward appearance, he does not allow this to annoy him and affect the rest of his game. He retains a smile.

There is a clergyman in America who, in the midst of a bout of the Black Yips, went to his Bible (1 Corinthians, 13) and, at a club dinner, produced this masterpiece of despair.

Though I speak with the tongues of Palmers and of Hogans, and cannot putt, I am become as sounding brass and a tinkling cymbal.

And though I have the gift of long drives, and understand all slices, and all hooks, and though I have chips to remove mountains, and cannot putt, I am nothing.

And though I bestow all my money to feed my family, and though I give my body to be spurned, and cannot putt, it profiteth me nothing.

Putts come long, and are very tricky. Putts envieth not, putts vaunteth not themselves, are not puffed up. They do behave unseemly, seeketh not the hole, are not easily involved, thinketh nothing.

Putts never faileth. But whether there be golfers, they shall fail; whether there be lies, they shall cease; whether there be the know-how, it shall vanish away.

For now we know in part, and we putt in part. But when that

which is perfect shall come, then that which is in putting shall be done away.

When I was a beginner, I spake with authority. I understood as a beginner, I thought as a beginner; but when I became a man I lost faith in my putter.

For now we see through a green darkly, but then face to face. Now I know I cannot putt, and what I know is also known.

And now abideth drives, chips, putts, these three: but the greatest of these is putts.

How well I understand the feelings of this golfing clergyman, especially those which prompted the lines: 'Now I know I cannot putt, *and what I know is also known.*' I, too, have seen the smirk, the sudden turn away, the heaving shoulders of my opponents. And in his unusual scripture exercise I recognize a plea to his Creator for succour and guidance.

Having grovelled in the mire, was he at last vouchsafed the understanding that he could be a happy golfer without being an expert putter? I like to think so.

The great paradox of the game – at least in my experience – is that when you wipe the dark glass clear and admit to yourself that you cannot putt, you become at once a better putter. And faith and hope return.

The Orkney Golf Match

from Duel on the Fairway

R.T. JOHNSTON

The majority of the famous golf courses in Scotland are on the mainland – Fife, Ayrshire, the North East and East Lothian providing most of the quality highlights. There are good full-length courses on the islands of Islay and Arran but, in general, the island courses are small and charming. The course belonging to the fictitious parish of Stenwick on Orkney is small too (only nine holes – 'as much as anyone wanted to play at one time', as the club's founder Godfrey Ritch wisely put it) but more 'rough and ready' than charming. R.T. Johnston's story, written in the 50s, is full of rather surreal action and the characters are a bit on the rough and ready side themselves, not to mention politically incorrect by modern standards. Johnston's rendering of the local dialect is splendid and the extremely coarse golfing action licks along nicely.

★ ★ ★

It is not generally known that there existed in Stenwick for a time, a golf club. It never really caught on to any great extent, and it is now defunct, the modest nine-hole course having returned to its natural state – from which, indeed, it had never very much departed – and having become once more over-run by real rabbits in place of the two-legged variety who occupied it during its brief heyday.

The club owed its inauguration to old Godfrey Ritch of Mucklegutter, as so many of Stenwick's institutions do. It was the outcome of a visit Godfrey had paid to a friend in St Andrews – not the East Mainland St Andrews, but the home of the Royal and Ancient game.

While he was there the friend had persuaded him to have a round of golf, and while the game itself did not greatly impress Godfrey, the subsequent session at the nineteenth hole roused him to the utmost enthusiasm. Tales are still told, I believe, of the bewhiskered Orkney veteran's carry-on in the august clubhouse. However that may be, Godfrey returned to Stenwick convinced that no Orkney parish should be without its golf clubhouse, and since one cannot very well have a clubhouse without having a club, he called a meeting of all interested and formed the Stenwick Golf Club. There were some twenty-five members, and the subscription was one guinea, the subscriptions being devoted to equipping the clubhouse with a bar, and those liquid commodities with which a bar is generally associated.

The club and the clubhouse functioned with great success for some two years, and then it was suggested by someone that the club ought to have a course, a suggestion which was put into force at the next annual general meeting.

There being few funds to spare on the construction of a really ambitious course, the course ultimately laid out was a somewhat rough and ready one, limited to nine holes which was, as Godfrey said, as much as anyone wanted to play at one time. The greens were small and there was little to distinguish them from the fairway, nor was there a great deal to distinguish the fairway from the rough. The course however, did not lack hazards. These it had in a profusion which would have made Henry Cotton or Bobby Locke take one look and withdraw, screaming, from the scene. The hazards included large clumps of stinging nettles, two extensive patches of bog (into one of which, it is said, Ronald Hourie vanished one night while playing a solitary round and was never seen again), four disused quarries, thirteen drystone dykes, a prehistoric earth dwelling (since taken over by the Office of Works), and an assortment of holes, ditches, cavities and what not.

This, however, is not a history of the Stenwick Golf Club, but rather the story of one particular match played during its existence.

Most of the club's membership was, naturally, male, but there was a small though active ladies' section, of which the leading lights were Mrs Boadicea Skea, the burly widow of Mucklebust, and Mrs Henrietta Kirkness, Godfrey Ritch's daughter, also a widow. Both these ladies took to golf like ducks to water, the more so, perhaps, as the male section of the club contained one or two eligible bachelors and widowers.

One of these bachelors, and by far the most eligible, was Bartholomew Spence of Sowfarrow, a robust, ruddy-faced individual with a liking for the ladies, but no liking for the halter of matrimony. Of all the members of the golf club, Bartholomew was the one who had been bitten most deeply by the insidious germ of the game. He became a golf fanatic. He assembled an array of clubs which, if placed end to end, would have stretched almost the length of the course, he would commandeer any discussion about fat stock prices and turn it into a saga of how he had done the tricky seventh hole in twelve, he could be seen flailing his way round the course at almost any hour between dawn and dusk, and he had presented three cups for competition by members of the club, all of which he had won himself with the greatest of ease.

Also, he had presented a cup for competition among the ladies' section, and it is upon this trophy that my story hangs. Four ladies, the full female membership, entered for the contest, namely Mrs Skea, Mrs Kirkness, Miss Janet Cutt (as she then was), the postmistress, and Mrs Delphine Budge of Snortquoy. Fate ordained that in the first round Mrs Skea should play Miss Cutt, and Mrs Kirkness Mrs Budge. Space does not allow me to go into detail about the games; suffice it to say that Boadicea thrashed Miss Cutt unmercifully, while Mrs Kirkness' victory over Mrs Budge was only a shade less emphatic.

Bartholomew Spence took the closest interest in the progress of the tournament, accompanying the players on their rounds and offering advice and criticism to every stroke played or missed. Probably this incessant babble on Spence's part had a good deal to do with the lamentable form displayed by Miss Cutt, an indifferent performer at the best of times and one who reacts badly to counsel, however wise and well-meant. For instance, when she swung ferociously on the first tee and sent the ball trickling only three inches, Bartholomew's comment of 'Michty, Chenet, if thoo hid gien doon ahint id on thee hands an' knees thoo could hiv blawn id further' was one which might have upset souls much less susceptible to criticism.

At all events Boadicea and Henrietta reached the final in the proverbial canter, and it was on the evening preceding the final that the incident occurred which gave the match its full atmosphere of drama.

Boadicea and Henrietta had been out on the course, independently of one another, getting themselves tuned up for the big contest, and on their return to the clubhouse they found there Bartholomew Spence, reclining in a cane chair, drinking home brewed ale, and boring three or four fellow members to tears with an account of how he had just missed doing the third hole in nine earlier in the evening.

'Weel,' bawled Bartholomew, as Boadicea Skea lumbered in, 'hoo wur thoo playin', Mrs Skea?'

'Oh middleen,' said the large lady, but her glum look clearly indicated that she had found her form far from satisfactory.

'Middleen,' echoed Spence. 'Desh, Mrs Skea thoo'll hiv tae dae better than that tae win the cup. Wur thoo keepin' thee heid steady like I telt thee?'

'Yaas,' said Boadicea.

'Weel whit wur wrang?'

'Oh noathing,' said Mrs Skea. 'I cheust wurno puttin' aafil weel.'

At that moment the second of the finalists entered. She too wore a significantly tight-lipped expression.

'Ay Henrietta,' Spence greeted her, 'thoo dinno luk aafil plazed wi' theesel ither. Wur thoo aff thee game teu?'

Henrietta Kirkness brightened a little at his indication that Mrs Skea had been playing badly.

'I don't ken whit wur wrang wi' me,' she said, 'bit I cheust couldno hit the ball strite.'

Bartholomew shook a disapproving head.

'That's no geud, Henrietta,' he said. 'Thoo kinno hit the ball aafil herd, bit thoo kin chenerally hit id strite. Desh, atween thee no hittin' the ball strite an' Boadicea no puttin' weel I kin see wur gaun tae hiv a final the morn that will no be worth a dochen.'

'Weel weel,' said Boadicea with a touch of irritation, 'whit aboot id? Id's cheust a peedie cup wur playin' for, an' id's no muckle differ whar wins id.'

'Cheust a peedie cup,' cried Bartholomew, stung to the quick. 'Desh, id's me trophy, an' id's up tae thee tae mak' a geud game o'd.'

Henrietta glanced at him and shrugged.

'Mrs Skea's right,' said she. 'Id's cheust a peedie insignifeecant bit o'cup an' thir's no yeuse gettan all wund up aboot id. Id's no as if wae wur playin' for something worth.'

Perhaps Bartholomew had been indulging in a little too much home brew. Perhaps this made him rash. At all events he now rose to his feet and burst out: 'Weel wid thoo consider me worth tae play for?'

There was a silence. Everyone in the clubhouse stared at him, and none more intently than Boadicea Skea and Henrietta Kirkness.

'Whit dis thoo mean?' asked Mrs Kirkness.

'This is whit I mean,' shouted Spence, hammering the top of the nearest table. 'Id's weel kent that thoo an' Mrs Skea is been lukkin' for a man iver since thoo lost thee hussbands. Weel, a'll mairry the wen whar wins the cup next night.Whit dis thoo say tae yin?'

There was a long, throbbing silence, in which a handicap might have been heard to drop. Then Boadicea and Henrietta simultaneously drew a deep, deep breath, and looked at one another, and then back at Bartholomew.

'Thoo're no – thoo're no gockan iss?' inquired Mrs Skea, suspiciously.

'Not I,' declared Spence. He rose solemnly to his feet, swayed a little, and drew his forefinger across his adam's apple. 'Cut me throt,' he stated. 'A'll mairry the winner, whariver shae is, if I shid niver go fae here.'

Henrietta Kirkness gulped. The thought that if she struck top form tomorrow night she would be rewarded with Bartholomew Spence and all his worldly goods almost made her imagination reel. Boadicea Skea felt the same. It was a moment large with destiny.

Henrietta snatched up the golfbag she had petulantly flung down on entering, and hurried out again, determination written large on her somewhat ferrety features.There was still sufficient light left for half an hour's golf and she meant to make the most of it. In a moment there came, from the direction of the first tee, the crack of a crisply-driven golfball.

'Yin soonded like a geud shot,' commented Eustace Rosie.

Boadicea Skea was tired, but the idea of Henrietta Kirkness getting practice while she was not was more than she could bear. With a grunt she opened her locker, dragged out her clubs, and lumbered in the wake of her rival into the gathering twilight.

Golf on Harris
from Crotal and White

FINLAY J. MACDONALD

★ ★ ★

'I have always maintained that, away back in the days of Creation, the Almighty, when he had finally remembered to place the Hebrides at all, had intended the undulating swathes of machair land which we had so unimaginatively commandeered for common grazing land, as a golf course.'

Finlay J. Macdonald wrote this memoir as the middle part of a trilogy in the 1980s. Televised more recently, it is a poignant rite of passage in the Presbyterian stronghold of the Island of Harris in the Outer Hebrides in the years leading up to World War II. Macdonald had a successful career as a journalist and broadcaster in Glasgow, the great magnet of advancement to people from the Long Island, but here he goes back to his roots. Crotal and White *is a reference to the dyeing process for the tweed produced in Harris, and this is a brilliant description of the interweaving of traditional threads of island life with the imported Sassenach (i.e. 'Southerner') game of golf. The clash as the village's small version of a plutocratic middle class meets the 'Grazings Committee' head-on is one to savour; communication between the two sides proved to be difficult since 'unfortunately they chose an evening when the crofters were suffering from a dose of bad English'.*

★ ★ ★

By the time I got back from listening to the men talking about the possibilities of war, mother had gone through to settle the baby and father was alone in the living room.

'Where's Donald?' I asked.

'Where you should be. In bed!'

Gone was the sympathy for my disappointment over the bursary result; gone was the feeling of bond on which we had parted when he had been so mysterious about Eilean na Caillich. I was fairly confident that I hadn't done anything wrong – for the simple reason that I hadn't been in the house – and I racked my brains to think of something that I had done in the recent past that was just redounding on me now. But no. My conscience was relatively clear and, in any case, the fact that Donald was in bed early suggested that it was he who had stirred up some trouble for which everybody else was suffering now.

'Has Donald been doing something wrong?' I asked hopefully.

'Probably. But I haven't discovered it yet.' It was a bad sign when he was being unforthcoming.

'Well, I haven't done anything; I haven't been in.'

'Precisely. Do you remember me asking you to do the greens before you went off gallivanting and nearly getting yourself drowned today? The last thing I said to you before you left was to do the greens when you came back. But I didn't mean when you came back at eleven o'clock at night with the Sabbath only an hour away!'

So that was it! And yet he had given me the get-out himself. 'Well that's all right, isn't it? Nobody's going to play golf on Sunday, and even if somebody does play on Monday it won't be till evening. Hardly anybody plays on Monday.'

'Smart thinking. But not smart enough. Monday's a Bank Holiday and there's a match starting at ten o'clock. That means I've got to be up at five in the morning to get the greens done before they arrive. I'll tell you something; you're going to be up too!'

It was on the tip of my tongue to point out that, after all, he was the one who was being paid to do the greens although I doubted if he could find Number Five without taking them in sequence, but I knew where to draw the line when he was in that kind of mood, and in any case I had more to lose than I had to gain by continuing the argument. I decided to slip off to bed where he couldn't score any fresh points without wakening the baby. The greens had been a source of argument for two years now.

I have always maintained that, away back in the days of Creation, the Almighty, when he had finally remembered to place the Hebrides at all, had intended the undulating swathes of machair land which we had so unimaginatively commandeered for common grazing land, as a golf course. But it took a long time for anybody to cotton on to the Almighty's purpose – a failure of communication which is not altogether peculiar to the Western Isles. But when the revelation came, it came (as the Good Book itself forever stresses) in an unexpected quarter. The doctor, the bank manager, the landlord, the road surveyor, and sundry other members of the leisured classes decided that our Atlantic coast should and would, indeed, be made into a golf course. And the policeman (for all that he was left-handed) concurred. But the *Gentry*, as they deemed themselves, were stymied before the first club was swung; indeed before the first green was made.

While the Articles of Surrender (or whatever they were called) drawn up between the dispossessed landlord and the Board of Agriculture decreed that the former retained the fishing and shooting rights on what had once been his land, in all other respects the jurisdiction over that land now rested with the democratically elected Grazings Committee which represented the crofters. And, while they could not stop the landlord exercising his wild animal and mineral rights, there was not – in that constitution – one fragment of clause which gave anybody the right to march over the common grazing firing hard white balls which could kill a spring lamb or damage an expectant sheep, or, come to that, an expectant mother who might conceivably be milking a cow in the middle of a fairway. So, fired with their newfound enthusiasm, there was nothing the gentry and the policeman could do except come cap in hand to the Grazings Committee to plead their case to a gaggle of horny-handed crofters who knew nothing about golf except that it involved a lot of balls. And, unfortunately, they chose an evening when the crofters were suffering from a dose of bad English. For once, in a manner of speaking, the ball was in their court.

Nowadays everybody in the country knows more about golf than the late Harry Vardon did, for the same reason that even frail old ladies clutching the Queen's telegram can see a snooker developing in the eyes of the man bending over the cue. But it is very difficult to define golf to people who have been conditioned to think all their lives that the highest score wins; it can be obscenely difficult to describe it in a language as capable of ambiguity as English to Gaelic-speaking natives who are accustomed to a language which calls a spade a spade and in which round objects have to be very specifically defined. But, at last, the general idea got through.

And the gentlemen could guarantee that this ball could always be made to travel in a dead straight line?

Well – er – not always, but pretty nearly always.

So there was a danger – just a slight danger – that this hard white ball could wander on to a croft and hit a hen or, Heaven forbid, a child?

The chances were minimal; like winning the football pools.

Like what?

There is a great deal to be said for bi-lingualism, and not least is the legitimate excuse it gives to plead for time to think in one language when one is talking in another. And so the crofters pled for time, which the gentry dreaded as an elastic commodity in the Hebrides; and the men of means began to see their chances of seaside links slipping away. So they tried the last resource of the moneyed classes. Money. Which was what the crofters had been waiting for; but, naturally, they couldn't resolve such a delicate problem haphazardly, however much might be on offer. They didn't want to spoil anybody's pleasure, and it wasn't as if this meant any great loss of amenity; not as if any of the grazing had to be scythed or anything like that.

Well, as a matter of fact, now that somebody had mentioned it there was a small matter of greens. Yes that had nearly been overlooked.

Greens?

Yes. Mown patches round those wee holes that the balls were ultimately going to land in.

But they could be down among the marram grass – the long stiff stuff growing out of the sand where there was no grazing for the sheep anyway.

Well, no. Not quite. It wasn't as easy as that. There had to be a fairly unobstructed run up to the – er – greens somewhere on this side of the marram, so that the marram could be a hazard for any balls which might, very occasionally, fly off course; just as it had been agreed that the crofts would be out of bounds for any balls which, once or twice a year, might go off course in that direction.

It was all becoming clearer now. Ideally the gentlemen wanted those green mown patches at intervals down the middle of the best green grazing. Was that it?

Well, that was one way of putting it.

But of course the greens – these mown patches – they would be very small?

O indeed yes. About – er – ten yards by ten.

About a hundred square yards?

That *was* another way of looking at it, yes.

And how many such patches would there be, very roughly?

That was *one* point there was no 'very roughly' about; there would be exactly nine. And nine things called tees which would be about sixteen square yards, but they wouldn't be mown as often as the greens. The divots usually saw to that.

The what?

Now, under pressure, divots *are* a bit difficult to explain without making them sound like miniature efforts at ploughing, and the gentlemen could not swear that occasional divots might not be uplifted accidentally from sundry other parts of the best grazing as well as from the designated area of the tees. All in all this was beginning to sound like a game with a fair incidence of accident. But an accommodation could surely be reached. In all fairness to the gentlemen though, they were overlooking some problems which might be more complicated to solve. For example, if those mown greens had to be so very smooth and flat, would the ever increasing incidence of rabbits (those very productive strong Dutch ones which had been introduced by the landlord himself) be rather a nuisance especially when they started making little practice burrows in the smoothly mown sward?

The landlord squirmed. He was now isolated. Not even his own cronies could be expected to support him when it came to an argument about the advantages of rabbits digging little shallow holes in golfing greens, and so it ended up with him practically pleading with the crofters to trap them, snare them, or ferret them, or do whatever the hell they liked with them. And that, except for the embarrassing business of the money, was all – apart from the matter of the flimsy little wooden bridge which the crofters had, at great cost to themselves, put across the river on the common grazing; but the golfers would be willing to wade (wouldn't they?) because these planks couldn't stand up to constant trafffic.

The district surveyor was a forceful man with access to wood and joiners. He was also getting fed up with the whole protracted argument. Yes, he would personally see to it that a solid new arched wooden bridge would be built across the river and would be regarded as a right of way. Now what about a token rental?

A crofter with an astonishingly good head for figures had worked out that nine hundred square yards (including of course those little tees) was not far off a quarter of an acre give or take a few square yards and those divot things, and put that way it sounded quite a lot. But, in view of the generosity of the gentlemen with regard to the bridge and the rabbits, a token rental of fifty-six pounds a year, payable to the Grazings Committee, would seem to be a modest sort of figure.

Fifty-six pounds a year! Good Heavens, that was about the total sum of the rental paid by the total sum of the eight crofters!

Well, well! Put that way, so it was!

And the crofters would be living rent free?

Only in a manner of speaking; the money would go into the coffers of the Grazings Committee. Naturally each crofter would hand over his own rent at term day as usual. But of course, if a score or so of salaried gentlemen were going to find it difficult to raise a pound and a couple of shillings a week between them . . .

Good Lord, there was no question of that. Of course the gentlemen would pay fifty-six pounds a year for the sake of good-will and all the rest of it . . .

Once the deal had been struck the only other thing that had to be seen to was the appointment of a greenkeeper whose function it would be to keep the nine greens neatly mown, and to keep any little rabbit holes which might appear on the greens from time to time neatly patched up, especially on Saturdays and Bank Holidays which were the only days on which salaried men could admit to being free to play golf – Sunday, of course, being out of the question. The role and salary of greenkeeper were, for reasons which I have never fathomed, allocated to my father, and, in due course the Golfing Committee presented the most unmechanically minded man I have ever known with a complicated petrol motor mower and an instrument for making neat round holes. The latter was to revolutionize the planting of early potatoes.

If my father was unmechanically minded, the boys of the village certainly were not, and if they'd had money they would have paid for the privilege of chuntering along behind a motor machine mowing large square and round patches called greens. We'd have mown the fairways too given a chance, but the Grazings Committee was adamant that that particular chore had to be left to the sheep since the sheepstock was still relatively important, now with the tweed trade improving – even to a crofting community living, technically, rent free.

It was an excellent golf course by any standards, designed, as I have indicated, by the Great Architect Himself. Not one single bunker nor artificial hazard of any kind had to be created. But natural hazards there were in plenty, ranging from wide-mouthed rabbit holes which could no longer be guaranteed not to have gin traps in them, to sand dunes and sand pits and stretches of thick marram grass. To say nothing of the river and sundry little burns.

Perhaps the most disconcerting hazard of all was a psychological one in the shape of a tiny knot of eagle-eyed urchins who followed each golfing pair or foursome at a safe distance and in total silence, watching and noting where each golf ball went, but sadly bereft of English when it came to telling. When the last golfer went home, we descended on the course. We kept the best of the recovered balls for ourselves, and, on the following Saturday sold the surplus ones to the most generous payers. We became rapidly addicted to the game. At first we had to make do with heavy walking sticks with the handles shaved to represent club faces, and with odd bits of light iron fencing droppers appropriately shaped. But, over the months, we managed to accumulate a motley set of clubs – usually hickory-shafted ones donated by the younger and friendlier members of the Golf Club; the landlord, in fact, presented a large selection of steel-shafted clubs to the school so that we could play in the intervals. By the time my first attempt at the bursary examination had come round I was playing off scratch even although my style might horrify Nicklaus and amuse Trevino.

Occasionally, in the summer and autumn, after I'd received the news of my failure, a flashy car would roll up at our gate and a well dressed tourist in plus-fours would come to enquire from my father, in his capacity as greenkeeper, if he could suggest somebody who might caddy and guide him round the course. The tourist was invariably accompanied by a lady, who was – or purported to be – his wife, whom he was always bent on impressing. His jaw would sag ever so slightly when my father produced me – in ragged trousers and muddy bare feet; in all my years of primary school we never graduated to shoes in summer or to long trousers at all.

These were, I think, the games I enjoyed most in all my golfing life. And the pattern of them was always remarkably the same. We would arrive on the first tee in silence, with the playing couple exchanging little doubtful upper-class glances which, translated in any language meant 'What the hell have we got here?'

Once on the tee I would point out where the first green was – a treacherous one on the lip of a twenty foot deep sandy crater – and

I would warn them about the sundry other hazards that lay ahead. The gentleman would always drive off first with great self-confidence; and regardless of whether he hooked, or sliced, or chopped a short one down the middle, he would throw his partner a smug little look which said 'Follow that if you can!' And, of course, she never could – or wouldn't dare.

The light on an Atlantic golf course is very deceptive for someone used to inland courses or east coast links. And golf on an unknown course with unmown fairways is a different ballgame from that on manicured expanses like Turnberry or Lytham St Anne's. I always mentally took my hat off to anybody getting down in under seven on that first green of ours on his first time out; of course I never saw a tourist play a second round. On the second tee I would timidly suggest that it might be quicker if I were allowed to play and indicate the lie of the fairways that way (all for the joy of being able to handle beautifully matched clubs) and the suggestion was always greeted sceptically till, invariably, the lady, if she was of the motherly type at all, would intercede on my behalf. From then on it was fun. I knew every blade of grass on that course, and I had the tremendous psychological advantage that plus-foured gentlemen never expected bare-foot scruffy and ungainly ragamuffins to play golf – far less play well. As the round progressed and I got used to the clubs my confidence would increase, and my opponent's morale would visibly begin to crumble, not only because he was being humiliated in front of his partner (who usually said 'O Charles!' or something to that effect every time he was one down) but because he was being beaten by somebody he was going to have to pay at the end of the round. In all my caddying days I rarely played golf with a good sportsman; in my adult life I played only once with a bad one. And I think the moral has something to do with ragged trousers and bare feet.

But, as that autumn wore on and the ground became water-logged, my spirits got heavier too as pressure from parents and teacher kept reminding me that I was now on my last chance; it was only by a matter of weeks that I had managed to meet the maximum age requirement that enabled me to have a second attempt at the bursary examination. This time if I failed, my option was quite clear; I would stay on at the village school and then leave to be a crofter or a weaver till such time as I found a job on the mainland. If I wanted a world of books I had eight months in which to ensure a glimpse of it. At the back of my mind I had begun to develop a feeling that though God might be a great designer of golf courses maybe he didn't see them as a guaranteed aid to scholastic success. And although my father had never said 'I told you so' after the shock of the first failure and the way it had come, it did linger in my young memory that on that August Bank Holiday morning – as we mowed the greens together in the dawn – he had said 'Golf's a bit like life you know; it's not getting to the green that really matters – it's how little fiddling about you have to do once you get there. You're on the green now and you've only got a short putt to sink! Remember that and be glad you've got another round to play.'

That was a long time ago. And now May was here again.

Oddly enough I can't remember how or when I went to Leverburgh for the second time. I remember nothing about the examination, except the rules that the teacher had made me learn by heart the day before. I can recite them still. 'Read the paper twice through. Make sure you understand the questions and then read it again. Choose the essay subject you know most about and don't try to write fancy stuff. Leave yourself time to read over what you've written. If you have to make a correction, make it carefully and neatly.'

The memory of Eilean na Caillich had stayed with me over the months and, peculiarly enough, it did something to wipe out the anger that I had felt for having had my prayers ignored. And so I had prayed again as diligently as before, and had found myself struggling hard to push away the thought 'but I'm not leaving it all to You this time'. Perhaps that's what worked.

This time there was no time for rumours. On 8 July I walked out of the village school for the last time as a pupil knowing that I had won, and that I would be going to Tarbert school and the future on 28 August.

On the evening before I left to take up lodgings with Big Grandfather I felt suddenly homesick for a home that I hadn't yet left, and I did what I always did when I wanted to be alone whether for joy or sadness. I walked up the peat road beside the river till I reached the old stone dyke which was the boundary of the croft, as, in the old days it had been the boundary of the big landlords who had held the people in thrall. The stone dyke enclosed, as it still does, the choicest piece of land on the west coast of Harris, known as Scarista Park, but by then the park had been divided between two of the men from the Great War – my father from the army, with a navyman beside him. The river ran down the middle of our croft and then became the boundary between us and the navyman on the left. At the point where I stood and looked back there was a worn step above a gully where my father had placed his feet every second day for nine years with a heavy bag of peat on his back, plodding his way through the kind of life that he had tried to teach me to escape in order that I might live the life he would have chosen for himself. A little further down from me, the river forked before meeting again round what my brother and I had always called 'the big island', where we played at crofts and planted 6 potatoes to represent a field, and a handful of corn to represent a harvest; they had always grown. Then on the river twisted to the spout in the cleft rock at which we filled the water pails; down past the little rectangle of stones with the three legged pot beside it where the white fleeces were dyed crotal to be married with the others in some blend of crotal and white.

Peeping up through a clump of nettles was a cairn of stones that I had forgotten all about; on that August Bank Holiday a year before, while the golf match was in progress, my father in a bout of enthusiasm – or perhaps wanting to take my mind off my failure – had decided that we should begin to collect stones for our new white house. I had laboured with a will for an hour or two and then something had diverted his attention, as had so often happened before. In Scotland cairns are frequently little memorials that people build on mountain tops to prove that they have climbed them; sometimes they're not . . .

Further down, the river passed the house and the pool where my mother used to rinse out the heavy tweeds when they had been thumped and cleaned and shrunk to the width beyond which they would shrink no more on moorland or on golf course. Then it left us, and passed below the road which hadn't been there when we came to the new village – or at least only the foundations of it had – and as the water reached the machair it widened out into a series of deep pools where we fished for sticklebacks. Two planks used to span it; now the golfers had supplied a beautiful arched bridge of wood which made it more than ever the Tiber of my imaginings from the poem that father had fired my imagination with when I was struggling with English years ago.

> *With weeping and with laughter*
> *Still is the story told . . .*

Unlike the Tiber, our river never reached the sea. Just after it got down to the white sands it filtered down into them to create patches of dangerous quicksands which one had to get to know, and not only know but try to keep a note of how they changed with excessive floods. You could read them when you got to know them. The quicksands weren't the ridged patches with treacherous looking shallow ditches of water lying between them. No, the quicksands were the peaceful looking flats that caught the light and looked as if one could step on them in perfect safety.

There had been 4 of us when father had built the little temporary house down below me; now we were 6 and the fact that I was moving out and, from now on, would only be coming home for holidays would take a bit of pressure off till father got round to building the new house now that things were getting better. And they were getting better. In 9 years a new village had grown up round the school and the church and the old manse up on the hill. The old manse which had seen the place change from an empty coast to an overcrowded coast, and then swing back to emptiness again, had seen the beginnings of a new village facing a new way of life with new hope. Now here it was, with all the amenities that were modern of their time – an aeroplane landing regularly on its white sands, radio in almost every home, a golf course, and a successful school with a brilliant teacher who could be guaranteed to send at least two pupils out into the world every year. Here was I leaving now – the first boy of the new village. Molly, the first girl, had gone. The trickle was to grow into a steady stream that would grow bigger and bigger, searching for its own bit of sea somewhere. Streams can grow into rivers for sure; they can reach their sea, or like ours sink into the sand. They rarely flow back because that way the hill is against them.

Erchie on Golf

from Erchie my Droll Friend

NEIL MUNRO

★ ★ ★

Erchie MacPherson, Neil Munro's comic invention, preceded the better-known Para Handy and was a perceptive observer of all aspects of early twentieth-century Glasgow life from the vantage point of a kirk beadle (or church officer), who also moonlighted as a waiter at civic receptions and other similar functions. Erchie is a great detector of trends and he is more than willing to share his views on the cult or 'craze' of golf. This story appeared in the Glasgow Evening News on 18 April 1904, in Munro's 'Looker On' column when the craze was reaching new heights. Erchie's wry observations include his description of the hapless beginner, when he 'hits Bonnie Scotland an awfu' welt'. Erchie's minister's golf clubs of choice are Western Gailes (founded 1897) and Royal Troon (founded back in 1878).

Two other 'sports', if we can call them that, are mentioned in this story: Moshey is a game of marbles played with target marbles in each of three hollows scooped in the ground; and more athletically, harriers are cross-country runners. As a footnote, Erchie never misses an opportunity to show how well read he is, and there are three literary quotations in this story: Duffy's 'sang' is normally Lord Byron's 'Dark Lochnagar', but on this occasion the quote has not been identified. Next is a quotation from Burns' 'To a Mountain Daisy On turning One down with the Plough, in April 1786':

> *Wee, modest crimson-tipped flow'r,*
> *Thou's met me in an evil hour;*
> *For I maun crush amang the stoure*

> *Thy slender stem:*
> *To spare thee now is past my pow'r,*
> *Thou bonnie gem.*

The third comes from Walter Scott's long narrative poem The Lay of the
Last Minstrel *(1805):*

> *O Caledonia stern and wild,*
> *Meet nurse for a poetic child!*
> *Land of brown heath and shaggy wood,*
> *Land of the mountain and the flood . . .*

*The land in question is made to 'dirl' or spin when hit by the tyro golfer.
Neil Munro was something of a golfer himself, although there is no
evidence that he became obsessive about it, nor does he give any
indication as to his prowess. His diary simply has a note to the effect that
he played his first ever round at Alexandra Park (still a nine-hole
course), in the Dennistoun area of Glasgow, in 1892.*

★ ★ ★

I was on my way to my customary game of golf on Saturday when I
met Erchie, who cast an understanding and, on the whole,
sympathetic eye on my bag of sticks.

'Ye're weel aff,' said he, 'that has the time for't. It's a fine game,
they tell me, and a' the doctors recommend it for want o' sleep, or
palpitation, or dyspepsy or onything that's wrang wi' ye. I was jist
readin' in the papers the ither nicht that if a wee, thin, peely-wally
chap no' able to disjeest his meat gaes oot to the gowfing for a
month or twa, he'll turn into a fair gladiator, that strong he'll no'
ken his ain strength, and he'll be able to eat onything the same as if
he was a connoshoor.'

'It's a wonder you never took up golf yourself, Erchie,' I said. 'It
would do you good.'

'I daursay,' said he; 'but I'm ower throng at my work; besides,
I'm savin' up for a yat. Yats is no' so common as gowf-bags.

They're no' a craze. There's something aboot gowf, I think, that gangs to your heid like beer, and I can see even in the vestry on Sunday, when oor minister's pittin' on his goon, that his mind's wanderin' oot aboot Gailes or Troon, where he aye gangs on a Monday. It's comin' tae't when the Toon Cooncils o' Gleska and Edinburgh neglect the interests o' the rate-payers for a hale day and gang doon to Ayrshire to chase a gutty ba'. It's nice, too; it shows there's nae ill-will between the places. But I'm vexed Edinburgh bate Gleska; surely the Gleska yins didna gi'e them enough to drink when they were at their lunch in George Square afore the game started.

'I see that yin o' the papers has been writin' to a wheen o' folks askin' them whit wye it is that gowf had such an attraction for clever men like them. Put like that, a paper was sure o' an answer frae onybody it wrote to, and some o' the clever men were so keen to explain the wye they felt aboot it that they made a breenge to the telegraph offfice and wired back the answer. It was plain from whit they said that gowf's the game for a' ages, a' complaints, and a' seasons. The only time ye canna play't is in the dark and even then ye can be lyin' in your bed keepin' your wife awake tellin' her hoo chawed Macphee was because ye bate him wi' three holes.

'Nae man's ower auld to learn gowfin'; at least if he's never likely to turn oot the champion at the age of 89, he can learn the wye to polish his clubs. I see auld chaps gaun to gowf that ye wad expect to be sittin' at hame readin' their Bibles, and the mair they gang gowfin' the mair they cling to this warld. It's awfu' aggravatin' to the friends that's waitin' for their money. The charm o' gowf, sae far as I could gaither frae the clever men that play't, and wrote their confessions on the way it effects genius, is that it's no' so relaxin' a game as dominoes, and still no' so violent an exercise as throwin' the hammer or playin' Rugby fitba'. It taks ye awa' frae yer business at the busiest time o' the day, awa' frae the worry and anxiety o' balancin' books and attendin' to customers in a stuffy atmosphere, oot into the glorious sunshine and face to face wi' the beauties o' nature and the problem o' gettin' your ba' oot o' the quarry near the ninth hole.

'There's no finer game for men that ha'e the doctor's advice to tak' plenty o' ootdoor exercise. Some o' them think the best way to mak' the maist o't is to drive in a cab to the links, ha'e twa caddies apiece – yin to cairry their bag, and anither for pittin' back the clods – ha'e a lie doon if the gress is dry, and smoke twa or three cigarettes between every hole. They come back to the warehouse in time to clear the tills, feelin' fine, at peace wi' all mankind, and awfu' glaury aboot the feet.

'It's a game ye can play by yoursel', too; it's no' like cricket, nor moshey, that wye. At the start, I believe, maist men prefer to play't themsel's when there's naebody lookin'. They like to rise at six in the mornin' or maybe nine, mak' themsel's desperate wi' a cup o' no' richt warm tea, and walk wi' a brisk step to the gowf course. At that 'oor o' the mornin', and under thae circumstances, a' nature smiles. Whiles it rains, but the gowfer that has newly catched the disease never heeds rain. Far awa' frae the haunts o' men, as Duffy's sang says, he reaches the place, looks roond to see the greenkeeper's no' in sight, for a greenkeeper mak's ye nervous; puts the bonny wee ba' in the tap o' as much sand as wad stock a grocer, spits on baith hands, swings his club, shuts baith his een to keep frae bein' blinded wi' the sand, and lets drive. He hits Bonnie Scotland an awfu' welt, then swears maist fearfu'. That's whit ye ca, I think, wan hole, and ninety-nine to play. He doesna mak' a hole every time, of course; noo and then he jist swipes the salubrious breeze.

'Ha'e ye noticed the sudden decline and fa' o' the daisy in Scotland? There'll soon be no' yin left, the result o' the deadly and unerrin' wallop o' the man new-started gowf, who goes up and down the land, practisin' the swing for the drive as explained in the different books. The modest crimson-tipped floo'ers perish in millions every time the lonely sportsman gangs oot, but the ba's, except when the tap's shaved clean off them, 's never ony the worse.'

'Faith, you seem to have studied the ardent amateur at pretty close range, and with some discernment, Erchie,' I said. 'I suspect you have at some time or other in your brilliant and versatile career banged the elusive wee ba' yourself.'

'Me!' cried Erchie. 'Catch me. A flet fit and a warm he'rt, but I never did a daisy ony hairm in a' my days, except maybe when I tramped on't. But I ken something aboot the gowfin' for a' that, for when the minister started first he used to tak' me wi' him on the Mondays to cairry his clubs. I never kent whit ministerial eloquence was afore then. When he topped his ba' or garred the land o' the mountain and the flood dirl, there was whit the papers ca' a weird silence that lasted five meenutes.

'And he kent less aboot gowf that I did, the minister, for efter he had sclaffed a dizzen or twa o' divots a yaird square aff the course, I tellt him it was considered the genteel thing to replace the turf.

'"Naething o' the kind,"' says he as snuffy as onything; "ye only replace clods if ye lift them aff the puttin'greens."'

'What did you say to that, Erchie?'

'I jist said "Holy Frost!" and looked at the scenery.

'I had only the a'e season actin' caddie for the minister; I found the experience was spilin' my respect for the Church o' Scotland, and I couldna' stand yon awfu' torrents o' silence efter he missed a four-inch putt so I tellt him I had plenty o' better-payin' jobs at my ain tred, and had to leave him. He took oot his wife then, to learn her the game when naebody was lookin', and it was a movin' sicht to see him and her comin' hame no' speakin' to yin anither, for she bate him easy frae the start – a thing nae man o' spirit cares to have happen to him.

'Oh, aye, that's anither advantage the game has ower fitba', or harriers; it's jist as weel suited for weemen as for men. I'm gled Jinnet's no' ta'en up wi't, though, for it's sae distractin'. If she took the craze my tea wad never be ready; she wad be like Duffy's wife when she nearly went aff her heid ower ping-pong.'

Golfers

ROBIN JENKINS

This is the first of two extracts taken from the work of Robin Jenkins, the prolific Scots novelist from Cambuslang in Lanarkshire. His writings are mostly set in Scotland, as here, or in places in the East, based on his work as a teacher in Afghanistan and Borneo. The story 'Golfers' is set at the fictitious Ayrshire golf club of Auchenskeoch, and in its opening section we are introduced to a threesome of local men who meet every Saturday, exhibiting a 'fanatical but necessary single-mindedness', reminiscent of the old joke about the man who asked to play through the match ahead, because his wife was in hospital and he was in a hurry to finish the game and see her.

★ ★ ★

A famous professional recently stressed the importance to golfers of shutting out the world and concentrating only on the game. That this is sound advice is known even to bunglers with handicaps of twenty-four. Whenever one of these muffs a shot and the ball stots feebly in the wrong direction, he will nevertheless have been trying very hard to think of absolutely nothing else but hitting it straight and far: his crude technique has simply let him down. Those figures in bright pullovers and spiked shoes, which can be seen walking about a golf course as determined as ants, are not human beings, they are golfers, concentrating on ball, stance and swing, to the exclusion of everything else. The best jokes in clubhouses celebrate this fanatical but necessary single-mindedness.

Of the three hundred members of Auchenskeoch Golf Club, on

the west coast of Scotland, none appreciated the necessity of total concentration more than a threesome that played together every Saturday morning. It consisted of William Lossit, manager of the local branch of the Caledonia Bank, Jack Killeyan, principal teacher of geography at Auchenskeoch High School, and Donald McLairg, proprietor of the Clydeview Hotel. They had met on the golf course and had taken care to keep their acquaintance purely a golfing one. They did not visit one another's houses and were not interested in one another's affairs. Their wives knew one another to nod to in the main street but were too well-trained ever to stop and gossip. Instinctively they knew that in some mysterious way their husbands' golf would suffer if they got to know one another well. Thus, after five years of playing together, the three men remained staunchly strangers.

Unless the rain was tempestuous or snow blanketed the course, they would meet on the first tee at half-past nine. After exchanging nods and good-mornings, they would toss to see who should have the honour of driving off first, and immediately begin. During the game they might mention, perfunctorily, some tournament of world-famous professionals taking place elsewhere, and the other two might grunt in commendation if the third brought off some spectacularly good shot; but for the most part they kept quiet and concentrated on the golf.

William Lossit had been a bank manager for ten years. Headquarters in Edinburgh, and some of his customers, now and then were not satisfied with his management, but in a time of fallen standards anyone not downright incompetent was secure. So he was content in his red-tiled bungalow with its fine view of Arran. He liked to work in the garden, taking care not to get calluses on his hands that might interfere with the proper gripping of his golf clubs. His grown-up son, happily married, was flourishing in Inverness as a chartered accountant. He had only one worry, if it could be called that. It concerned his wife, Agnes. For months on end she would be the perfect wife, obedient, dutiful, thrifty and self-effacing; then suddenly she would go and do something odd. It was never anything sensational, indeed it was always trifling. For instance, he would plant some gladioli in some spot he had carefully chosen. In a day or two he would discover she had dug them up and replanted them in some other place quite unsuitable. Then again, he was fond of a certain brand of sauce. Once when the bottle was empty she replaced it with a different brand altogether, one she must have known he would not like. Over the years there had been many such oddities of behaviour on her part. Sometimes he wondered if their purpose could be to spite him, perhaps in revenge for his devoting more time to golf than to her.

As a teacher, Jack Killeyan was no more and no less successful than the majority of his colleagues. Given a bright class, he got good results; given a dull one, his results were poor.

He had been glad when he had got the post at Auchenskeoch: there was an increase in salary; the troublemakers of Auchenskeoch were less vicious and enterprising than those of Glasgow, whence he had come and where he had been born; the seaside air was healthier for his two daughters, and the golf course at Auchenskeoch was a splendid one, running alongside the sea.

After eight years at Auchenskeoch, his contentment was ruined when he noticed, or rather when his wife Bessie noticed, that contemporaries of his, in no observable way superior, were being promoted to headmasterships. He thereupon began to apply for every appropriate post he saw advertised, from Thurso in the north to Kelso in the south. Bessie helped him to fill in the forms. Unfortunately, she could not be with him at his interviews, to tell him what to say and, still more important, what not to say. Unknown to him, she wrote to their daughters, one by this time a nurse in Glasgow and the other a student in Edinburgh, that Dad was getting a bit depressed about being rejected so often, but they weren't to mention it, and anyway he had his golf to console and sustain him.

Donald McLairg had inherited Clydeview Hotel from his father. It was large, and occupied an enviable position near the harbour, though the roses in its front gardens seemed to smell of seaweed. Like Auchenskeoch itself, it was a little run down, suffering, like all Clydeside hotels, from the preference of Glaswegians for the sunshine of Majorca to the rain and midges of the Scottish Riviera.

In his young days Donald had loved to go off to watch the Open Championship wherever it was being played. He had stayed in the same five-star hotels as some of the famous competitors, and spent a lot of money. He had also been fond of pinching the bottoms of the Clydeview maids. Since then he had unaccountably married Martha, as skinny as she was devout. There was no mention of golf in the Bible, so she couldn't make up her mind whether or not the Lord approved of it. Consequently, Donald was allowed to continue, though he was obliged to wear less flamboyant pullovers and hats. After a while, his bottom-pinching was resumed, furtively . . .

Donald Cleans Up
from England, their England

A.G. MACDONELL

In the first chapter of England, their England *(pub. 1933) we met Donald, the ingenue Scotsman set loose in London and on a Kentish village cricket ground. This time he is more at home, so to speak, because he finds himself on a golf course. The characters he meets on this escapade are even more eccentric and Macdonell's uniquely 'sympathetic' satire is given free rein – for example, Sir Ludovic's inability to talk about anything other than the iniquities, as he saw it, of 'the dole' and those who draw it or attempt to draw it. Like many a young Scot, Donald once had been 'more interested in golf than religion', but that was before the War and he had not taken it up again until the comic episode described in this chapter. Particularly amusing is the encounter with the expatriate professional masquerading as a 'rare old character', so as to meet the expectations of the upper class twits who shell out large sums of money for his golf equipment. Macdonell's satire is beautifully multi-layered and his line of fire can be adjusted to suit the context, not ruling out, for example, a side-swipe at the bickering of different Presbyterian sects back home in Scotland.*

★ ★ ★

A few days after this curious experience on the cricket field, Donald's attention was drawn away from the problem of the Englishman's attitude towards his national game by a chance paragraph in a leading newspaper on the subject of Golf. And golf was matter of grave temptation to Donald at this period of his life.

Both Sir Ethelred Ormerode, M.P., and Sir Ludovic Phibbs, M.P., had invited him to a day's golf at one or other of the large clubs near London to which they belonged; but Donald had made excuses to avoid acceptance, for the following reason. He had played no golf since he had been a lad of eighteen at Aberdeen, and as he had not enough money to join a club in the south and play regularly, he was unwilling to resurrect an ancient passion which he had no means of gratifying. Up to the age of eighteen golf had been a religion to him far more inspiring and appealing than the dry dogmatics of the various sections of the Presbyterian Church which wrangled in those days so enthusiastically in the North-East of Scotland. Since that time, of course, there has been a notable reunion of the sections and public wrangling has perforce come to an end, an end regretted so passionately that the phrase 'a peace-maker' in that part of the world is rapidly acquiring the sense of a busy-body or a spoil-sport. As one ancient soldier of the Faith, whose enthusiasm for the Word was greater than his knowledge of it, was recently heard to observe bitterly into the depths of his patriarchal beard, 'Isn't it enough for them to have been promised the Kingdom of Heaven, without they must poke their disjasket nebs into Buchan and the Mearns?'

But whatever the rights and wrongs of the once indignant and now cooing Churches, it is a fact that Donald before the War was more interested in golf than in religion, and a handicap of plus one when he was seventeen had marked him out as a coming man. But first the War and then the work of farming the Mains at Balspindie had put an end to all that, and Donald was reluctant to awaken the dragon.

But one day he happened to read in one of the most famous newspapers in the world the following paragraph column written by 'Our Golf Correspondent':

Our recent defeat at the hands of the stern and wild Caledonians was, no doubt, demnition horrid, as our old friend would have said, and had it not been for the amazing series of flukes by which the veteran Bernardo, now well advanced in decrepitude, not only managed to hang on to the meta-phorical coat-tails of his slashing young adversary, but even to push his nose in front on the last green, the score of the Sassenachs would have been as blank as their faces. For their majestic leader was snodded on the fourteenth green, and even the Dumkins and the Podder of the team, usually safe cards, met their Bannockburn. And that was that. The only consolation for this unexpected 'rewersal' lies in the fact that the Northerners consisted almost entirely of what are called Anglo-Scots, domiciled in England and products of English golf. For there is no doubt that the balance of golfing power has shifted to the south, and England is now the real custodian of the ancient traditions of the game. Which, as a consolation prize, is all wery capital.

Donald read this Pickwickian parody through carefully several times, for it seemed to be a matter of importance to him and his work. He had seen, at very close quarters, the English engaged upon their own ancient, indigenous national pastime, and he had been unable to make head or tail of it.

But it was worth while going out of his way to see how they treated another nation's national game which, according to the golf correspondent, they had mastered perfectly and had, as it were, adopted and nationalized.

The matter was easily arranged, and, on the following Sunday, he was picked up at the corner of Royal Avenue and King's Road by Sir Ludovic Phibbs in a Rolls-Royce limousine car. Sir Ludovic was wearing a superb fur coat and was wrapped in a superb fur rug. On the way down to Cedar Park, the venue of the day's golf, Sir Ludovic talked a good deal about the scandal of the dole. It appeared to be his view that everyone who took the dole ought to be shot in order to teach them not to slack. The solution of the whole trouble was the abolition of Trades Unionism and harder work all round, including Saturday afternoons and a half-day on Sundays.

This theme lasted most of the journey, and Donald was not called upon to contribute more than an occasional monosyllable.

Cedar Park is one of the newest of the great golf clubs which are ringed round the north, west, and south of London in such profusion, and what is now the club-house had been in earlier centuries the mansion of a venerable line of marquesses. High taxation had completed the havoc in the venerable finances which had been begun in the Georgian and Victorian generations by high gambling, and the entire estate was sold shortly after the War by the eleventh marquess to a man who had, during it, made an enormous fortune by a most ingenious dodge. For, alone with the late Lord Kitchener, he had realized in August and September of 1914 that the War was going to be a very long business, thus providing ample opportunities for very big business, and that before it was over it would require a British Army of millions and millions of soldiers. Having first of all taken the precaution of getting himself registered as a man who was indispensable to the civil life of the nation during the great Armageddon, for at the outbreak of hostilities he was only thirty-one years of age, and, in order to be on the safe side, having had himself certified by a medical man as suffering from short sight, varicose veins, a weak heart, and incipient lung trouble, he set himself upon his great task of cornering the world's supply of rum. By the middle of 1917 he had succeeded, and in 1920 he paid ninety-three thousand pounds for Cedar Park, and purchased in addition a house in Upper Brook Street, a hunting-box near Melton, a two-thousand-ton motor-yacht, Lochtarig Castle, Inverness-shire, and the long leases of three luxurious flats in Mayfair in which to entertain, without his wife knowing, by day or night, his numerous lady friends. He was, of course, knighted for his public services during the War. It was not until 1925 that the rum-knight shot himself to avoid an absolutely certain fourteen years for fraudulent conversion, and Cedar Park was acquired by a syndicate of Armenian sportsmen for the purpose of converting it into a country club.

An enormous man in a pale-blue uniform tricked out with thick silver cords and studded with cart-wheel silver buttons, opened the door of the car and bowed Sir Ludovic, and a little less impressively, Donald Cameron into the club-house. Donald was painfully conscious that his grey flannel trousers bagged at the knee and that his old blue 1914 golfing-coat had a shine at one elbow and a hole at the other.

The moment he entered the club-house a superb spectacle met his dazzled gaze. It was not the parquet floor, on which his nail-studded shoes squeaked loudly, or the marble columns, or the voluptuous paintings on the ceiling, or the gilt-framed mirrors on the walls, or the chandeliers of a thousand crystals, or even the palms in their gilt pots and synthetic earth, that knocked him all of a heap. It was the group of golfers that was standing in front of the fire-place. There were purple jumpers and green jumpers and yellow jumpers and tartan jumpers; there were the biggest, the baggiest, the brightest plus-fours that ever dulled the lustre of a peacock's tail; there were the rosiest of lips, the gayest of cheeks, the flimsiest of silk stockings, and the orangest of finger-nails and probably, if the truth were known, of toe-nails too; there were waves of an unbelievable permanence and lustre; there were jewels, on the men as well as on the women, and foot-long jade and amber cigarette-holders and foot-long cigars with glistening cummer-bunds; and there was laughter and gaiety and much bending, courtier-like, from the waist, and much raising of girlish, kohl-fringed eyes, and a great chattering. Donald felt like a navvy, and when, in his agitation, he dropped his clubs with a resounding clash upon the floor and everyone stopped talking and looked at him, he wished he was dead. Another pale-blue-and-silver giant picked up the clubs, held them out at arm's length and examined them in disdainful astonishment – for after years of disuse they were very rusty – and said coldly, 'Clubs go into the locker-room, sir,' and Donald squeaked his way across the parquet after him amid a profound silence.

The locker-room was full of young gentlemen who were

discarding their jumpers – which certainly competed with Mr. Shelley's idea of Life Staining the White Radiance of Eternity – in favour of brown leather jerkins fastened up the front with that singular arrangement which is called a zipper. Donald edged furtively, hazily watched the flunkey lay the clubs down upon a bench, and then fled in panic through the nearest open door and found himself suddenly in a wire-netted enclosure which was packed with a dense throng of caddies. The caddies were just as surprised by his appearance in their midst as the elegant ladies and gentlemen in the lounge had been by the fall of the clubs, and a deathly stillness once again paralysed Donald.

He backed awkwardly out of the enclosure, bouncing off caddy after caddy like a cork coming over a rock-studded sluice, and was brought up short at last by what seemed to be a caddy rooted immovably in the ground. Two desperate backward lunges failed to dislodge the obstacle and Donald turned and found it was the wall of the professional's shop. The caddies, and worse still, an exquisitely beautiful young lady a cupid's-bow mouth and practically no skirt on at all, who had just emerged from the shop, watched him with profound interest. Scarlet in the face, he rushed past the radiant beauty, and hid himself in darkest corner of the shop and pretended to be utterly absorbed in a driver which he picked out at random from the rack. Rather to his surprise, and greatly to his relief, no one molested him with up-to-date go-getting salesmanship, and in a few minutes he had pulled himself together and was able to look round and face the world.

Suddenly he gave a start. Something queer was going on inside him. He sniffed the air once, and then again, and then the half-forgotten past came rushing to him across the wasted years. The shining rows of clubs, the boxes of balls, the scent of leather and rubber and gripwax and pitch, the club-makers filing away over the vices and polishing and varnishing and splicing and binding, the casual members waggling a club here and there, the professional listening courteously to tales of apocryphal feats, all the old familiar scenes of his youth came back to him. It was eleven years since he had played a game of golf, thirteen years since he had bought a club. Thirteen wasted years. Dash it, thought Donald, damn it, blast it, I can't afford a new club – I don't want a new club, but I'm going to buy a new club. He spoke diffidently to one of the assistants who was passing behind him, and enquired the price of the drivers.

'It's a new lot just finished, sir,' said the assistant, 'and I'm not sure of the price. I'll ask Mr. Glennie.'

Mr. Glennie was the professional himself. The great man, who was talking to a member, or rather was listening to a member's grievances against his luck, a ritual which occupies a large part of a professional's working day, happened to overhear the assistant, and he said over his shoulder in the broadest of broad Scottish accents, 'They're fufty-twa shullin' and cheap at that.'

Donald started back. Two pounds twelve for a driver! Things had changed indeed since the day when the great Archie Simpson had sold him a brassy, brand-new, bright yellow, refulgent, with a lovely whippy shaft, for five shillings and nine-pence.

His movement of Aberdonian horror brought him out of the dark corner into the sunlight which was streaming through the window, and it was the professional's turn to jump.

'It's Master Donald!' he exclaimed. 'Ye mind me, Master Donald – Jim Glennie, assistant that was at Glenavie to Tommy Anderson that went to the States?'

'Glennie!' cried Donald, a subtle warm feeling suddenly invading his body, and he grasped the professional's huge red hand.

'Man!' cried the latter, 'but I'm glad to see ye. How lang is't sin' we used to ding awa at each other roon' Glenavie? Man, it must be years and years. And fit's aye deein' wi' yer game? Are ye plus sax or seven?'

'Glennie,' said Donald sadly, 'I haven't touched a club since those old days. This is the first time I've set foot in a professional's shop since you took me that time to see Alec Marling at Balgownie the day before the War broke out.'

'Eh man, but you're a champion lost,' and the professional shook his head mournfully.

'But, Glennie,' went on Donald, 'where did you learn that fine

Buchan accent? You never used to talk like that. Is it since you came south that you've picked it up?'

The big professional looked a little shamefaced and drew Donald back into the dark corner.

'It's good for trade,' he whispered in the pure English of Inverness. 'They like a Scot to be real Scottish. They think it makes a man what they call 'a character.' God knows why, but there it is. So I just humour them by talking like a Guild Street carter who's having a bit of back-chat with an Aberdeen fish-wife. It makes the profits something extraordinary.'

'Hi! Glennie, you old swindler,' shouted a stoutish red-faced man who was smoking a big cigar and wearing a spectroscopic suit of tweeds. 'How much do you want to sting me for this putter?'

'Thirty-twa shullin' and saxpence, Sir Walter,' replied Glennie over his shoulder, 'but ye'll wastin yer siller for neither that club nor any ither wull bring ye doon below eighteen.'

A delighted laugh from a group of men behind Walter greeted this sally.

'You see,' whispered Glennie, 'he'll buy it and he'll tell his friends that I tried to dissuade him, and they'll all agree that I'm a rare old character, and they'll all come and buy too.'

'But fifty-two shillings for a driver!' said Donald. 'Do you mean to say they'll pay that?'

'Yes, of course they will. They'll pay anything so long as it's more than any other professional at any other club charges them. That's the whole secret. Those drivers there aren't a new set at all. They're the same set as I was asking forty-eight shillings for last week-end, but I heard during the week from a friend who keeps an eye open for me, that young Jock Robbie over at Addingdale Manor had put his drivers and brassies up from forty-six shillings to fifty, the dirty young dog. Not that I blame him. It's a new form of commercial competition, Master Donald, a sort of inverted price-cutting. Na, na, Muster Hennessey,' he broke into his trade voice again, 'ye dinna want ony new clubs. Ye're playin' brawly with yer auld yins. Still, if ye want to try yon spoon, tak it oot and play a couple of roons wi' it, and if ye dinna like it put it back.'

He turned to Donald again.

'That's a sure card down here. They always fall for it. They take the club and tell their friends that I've given them on trial because I'm not absolutely certain that it will suit their game, and they never bring it back. Not once. Did you say you wanted a driver, Master Donald?'

'Not at fifty-two shillings,' said Donald with a smile.

Glennie indignantly waved away the suggestion.

'You shall have your pick of the shop at cost price,' he said; and then, looking furtively round and lowering his voice until it was almost inaudible, he breathed Donald's ear, 'Fifteen and six.'

Donald chose a beautiful driver, treading on air all the while and feeling eighteen years of age, and then Sir Ludovic Phibbs came into the shop.

'Ah! There you are, Cameron,' he said genially; 'there are only two couples in front of us now. Are you ready? Good morning, Glennie, you old shark. There's no use trying to swing the lead over Mr. Cameron. He's an Aberdonian himself.'

As Donald went out, Glennie thrust a box of balls under his arm and whispered, 'For old times' sake!'

On the first tee Sir Ludovic introduced him to the other two players who were going to make up the match. One was a Mr. Wollaston, a clean-shaven, intelligent, large, prosperous-looking man of about forty, and the other was a Mr. Gyles, a very dark man, with a toothbrush moustache and a most impressive silence. Both were stockbrokers.

'Now,' said Sir Ludovic heartily, 'I suggest that we play a four-ball foursome, Wollaston and I against you two, on handicap, taking our strokes from the course, five bob corners, half a crown each birdie, a dollar an eagle, a bob best ball and a bob aggregate and a bob a putt. What about that?'

'Good!' said Mr. Wollaston. Mr. Gyles nodded, while Donald, who had not understood a single word except the phrase 'four-ball foursome' – and that was incorrect – mumbled a feeble affirmative. The stakes sounded enormous, and the reference to birds of the air

156

sounded mysterious, but he obviously could not raise any objections.

When it was his turn to drive at the first tee, he selected a spot for his tee and tapped it with the toe of his driver. Nothing happened. He looked at his elderly caddy and tapped the ground again. Again nothing happened.

'Want a peg, Cameron?' called out Sir Ludovic.

'Oh no, it's much too early,' protested Donald, under the impression that he was being offered a drink. Everyone laughed ecstatically at this typically Scottish flash of wit, and the elderly caddy lurched forward with a loathsome little contrivance of blue and white celluloid which he offered to his employer. Donald shuddered. They'd be giving him a rubber tee with a tassel in a minute, or lending him a golf bag with tripod legs. He teed his ball on a pinch of sand with a dexterous twist of his fingers and thumb amid an incredulous silence.

Donald played the round in a sort of daze. After a few holes of uncertainty, much of his old skill came back, and he reeled off fairly good figures. He had a little difficulty with his elderly caddy at the beginning of the round, for, on asking that functionary to hand him 'the iron,' he received the reply, 'Which number, sir?' and the following dialogue ensued:

'What number what?' faltered Donald.

'Which number iron?'

'Er – just the iron.'

'But it must have a number, sir.'

'Why must it?'

'All irons have numbers.'

'But I've only one.'

'Only a number one?'

'No. Only one.'

'Only one what, sir?'

'One iron!' exclaimed Donald, feeling that this music-hall turn might go on for a long time and must be already holding up the entire course.

The elderly caddy at last appreciated the deplorable state of affairs. He looked grievously shocked and said in a reverent tone:

'Mr. Fumbledon has eleven.'

'Eleven what?' enquired the startled Donald.

'Eleven irons.'

After this revelation of Mr. Fumbledon's greatness, Donald took 'the iron' and topped the ball hard along the ground. The caddy sighed deeply.

Throughout the game Donald never knew what the state of the match was, for the other three, who kept complicated tables upon the backs of envelopes, reckoned solely in cash. Thus, when Donald once timidly asked his partner how they stood, the taciturn Mr. Gyles consulted his envelope and replied shortly after a brief calculation, 'You're up three dollars and a tanner.'

Donald did not venture to ask again, and he knew nothing more about the match until they were ranged in front of the bar in the club-room, when Sir Ludovic and Mr. Wollaston put down the empty glasses which had, a moment ago, contained double pink gins, ordered a refill of the four glasses, and then handed over to the bewildered Donald the sum of one pound sixteen and six.

Lunch was an impressive affair. It was served in a large room, panelled in white and gold with a good deal of artificial marble scattered about the walls, by a staff of bewitching young ladies in black frocks, white aprons and caps, and black silk stockings. Bland wine-stewards drifted hither and thither, answering to Christian names and accepting orders and passing them on to subordinates. Corks popped, the scent of the famous club fish-pie mingled itself with all the perfumes of Arabia and Mr. Coty, smoke arose from rose-tipped cigarettes, and the rattle of knives and forks played an orchestral accompaniment to the sound of many voices, mostly silvery, like April rain, and full of girlish gaiety.

Sir Ludovic insisted on being host, and ordered Donald's half-pint of beer and double whiskies for himself and Mr. Gyles. Mr. Wollaston, pleading a diet and the strict orders of Carlsbad medicos, produced a bottle of Berncastler out of a small brown handbag, and polished it off in capital style.

The meal itself consisted of soup, the famous fish-pie, a fricassee of chicken, saddle of mutton or sirloin of roast beef, sweet, savoury, and cheese, topped off with four of the biggest glasses of hunting port that Donald had ever seen. Conversation at lunch was almost entirely about the dole. The party then went back to the main club-room where Mr. Wollaston firmly but humorously pushed Sir Ludovic into a very deep chair, and insisted upon taking up the running with four coffees and four double kümmels. Then after a couple of rubbers of bridge, at which Donald managed to win a few shillings, they sallied out to play a second round. The golf was only indifferent in the afternoon. Sir Ludovic complained that, owing to the recrudescence of what he mysteriously called 'the old trouble,' he was finding it very difficult to focus the ball clearly, and Mr. Wollaston kept on overswinging so violently that he fell over once and only just saved himself on several other occasions, and Mr. Gyles developed a fit of socketing that soon became a menace to the course, causing, as it did, acute nervous shocks to a retired major-general whose sunlit nose only escaped by a miracle, and a bevy of beauty that was admiring, for some reason, the play of a well-known actor-manager.

So after eight holes the afternoon round was abandoned by common consent, and they walked back to the club-house for more bridge and much-needed refreshment. Donald was handed seven-teen shillings as his inexplicable winnings over the eight holes. Later on, Sir Ludovic drove, or rather Sir Ludovic's chauffeur drove, Donald back to the corner of King's Road and Royal Avenue. On the way back, Sir Ludovic talked mainly about the dole.

Seated in front of the empty grate in his bed-sitting-room, Donald counted his winnings and reflected that golf had changed a great deal since he had last played it.

Off My Game

ANDREW LANG

★ ★ ★

Andrew Lang was a Scots man of letters, a great friend of Robert Louis Stevenson, and known for his literary versatility. Lang was accomplished in poetry (his verses included those to be found in his amazingly popular 'fairy books') and essays, as well as being highly regarded in Scotland and beyond for his translations of Homer. It would appear that he also was a bit of an all-rounder in his sporting pursuits, writing poems about fishing and country sports as well as golf, as in this splendid composition.

★ ★ ★

'I'm off my game,' the golfer said,
And shook his locks in woe;
'My putter never lays me dead,
My drives will never go;
Howe'er I swing, howe'er I stand,
Results are still the same,
I'm in the burn, I'm in the sand –
I'm off my game !

'Oh, would that such mishaps might fall
On Laidlay or Macfie,
That they might toe or heel the ball,
And sclaff along like me!
Men hurry from me in the street,
And execrate my name,

Old partners shun me when we meet –
I'm off my game!

'Why is it that I play at all?
Let memory remind me
How once I smote upon my ball,
And bunkered it – *behind me*
I mostly slice into the whins,
And my excuse is lame –
It cannot cover half my sins –
I'm off my game!

'I hate the sight of all my set,
I grow morose as Byron;
I never loved a brassey yet,
And now I hate an iron.
My cleek seems merely made to top,
My putting's wild or tame;
It's really time for me to stop –
I'm off my game!'

Song in Praise of Gowfing

ANDREW DUNCAN

★ ★ ★

Duncan, a Scot, wrote this nice little poem in 1813 for the Blackheath Golf Club on the outskirts of London, a club which lays claim to being the oldest established in the world. Although it is to be hoped that the claim is inaccurate, James VI is recorded as playing there in 1608 after taking the road south following the Union of the Crowns in 1603. Everything and everyone in the poem seems perfectly amiable and accomplished, and Angus MacVicar would no doubt be envious of the 'well-directed' putts. Verse 2 seems to view golf as a substitute not only for life but also for war, and the final verse has a ring of James Bond about it.

★ ★ ★

O' rural diversions, too long has the chace
All the humours usurp'd, and assum'd the chief place;
But truth bids the Muse from henceforward proclaim,
That Gowf, first of sports, shall stand foremost in fame.

At Gowf we contend, without rancour or spleen,
And bloodless the laurels we reap on the green;
From vig'rous exertion our pleasures arise,
And to crown our delights no poor fugitive dies.

O'er the heath see our heroes in uniform clad,
In parties well match'd, how they gracefully spread;
While with long strokes and short strokes they tend to the goal,
And with putt well-directed plump into the hole.

From exercise strong, from strength active and bold,
We'll traverse the green, and forget to grow old.
Blue devils, diseases, dull sorrow and care,
Knock'd down by our balls as they whizz thro' the air.

Health, happiness, harmony, friendship, and fame,
Are the fruits and rewards of our favourite game;
A sport so distinguish'd, the fair must approve,
Then to Gowf give the day, and the evening to love.

3

UTTERLY CRYIT DOON
(The Different Codes of Football)

Introduction

★ ★ ★

Scotland is like Uruguay. Both are small countries obsessed by football; both at one time or another have reached a peak of achievement in the game surpassed only by the elite like Brazil and Germany and Argentina. Early Scottish missionaries of football carried the flame to Uruguay and elsewhere in South America. Uruguay won the first World Cup in 1930, Scotland defeated England in the first ever football international. At the start of the twenty-first century, both have their great days, it seems, far behind them. Or at least that is true of Scotland.

One of the Stewart kings, James I, has already made an appearance in this book, as an *aficianado* of real tennis, a pastime for the elite. This chapter is about something more to the taste of the common folks then and now: football. The proclamation of his son James II's Parliament of March 1457 runs:

> It is decreyet and ordanyt . . . that the futball and golf be utterly cryit downe, and not to be usit.

Medieval football seems to have been obsessive indeed – in 1511 the Privy Council described it as 'wood' (or mad) football – evidence perhaps that there has always been a hooligan element. In

1607, for example, youths in Aberdeen were had up before the
sheriff for profaning the Sabbath by: 'Drinking, playing football,
dancing and roving from parish to parish.' Even today the 'town
games' which survive, like the 'Ba' game in Kirkwall, are thoroughly
uninhibited in action and the talk of the town for days on end. Once
or twice a year these games raged up and down the town streets and
pends, gigantic heaving scrums in which rules were minimal and
goals rare – a kind of primeval chaos, from which the separate codes
of soccer and rugby (and American football) slowly emerged in the
nineteenth century. These were games as enthusiastic communal
activities on high days and holidays, involving all or most of the
able-bodied, not, as now, regular weekly occurrences for a few
skilled participants and many observers. So, many of the folk were
enthusiastic participants, not to say obsessive. In the eighteenth
century the Reverend John Skinner from Aberdeenshire gave a vivid
description of such a game in his poem *The Christmas Bawing of
Monimusk*. Skinner wrote it when he was an eighteen-year-old
assistant schoolmaster at Monymusk, so it is entirely possible that
he had taken part in the game of ba'ing. Here is a flavour of it:

> Has never in a' this country been
> Sic shoudering and sic fawing,
> As happent twa, three days senseen,
> Here at the Christmas Ba'ing:
> At evening syne the fellows keen,
> Drank till the neist day's dawing
> Sae snell that some tint baith their e'en,
> And couldna pay their lawing   bill
> For a' that day.

> The hurry-burry now began,
> Was right well worth the seeing,
> Wi' bensils bauld tweish man and man,   blows
> Some getting fa's some gieing,
> And a' the tricks o' foot and hand,
> That ever were in being:

> Sometimes the ba' a yirdlins ran,   along the ground
> Sometimes in air was fleeing
> Fou heigh that day.

The shoulder charge and other rough tactics evidently had not been outlawed, but even so there was latitude for the tanner-ba' tricks beloved of generations of Scots footballers.

The unlikely figure of Walter Scott also had a shot at capturing our obsessive love of the sport generically known as 'football'. In a poem composed to mark a 'grand match' he sponsored between Selkirk and Yarrow in 1815, in the unlikely surroundings of Ettrick Forest, he urged:

> Then strip lads and to it, though sharp be the weather
> And if by mischance you should happen to fall
> There are worse things in life than a tumble on heather
> And *life is itself but a game of football*

Notice that he calls it a 'game' – an echo (or anticipation) of the 'Beautiful Game' of our day. No half measures, and Bill Shankly-like, Sir Walter places the game of football right at the heart of the meaning of life, no less. Even the present-day Scottish Executive has a tremulous moment of uncommon excitement in their website called 'The Game': .

> Welcome. The founding of Queen's Park Football Club in 1867 was the formal beginning of the swift rise of football to its pre-eminent place in Scottish sport. Over a hundred years later the game is essentially the same as that played in the late 19th century: two teams, one ball, two goals. The aim of the game to put the ball more times in your opponent's net than they do in yours. While Scotland cannot claim to have invented the game, its role in the development of world football cannot be questioned.

The story of modern or association football, so-called because it followed the rules laid down in the 1860s by an association of clubs under the distinguished leadership of Oxford University, is a curious regression within a century from blazered toffs through cloth caps to bare painted chests and tribal chants – a case of reverting to its primitive roots perhaps? The nineteenth century did see many changes in the game, like the rise of professionalism. And in this move towards a paid profession, as you might expect, there were Scotsmen on the make. In 1878, a team that included two professionals from Partick ran out to play in the FA Cup fourth round, at the Kennington Oval, versus an Old Etonians eleven.

This was also, however, the heyday of the villages and small towns, when a team like Dumbarton could share the league championship with Glasgow Rangers in 1890 (and win it outright the following year) or Renton (not even a league club in many a long day) defeat Preston North End in a challenge match between the Scottish and English cup winners. The men from the Vale of Leven village celebrated their 1888 victory with no great degree of modesty:

Tonight the conqueror's banner in Renton town's unfurled
To welcome home their heroes, the champions of the world;
The band in triumph playing – the busy stir's began
And the fire of victory's blazing on the braes of old Carman.

For we, as honest Scotchmen, should honour and admire
The hardy lads we've reared and trained in old Dumbartonshire;
And when you meet the Preston team, be careful how you
play,
And beat them, as you played and beat your Southern foes to-
day.

As has been said, the Scots footballers were among the first to sally forth as mercenaries. Neil Munro's story in *Erchie, My Droll Friend* gives a curiously modern account of a transfer, involving the vast sum of £4,500 in the 1920s.

Tom Hamilton doesna' handle a' that money; it maistly gangs
to the Kilmarnock club that sold him. A' he gets frae the

Preston North End is his wages and expenses. Bein' a champion fitba player's no great catch; he's the last relic o' slavery left in modern times. He has nae sooner settled doon in a nice wee hoose wi' a bit o' gairden than somebody comes and buys him and cairts him awa' to anither pairt o' the country where he doesna ken a livin' soul and has to learn the language.

By the 1920s there was a fair representation of Scots operating at the highest level in England. At this point came Scotland's international team's greatest day:

THE WEMBLEY WIZARDS

Decisive victories have marked the two great athletic contests of the weekend. At Wembley Scotland triumphed over England in the Association Football International. At Putney Cambridge scored a runaway victory over Oxford. The interest taken by Scotsmen in the International match may be gauged from the fact that some 8,000 travelled to London specially to see it. They had their reward for the Scottish team, in spite of the rain, gave an exhibition of artistic and scientific play which has seldom been surpassed, and which the English spectators, always generous in defeat, applauded with enthusiasm. There is no question that Scotland's overwhelming victory by five goals to one was fully earned. The English team played well and pluckily, but they were no match for the superlative brilliance of their opponents. The result of one of the most thrilling international matches ever played is a striking tribute to the soundness of Scottish football.

Glasgow Herald, 2 April 1928

A footballer from our own era with a career as a mercenary (like Tom Hamilton) – indeed one who has been compared to D' Artagnan because of his flashing, rapier-like style – is the Aberdonian forward, Denis Law. Law became a starring figure in European soccer at a very young age. A prolific scorer throughout his career, he turned professional at the age of sixteen straight from school with Huddersfield Town. At eighteen he scored in his Scotland debut. In one game for his club Law scored an incredible six goals against Luton. Word of his scoring prowess soon spread however and he went on to play at the highest level with both Manchester clubs and Torino in Italy. He won two English league titles and the 1963 FA Cup, and was awarded the title of 1964's European Footballer of the Year; and thus the statistics tell the story. However, for those who saw Denis Law, or indeed any other great footballer, a fitter description of their prowess than any statistics is given in a sentence taken from the superior journalism of Hugh McIlvanney:

> The game's extraordinary grip on the imagination of countless millions is exerted not through score-lines but through the images of grace and skill, of courage and inventiveness, it leaves to shimmer in the memory.

There can be no 'images of grace and skill' better and more memorable than Law's flashing interceptions in the penalty area, and the sight of him leaping like a salmon to meet the ball with his head.

Of course, Law's status as an iconic figure depended on other things as well. He is well-known for a quite disproportionate degree of patriotism for one who has spent most of his career outside Scotland – returning for the birth of his son to ensure Scottish citizenship, or describing through gritted teeth a game of golf he played one day in 1966:

> As we came round the corner from the eighteenth green a crowd of members were at the clubhouse window cheering and waiting to tell me that England had won the World Cup. It was the blackest day of my life.

Scotland wasn't even involved, but he makes it seem as bad, or worse, than the most humiliating of defeats. As a matter of fact, Law had been 'present' at the 9–3 Wembley debacle five years previous to the English victory. One journalist blamed the 'Flodden' mainly on him and another Anglo-Scot.

SCOTLAND'S HEAVIEST DEFEAT TO DATE
England 9 – Scotland 3

The International at Wembley on Saturday was the 213th played by Scotland against one of the other British countries but never before have so many goals as the nine which were shot or flicked past Haffey been scored against a Scottish team . . . But what a deplorable display was that of Scotland on Saturday. I have not the slightest doubt what the principal reason was, apart from the fact that England were, as they have appeared be throughout this season, much the better team. Such effort as Mackay and Law expended – and one is bound to say that this was considerable – was to their side's great disadvantage, and it was on those two Anglo-Scots, supposedly wise in the ways of English football and more than ordinarily capable players, that so much depended. Not for the first time Mackay and Law must be charged with putting their own whims and fancies before the good of the team as a whole. When England scored their first three goals all in the first half-hour, Mackay was as far away from the breaching of the defence as some of the spectators on the terracing; indeed when Greaves side-footed the third almost on the Scottish goal-line this assiduous promoter of attack was still in the English half of the field. If this has any connection with common-sense wing-half play I am the Queen of Sheba . . .
(England – Springett; Armfield and McNeil; Robson, Swan and Flowers; Douglas and Greaves; Smith; Haynes and Charlton. Scotland – Haffey; Shearer and Caldow; Mackay, McNeill and McCann; McLeod and Law; St John; Quinn and Wilson.)
Glasgow Herald, Monday, 17 April 1961

Arrogance very often accompanies great talent, but one thing is certain: Law was a member of a group of footballers seldom seen nowadays – those who put country before club.

The growth of the professional game in the twentieth century was accompanied by the massive increase in the spectator element of football – mass participation in a weekly ritual that gave shape and meaning to working-class lives. Every Saturday, across Scotland and England (and especially when workers won their freedom in the afternoons), hundreds of thousands of people streamed towards football grounds in pilgrimages of an almost medieval scale. Huge cauldrons of the game like Hampden Park (with crowds at times approaching 150,000 people) and Ibrox were the biggest stadia in the world at the time, and for many years to come.

'Catch the red car to Mount Florida!' These are the directions given to Neil Munro's Jimmy Swan for getting to Hampden to see a football international. Jimmy has lived in Glasgow all his life and might be expected to know which tramcar to catch from the city centre to reach the great stadium – but Jimmy is a sensitive soul and much prefers singing in a choir to going to football matches. As a commercial traveller visiting many country towns and villages in Scotland just before the Great War, he uses talk about football, the players and the games, as part of his common currency of salesman's patter along with jokes and snatches from the music hall. The story *Jimmy's Sins Find Him Out* tells what happens when a country customer unexpectedly arrives in town and Jimmy's happy indifference to everything about football – apart from what he gleans from the sporting papers when he has to – is in danger of being revealed.

Mount Florida, a pleasant hilly suburb on Glasgow's South Side, has been for more than a century the scene of many great international sporting occasions (and not a few religious revivalist gatherings). In one of our extracts the novelist Robin Jenkins compares the vast edifice to a secular cathedral. Certainly for most of the year, proceedings at Hampden are incredibly sedate, as a tiny sprinkling of devotees gather on the mighty slopes (now seated) to watch the Amateurs of Queen's Park playing at home. On big occasions like internationals and cup finals, however, the surrounding streets become clogged with thousands of intending spectators. Families and friends such as those following the Drumsagart Thistle (in Jenkins's *The Thistle and the Grail*) are wise to stick closely together, in case they are forcibly parted from each other. This of course is what happened to Jimmy Swan and his customer up from the country.

One of the most venerable of clichés is the comparison between football and war and nowhere is it more likely to be used than when talking about Glasgow's and Scotland's two biggest clubs. In his poem, *You Lived in Glasgow*, Iain Crichton Smith speaks of the 'divided city of the green and blue', although oddly enough, the collective term for Celtic and Rangers – 'The Old Firm' – is actually quite innocuous and unwarlike. Perhaps the epithet 'Old Firm' is a gentle harking back to the city's mercantile past. More typically, however, the impressions many have of the clubs is of passion and skill certainly, but passion mixed with bigotry, and what most supporters get from the game is a lot less innocuous than entertainment or recreation. This is all too clear in an extract from a 1935 novel by George Blake, *The Shipbuilders*, which describes a clash of 'the green and blue' at Ibrox Park.

Following World War II, there was a dawning recognition that Scotland's days of world leadership of the game had gone. New and exotic names like Moscow Dynamo and Inter Milan now formed part of conversations in pub and factory, along with a growing respect for the silky skills of the 'Continentals'. A brief flourish of the old hegemony came in 1967, when Celtic won the European Cup and created legends of the 'lost legions' who never returned from Lisbon.

By then, and by the time that Denis Law was playing, the game had indeed assumed a global significance – not just players but spectators were becoming increasingly mobile, and in the case of Scottish international supporters, they were prepared to journey far, even to the Southern Hemisphere, to experience defeat. Walter Scott, the 'Wizard of the North', in his capacity as an admirer of

Scotland's history, would have recognised certain aspects of the age into which football now moved. For this was the era of the 'Tartan Army'. Looking and behaving like participants in an event organised by the Sealed Knot Society, the supporters of the national team took on a sort of historical re-enactment of battles from Scotland's past. Those who stood or sat on the stadium slopes took refuge in a kind of self-conscious romanticism – a curious echo of the last great military campaign on British soil. There were tartan-clad hordes in place of the Jacobites of the '45 Rebellion and the matches of the 1978 Argentina World Cup as a symbolic rendering of the battles of that doomed army. To be even more fanciful, there was a Pretender in the shape of Ally Macleod, the national manager, and Argentina was his Culloden. Many sports journalists, the notorious 'fans with typewriters', turned on their former heroes, although others, like Hugh McIlvanney, had a shrewder view of the whole nation's complicity in the disappointment:

> Some of us have been acknowledging through most of our lives that the game is hopelessly ill-equipped to carry the burden of emotional expression the Scots seek to load upon it. What is hurting so many now is the realisation that something they believed to be a metaphor for their pride has all along been a metaphor for their desperation.
>
> *McIlvanney on Football*

In the aftermath of the 'disaster', the other McIlvanney also called for a rational reassessment of the way Scots look at their national game:

> It's not that we lost, but that it meant so much. Losing a football match shouldn't be confused with loss of identity. I suspect that the kind of commitment Scots invest in football means that there's less left for more important concerns.
>
> *Surviving the Shipwreck*

Twenty-five years on and things are quieter and less desperate, perhaps because political change in Scotland has recovered some of that identity. The Tartan Army survives, but has now developed an almost completely humorous and ironic form of existence. That apart, outside of the undiminished ranks of the 'Old Firm' followers, Scots have opted for the role of couch potato, rather than active supporter.

So much for soccer, then, that is the undisputed 'world game'. There is interesting Scottish writing about other members of the football family – from the old ballad of the 'Bonny Earl o' Moray', who 'played at the ba'', to the modern game of 'Rugby Football'. (We include examples from the classy pair of Buchan and Conan Doyle.) Rugby football is from its name clearly a first cousin of the game with the round ball, but arguably still a manifestation of an aspect of the Scottish class structure, or to use the old cliché as did Buchan's Mrs McCunn – 'a game for hooligans played by gentlemen'. This is of course in contrast to football's description as 'a game for gentlemen played by hooligans' – except in the Borders enclave where people from all social strata play or follow the game with the oval ball.

This view is somewhat outdated. It is difficult to imagine a contemporary definition of a 'gentleman' anyway, and in the television age the cult of sport transcends so-called class barriers. It is possible now for a Scottish rugby supporter not to have the 'old school' or equivalent social background. All sorts of people watch the international matches on television these days, at least when Scotland are having a good run. And rugby even shares with soccer an 'anthem' which combines bad grammar with shaky history.

As a postscript, this anthology includes some writing about the strange anachronistic offshoot of the 'Beautiful Game', the really quite unlovely but characterful junior football. The previously mentioned novel by Robin Jenkins, *The Thistle and the Grail*, is an amusing mock-epic tale of a progress to the final of the Scottish Junior Cup, 'the juniors' being a game of a very different colour from the seniors.

The 1883 Final

from The Sons of the Rock

ARTHUR JONES

★ ★ ★

*Arthur Jones is a librarian and follower of Dumbarton Football Club, the
'Sons of the Rock' (founded 1872). His history (with Jim McAllister) of
the club includes this description of the replayed Scottish Cup Final of
1883, and it gives a flavour of the game as it was in the 1880s –
Dumbarton had defeated the mighty Queen's Park on the way to the
final. In challenge matches that year they had also accounted for English
giants Blackburn Rovers and Bolton. On the day of the final at
Hampden the result was a 2-each draw. The replay took place on 7 April.
Rumours that some Dumbarton players had had a dram too many before
the first match were reflected in the chant:*

> *As lang's oor chaps keep a' T.T.*
> *Naething can beat the D.F.C.*

★ ★ ★

On the following Saturday, April 7th; the two teams assembled at
Hampden for the replay. The line-ups were:

Dumbarton: McAulay; Hutcheson & Paton; Miller & Keir; Brown
(1) & Brown (2), Miller & Lindsay; Anderson & McArthur.

Vale of Leven: McIntosh; Mcintyre & Forbes; McLeish & McPherson;
Gillies & McCrae; Johnstone & Friel, Kennedy & McFarlane.

Again about 15,000 spectactors turned up. Many of the spectators only caught glimpses of play. Improvements had, however, been made for the spectators, particularly those in the stand, and the weather too was favourable. R Anderson from the reserves in place of W Lang was the only alteration to either side from the previous game.

Both keepers had to look lively in the early stages. Play was often confined to the midfield during the first half – but there were also end-to-end spells when over-hasty or inaccurate shooting spoiled chances at both ends. James McAulay made a fine save just before halftime.

There was an interval of two minutes! A minute into the second half, the Sons profited by a long clearance and the ever-alert 'Plumber' Brown shot Dumbarton into the lead. Not long after 'Sparrow' Brown tried his luck with a long shot, which McIntosh misjudged. The Vale keeper tried to kick clear without using his hands – this was then quite usual; however, he missed it and Dumbarton were two up. Not content with this, the Sons continued to bombard the Vale defence; however, with only five minutes to go the Vale men, as a result of one of their occasional forays, scored with a shot which went in off the post. In spite of intense Vale pressure in the last few minutes the Sons held out and so the great moment had arrived! Dumbarton had won the Scottish Cup.

Back in the town of Dumbarton itself some 2,000 people had collected near the Post Office with others milling around Dumbarton Cross. Rumours were spreading but not all believed. Then a public telegram with the final result was read out in the High Street. The level of excitement was very high. Hats were thrown in the air and loud cheering resounded throughout the burgh. Before 9.30pm a huge number of people collected near the station to cheer the returning team. The three brass bands in the town were present: the Dumbarton Rifle Volunteers Band, the Academy Band, and the Catholic Brass Band. When the train arrived, 'See the conquering hero comes' was played. The team were then transported in a wagonette decorated with flags. The bands formed a procession through the streets of the town; the wagonette, having been unyoked, was pulled by some of the crowd. Handkerchiefs were waved from the tenement windows. At the Elephant Hotel the team were received and offered refreshments. They appeared at one of the windows, and each member in turn received the cheers of the crowd.

On a sporting note, it should be noted that the Vale team cheered the Sons at Dumbarton station, and when the runners-up arrived at Alexandria a fine reception awaited them too.

This note was somewhat spoiled on the following Monday when some of the Dumbarton team, with their friends, were returning from Loch Lomond on two wagonettes. As they passed through the Vale, and, it seems, emboldened by excessive refreshment, the players made plain to the locals how proud they were of their victory on Saturday. The Valeites took exception to this effrontery and some rough and unseemly scenes followed, including the pouring of two pails of slaughterhouse blood over the occupants of the wagonette.

However, the general atmosphere was a sporting one. It was recognised that Dumbarton had fought the last three finals and deserved to win at last.

The Old Firm

from The Shipbuilders

GEORGE BLAKE

★ ★ ★

George Blake's 1935 novel The Shipbuilders *is the story of a Glasgow shipyard, 'Pagan's', told mainly through the interwoven lives of the yard owner Leslie Pagan and the riveter Danny Shields. This excerpt focuses on the latter and is part of a longer section called 'Saturday in Glasgow'. The episode revolves around a Saturday spent by Danny. In the morning he goes to his work, as was customary right up until the Fifties, but because the only ship on order at Pagan's yard is nearing completion, there is no real work for a riveter. Danny's afternoon is spent in what we would now call a form of escapism, at Ibrox Park on the South Side, watching his team, Rangers, at home to their deadly rivals, Celtic. Set in the Depression years but characteristic of this particular confrontation at any time over more than 100 years, the book presents a sectarian picture familiar to anyone brought up in the West of Scotland, and, as Blake tells us, even farther afield: 'Blue for the Protestants of Scotland and Ulster, green for the Roman Catholics of the Free State'. The description of the game is in many ways intended as a form of social record, with the religious divide symbolised by the separation of the supporters, or 'enthusiasts', in different areas of the ground. 'All the social problems of a hybrid city were to be sublimated in the imminent clash of mercenaries.' There is more than just an undercurrent of violence, but Blake's view seems to be that in this way, Danny and others like him find release or, more explicitly, 'orgasm'.*

Only in one case is any of the 'mercenaries' named. Alan Morton, the 'Wee Blue Devil', who is described in some detail, was a real person and played for all of his career for Rangers in the city where he was born. He also won thirty-one caps on the left wing for Scotland in an era when there were few international matches, and he was a member of the famous 1928 'Wembley Wizards'.

A large tea inside him, including a black pudding of considerable size, Danny achieved peace of mind. The alcoholic anger melted from his consciousness and left him the friendly glow of repletion. Agnes did not return once to the obsession about Lizzie and Jim and the pictures. Before the meal was over he was boasting to her of his unique immunity in the matter of the pay-off at Pagan's and she, after her fashion, was complimenting him on the distinction and exclaiming at her own luck. Then, when she had gone, Peter stayed behind and assisted in the filling up of the coupon, revealing a particularly helpful knowledge of the form in the South sub-section of the Third Division of the English League; and he stayed in while Danny went out for a final drink at half-past nine. Billy sat like a mouse by the fire, reading, and went to bed when he was told. Wee Mirren slept the evening through and stirred only when her mother returned at the back of eleven, her face flushed.

Agnes, too, had passed an agreeable time. She had seen Ronald Coleman on the screen of one of the swell picture houses in Sauchiehall Street, and Jim had risen to balcony seats and ices. He had had his car parked in Holland Street, and after the show, had run them down to the lounge of the Adelphi for a round or two of drinks, in which Agnes's favourite wee ports figured pleasantly, and then had run her home as far as Partick Cross.

'Oh, and Dan!' she blurted out finally, 'They're awful keen for us to go out the morn's night. Not to the Pictures, but a wee supper. Jim's got a friend from England coming up, and they want to give him a night out. Could you not come after the match?'

A sudden shadow of resentment clouded Danny's mind. He could not like Lizzie and her husband, and he vaguely distrusted their influence on Agnes. But there some something in her eagerness that melted him, something that his Friday evening complaisance could not resist – and she had by an implication more cunning than he quite appreciated indicated that she would not nag him if he wished to go to the match.

'Ach to hell! I suppose we might as well,' said Danny.

If he regretted that desperate affability by breakfast time on Saturday, he did not confess the fact. There was never time for argument in the rush of getting to the Yard by eight o'clock, nor did Agnes ever quite emerge from sleep while he made his own breakfast, gulped it down, and hurried out. And on this great day of the Rangers–Celtic match at Ibrox, Danny was almost incapable of thinking beyond the thrills of the afternoon.

Anticipation of the game was indeed an obsession. An honest, keen workman, he found his labour in the Yard that morning an irritating irrelevance. If he worked hard, it was so that the hour of release might seem to come more quickly. Unhappily for him, his position as one who was there by favour, as a riveter for whom no task of riveting remained, was uneasy.

'I suppose I'll have to make work for you,' the foreman sneered. 'A riveter's no damned use to me. Och, go and give old Tom a hand in the store there. We'll see on Monday. . .'

The man went off grumbling, and Danny was left with a double burden. He knew there was nothing for him to do in the Store that would keep him decently occupied; and the weakness of his supernumerary position had been emphasised. He greatly feared that particular foreman and his prejudices. What if the Major should forget the promise? A blue lookout indeed, and a nice come-down from the triumphs of yesterday!

These anxieties he quickly forgot in friendly chat with brosy old Tom, who had himself not sufficient work to keep him going, and his heart leaped when the foreman popped his head over the half-door of the store about eleven and called on Danny to run across to the engine-shop with a message to the foreman there. For this meant a licensed escape from the yard at a vital hour – and Danny had just remembered his need of something necessary to his enjoyment of the afternoon.

In their wisdom, the Magistrates of that part of the world in which Pagan's was situated had long ordained that public-houses should open at ten and close at noon on Saturdays. The ordinance was based on the theory that the working-man should not be tempted to squander his wages on strong drink on his way home, and had no doubt a bearing on public behaviour at the afternoon football games; but as the artisan had for many a day past been paid on Fridays it was only an interesting anachronism of local administration and bore hardly on such as Danny who desired refreshment in anticipation of other enjoyments. So the foreman's gruff order rejoiced him. It was easy to slip into Mackenzie's between Yard and engine-shop, swallow a quick half and half-pint, buy a flat half-mutchkin of whisky for the pocket and the cold vigil on the terraces, and time his return to the store almost as the whistle boomed the signal for the week-end release.

Thereafter there was nothing in the world for him but the Game. He hurried home, hurried through his washing and changing and eating, and, as if all the claims of family and hearth were nothing now, was out on the streets again half an hour before two o'clock, a unit of one of the stream of men converging from all parts of the city and from all its outliers on the drab embankments round an oblong of turf in Ibrox.

The surge of the stream was already apparent in the Dumbarton Road. Even though only a few wore favours of the Rangers blue, there was that of purpose in the air of hurrying groups of men which infallibly indicated their intention. It was almost as if they had put on uniform for the occasion, for most were attired as Danny was in decent dark suits under raincoats or overcoats, with great flat caps of light tweed on their heads. Most of them smoked cigarettes that shivered in the corners of their mouths as they fiercely debated the prospects of the day. Hardly one of them but had his hands deep in his pockets.

The scattered procession, as it were of an order almost religious, poured itself through the mean entrance to the Subway station at Partick Cross. The decrepit turnstiles clattered endlessly, and there was much rough, good-humoured jostling as the devotees bounded down the wooden stairs to struggle for advantageous positions on the crowded platform. Glasgow's subway system is of high anti-quarian interest and smells very strangely of age. Its endless cables, whirling innocently over the pulleys, are at once absurd and fasci-nating, its signalling system a matter for the laughter of a later generation. But to Danny and the hundreds milling about him there was no strange spectacle here: only a means of approach to a shrine; and strongly they pushed and wrestled when at length a short train of toylike dimensions rattled out of the tunnel into the station.

It seemed full to suffocation already, but Danny, being alone and ruthless in his use of elbow and shoulder, contrived somehow to squeeze through a narrow doorway on to a crowded platform. Others pressed in behind him while official whistles skirled hopelessly without, and before the urgent crowd was forced back at last and the doors laboriously closed, he was packed tight among taller men of his kind, his arms pinned to his sides, his lungs so compressed that he gasped.

'For the love o' Mike . . .' he pleaded.

'Have ye no' heard there's a fitba' match the day, wee man?' asked a tall humorist beside him.

Everybody laughed at that. For them there was nothing odd or notably objectionable in their dangerous discomfort. It was, at the worst, a purgatorial episode on the passage to Elysium.

So they passed under the River to be emptied in their hundreds among the red sandstone tenements of the South Side. Under the high banks of the Park a score of streams met and mingled, the streams that had come by train or tram or motor car or on foot to see the Game of Games.

Danny ran for it as soon as his feet were on the earth's surface again, selecting in an experienced glance the turnstile with the shortest queue before it, ignoring the mournful column that waited without hope at the Unemployed Gate. His belly pushed the bar precisely as his shilling smacked on the iron counter. A moment later he was tearing as if for dear life up the long flight of cindered steps leading to the top of the embankment.

He achieved his favourite position without difficulty: high on one of the topmost terraces and behind the eastern goal. Already the huge amphitheatre seemed well filled. Except where the monstrous stands broke the skyline there were cliffs of human faces, for all the world like banks of gravel, with thin clouds of tobacco smoke drifting across them. But Danny knew that thousands were still to come to pack the terraces to the point of suffocation, and, with no eyes for the sombre strangeness of the spectacle, he proceeded to establish himself by settling his arms firmly along the iron bar before him and making friendly, or at least argumentative, contact with his neighbours.

He was among enthusiasts of his own persuasion. In consonance with ancient custom the police had shepherded supporters of the Rangers to one end of the ground and supporters of the Celtic to the other: so far as segregation was possible with such a great mob of human beings. For this game between Glasgow's two leading teams had more in it than the simple test of relative skill. Their colours, blue and green, were symbolic. Behind the rivalry of players, behind even the commercial rivalry of limited companies, was the dark significance of sectarian and racial passions. Blue for the Protestants of Scotland and Ulster, green for the Roman Catholics of the Free State; and it was a bitter war that was to be waged on that strip of white-barred turf. All the social problems of a hybrid city were to be sublimated in the imminent clash of mercenaries.

Danny was as ready as the next man to fight a supporter of the other team, but he had no opportunity of doing so. They were solid for Rangers within a radius of twenty yards from where he stood, and time until the kick-off was pleasantly taken up with discussion of the miracles their favourites could perform. They needed no introductions to one another. Expertise was assumed. The anxiety was that the Rangers team, as announced and on form, could be relied on to beat the men from the East. It was taken for granted that the Rangers were in normal circumstances the superiors of the

Celts; but here, it seemed, were special circumstances to render the issue of the afternoon's match peculiarly obscure.

Danny had some heartening exchanges with a man, smaller and older and grimmer than himself, who at his elbow smoked a clay pipe with a very short stem. The small man was not prepared to be unduly optimistic. Rangers were a fine bunch of boys, but the Celtic had been playing up great these last few Saturdays.

'It's a' in the melting-pot,' declared the small man, who had been reading the newspapers. 'I'm tellin' ye – it's a' in the bloody melting-pot.'

'Melting-pot, my foot!' Danny insisted gallantly. 'It's all in Alan Morton's left toe – out on the wing there. Wait till ye see the wee dandy.'

'Alan's fine,' the small man allowed gravely. 'Alan's a dandy. Alan's the best bloody outside left in fitba' the day. But I've been studying form, see?' He paused to let an attenuated dribble of saliva fall between his feet, and it took him a long time to wipe clean the stem of his short pipe. 'I've been studying form. Aye, I've been studying form – reading a' the papers, looking back a' the records – and it's like this. When ye've the Rangers here and the Celtic there and there's no much between them in the League –'

His discourse was interrupted by the irreverent voice of a youth behind. 'Does the wife know ye're out, old man?' it asked.

Laughter, half-friendly, half-derisive rose about them.

'I'll knock your block off, young fella,' said the old fellow, turning gravely on the youth and slowly removing the pipe from his wet mouth.

'Please, teacher, I'm sorry I spoke,' his tormentor assured him, mock-afraid.

They all laughed again; and so it went on – rough give-and-take, simple wisdom and facetious nonsense, passion and sentiment, hate and friendly laughter – while a brass band pumped out melody in the lee of the grandstand and press photographers hovered restlessly in anticipation of the appearance of the teams.

The Celtic came first, strangely attractive in their white and green, and there was a roar from the western end of the ground ('Hefty-looking lot o' bastards,' admitted the small, old man at Danny's side.) They were followed by a party of young men in light blue jerseys; and then it seemed that the low-hanging clouds must split at the impact of the yell that rose to greet them from forty-thousand throats. The referee appeared, jaunty in his shorts and khaki jacket; the linesmen, similarly attired, ran to their positions. In a strange hush, broken only by the thud of footballs kicked by the teams uneasily practising, the captains tossed for ends. Ah! Rangers had won and would play with the sou' westerly wind, straight towards the goal behind which Danny stood in his eagerness.

This was enough to send a man off his head. Good old Rangers – and to hell with the Pope! Danny gripped the iron bar before him. The players trotted limberly to their positions. For a moment there was dead silence over Ibrox Park. Then the whistle blew, a thin, curt, almost feeble announcement of glory.

For nearly two hours thereafter Danny Shields lived far beyond himself in a whirling world of passion. All sorts of racial emotions were released by this clash of athletic young men; the old clans of Scotland lived again their ancient hatreds in this struggle for goals. Not a man on the terraces paused to reflect that it was a spectacle cunningly arranged to draw their shillings, or to remember that the twenty-two players were so many slaves of a commercial system, liable to be bought and sold like fallen women, without any regard for their feelings as men. Rangers had drawn their warriors from all corners of Scotland, lads from mining villages, boys from Ayrshire farms, and even an undergraduate from the University of Glasgow. Celtic likewise had ranged the industrial belt and even crossed to Ulster and the Free State for men fit to win matches so that dividends might accrue. But for such as Danny they remained peerless and fearless warriors, saints of the Blue or Green as it might be; and in delight in the cunning moves of them, in their tricks and asperities, the men on the terraces found release from the drabness of their own industrial degradation.

That release they expressed in ways extremely violent. They

exhorted their favourites to dreadful enterprises of assault and battery. They loudly questioned every decision of the referee. In moments of high tension they raved obscenely, using a language ugly and violent in its wealth of explosive consonants – f's and k's and b's expressing the vehemence of their passions. The young man behind Danny, he who had chaffed his scientific neighbour, was notable in foulness of speech. His commentary on the game was unceasing, and not an observation could he make but one primitive Anglo-Saxon epithet must qualify every noun – and serve, frequently, as a verb. It was as if a fever of hate had seized that multitude, neutralising for the time everything gracious and kindly.

Yet that passionate horde had its wild and liberating humours. Now and again a flash of rough jocularity would release a gust of laughter, so hearty that it was as if they rejoiced to escape from the bondage of their own intensity of partisanship. Once in a while a clever movement by one of the opposition team would evoke a mutter of unwilling but sincere admiration. They were abundantly capable of calling upon their favourites to use their brawn, but they were punctilious in the observation of the unwritten laws that are called those of sportsmanship. They constituted, in fact, a stern but ultimate reliable jury, demanding of their entertainers the very best they could give, insisting that the spectacle be staged with all the vigour that could be brought to it.

The Old Firm – thus the evening papers conventionally described the meeting of Rangers and Celtic. It was a game fought hard and fearless and merciless, and it was but the rub of the business that the wearers of the Blue scored seven minutes from half-time.

The goal was the outcome of a movement so swift that even a critic of Danny's perspicacity could hardly tell just how it happened. What is it to say that a back cleared from near the Rangers' goal; that the ball went on the wind to the nimble feet of Alan Morton on the left wing; that the small but intense performer carried it at lightning speed down the line past this man in green-and-white and then that; that he crossed before the menace of a charging back, the ball soaring in a lovely curve to the waiting

186

centre; and that it went then like a rocket into a corner of the Celtic net, the goalkeeper sprawling in a futile endeavour to stop it?

It was a movement completed almost as soon as it was begun and Danny did not really understand it until he read his evening paper on the way home. But it was a goal, a goal for Rangers, and he went mad for a space.

With those about him he screamed his triumph, waving his cap wildly above his head, taunting most foully those who might be in favour of a team so thoroughly humiliated as the Celtic.

From this orgasm he recovered at length.

'Christ!' he panted. 'That was a bobbydazzler.'

'Good old Alan!' screeched the young man behind. 'Ye've got the suckers bitched!'

'A piece of perfect bloody positioning,' gravely observed the scientist on Danny's left.

'Positioning, ma foot!' snorted Danny. 'It was just bloomin' good fitba! Will ye have a snifter, old fella?'

So they shared the half-mutchkin of raw whisky, the small man politely wiping the neck of the bottle with his sleeve before handing it back to Danny.

'That's a good dram, son,' he observed judicially.

Half-time permitted of discussion that was not, however, without its heat, the young man behind exploiting a critical theory of half-back play that kept some thirty men about him in violent controversy until the whistle blew again. Then the fever came back on them with redoubled fury – One-nothing for Rangers at half-time made an almost agonising situation; and as the Celtic battled to equalise, breaking themselves again and again on a defence grimly determined to hold its advantage, the waves of green hurling themselves on rocks of blue, there was frenzy on the terraces.

When, five minutes before time, the men from the East were awarded a penalty kick, Danny's heart stopped beating for a space, and when the fouled forward sent the ball flying foolishly over the net, it nearly burst. The Rangers would win. 'Stick it, lads!' he yelled again and again. 'Kick the tripes out the dirty Papists!' The

Rangers would win. They must win . . . A spirt of whistle; and, by God, they had won!

In immediate, swift reaction, Danny turned then and, without a word to his neighbours, started to fight his way to the top of the terracing and along the fence that crowned it to the stairs and the open gate. To the feelings of those he jostled and pushed he gave not the slightest thought. Now the battle was for a place in the Subway, and he ran as soon as he could, hurtling down the road, into the odorous maw of Copland Road station and through the closing door of a train that had already started on its journey northwards.

He even got a seat and was glad of it. Now he felt tired and flat after that long stand on a step of beaten cinders and nearly two hours of extreme emotional strain. It had been a hell of an afternoon, right enough! At Partick Cross he paused only to buy an evening paper before darting into the public-house nearest at hand. It was disappointing that the barman already knew the result, thanks to the daily miracle of the Press, and he saw in a glance at the stop-press that his coupon was burst again – Queen's Park down to St Mirren at home, the bunch of stiffs! But the accumulator looked good, his team having nine goals to their credit in two matches and a 2-1 victory as like as possible next Saturday. And there was the glory of telling with authority how Rangers, those shining heroes, had won at Ibrox that very afternoon.

Danny was happy and in his contentment thought kindly of Agnes at home. There remained in his mind the substance of his promise to her, and he did not linger unduly over his glass and pint. She too would welcome his news of victory, and he hurried home to tell her.

'My, that's fine, Dan!' she triumphed with him. 'It must have been great. But I've left your good clothes ben in the room, and ye'd best go and change now. We're to be at the Commodore at six.'

On the Sidelines

from Walking Wounded

WILLIAM McILVANNEY

★ ★ ★

The theme in fiction and film of father and son working out attitudes and affections through the medium of sport is a familiar one, as in this excerpt from William McIlvanney's 1989 collection of short stories Walking Wounded. *Whether tossing an American football around, swinging a baseball bat or going together to a boys' football game, like here, novelists and film-makers find sport a suitable setting for rites of passage and male bonding. McIlvanney's hero, John Hannah, accompanies his son Gary to a Boys' Brigade match and as he watches, muses on life and his own memories of playing football, someone who could have made good at the game but whose 'refusal to take football seriously as a career had come back to haunt him'. The story takes place in Kilmarnock, McIlvanney's own birthplace, where the Dean Park does indeed have many football pitches. An amusing feature of the story is the reference to 'four-two-four' as a tactic being imposed on the boys' game: 'the imposition of sterile theory upon the most creatively fluid ball-game in the world'. Yet again McIlvanney finds a telling phrase to capture the rich complexity of sport.*

★ ★ ★

British Summer Time had officially begun but, if you didn't have a diary, you might not have noticed. The few people standing around in the Dean Park under a smirring rain didn't seem to be convinced. They knew the clocks had been put forward an hour – that was what enabled these early evening football matches to take place. But the arbitrary human decision to make the nights lighter hadn't outwitted the weather. The Scottish climate still had its stock of rain and frost and cold snaps to be used up before the summer came, assuming it did.

Two football pitches were in use. On one of them a works' game was in progress. On the adjoining pitch two Boys' Brigade teams were playing. Standing between touchlines, John Hannah, his coat collar up, paid most attention to the Boys' Brigade game – he was here to see Gary – but the works' match, so noisy and vigorous and expletive, was impossible to ignore. It impinged on the comparative decorum of the boys' game like the future that was coming to them, no matter what precepts of behaviour the Company Leaders tried to impose on them. John had heard some of the other parents complaining ostentatiously at half-time about the inadvisability of booking a pitch beside a works' game. 'After all, it's an organisation to combat evil influences, not arrange to give them a hearing,' a woman in a blue antartex coat and jodhpurs and riding-boots had said. Presumably the horse was a white charger.

John found the contrast between the games instructive. It was like being sandwiched between two parts of his past. The works' game was an echo of his own origins. He had himself played in games like that often enough. Standing so close to the crunch of bone on bone, the thud of bodies, the force of foot striking ball, he remembered what a physically hard game football is. Watching it from a grandstand, as he had so often lately, you saw it bowdlerised a little, refined into an aesthetic of itself. The harshness of it made him wonder if that was why he hadn't pursued the game as determinedly as his talent might have justified. He hoped that wasn't the reason but lately the sense of other failures had made him quest back for some root, one wrong direction taken that had led on to all the others. He had wondered if he had somehow always been a quitter, and his refusal to take football seriously as a career had come back to haunt him.

Three separate people whose opinions he respected had told him he could be a first-class professional footballer. The thought of that had sustained him secretly at different times of depression for years, like an option still open, and it was only fairly recently that he had forced himself to throw away the idea out of embarrassment. He was forty now. For years the vague dream of playing football had been like a man still taking his teddy-bear to bed with him. He might still occasionally mention what had been said to him but, whereas before he had named the three men and sometimes described the games after which they had said it, now the remark had eroded to a self-deprecating joke: 'A man once told me . . . At least I think that's what he said – I couldn't be sure because his guide-dog was barking a lot at the time'. The joke, like a lot of jokes, was a way of controlling loss.

'Oh, well done, Freddie!' the woman in the jodhpurs whinnied.

John supposed that Freddie was her son. The kind of parents who attended these games were inclined to see one player in sharp focus and twenty-one meaningless blurs, as if parenthood had fitted their eyes with special lenses. What Freddie had done was to mis-head the ball straight up into the air so that it fell at the feet of an opponent. It had to he assumed that the expression of admiration that was torn involuntarily from the mouth of Freddie's mother was due to the surprising height, about thirty feet, the ball had achieved by bouncing off Freddie's head. Freddie's mother was apparently not scouting for one of the senior clubs.

Gary, John decided after applying rigorous rules of non-favouritism to his judgment, was playing quite well. At ten, he had already acquired basic ball control and he wasn't quite as guilty as most of them were of simply following the ball wherever it went, as if they were attached to it by ropes of different lengths. John had been following Gary's games religiously all season, as a way of showing him that he was still very much involved in his life though he might not live in the same house, and the matches had acquired the poignancy of a weekly recital for John, a strange orchestration of his past and his present and his uncertain future.

The movingness was an interweave of many things. Part of it was memory. A municipal football park in Scotland is a casually haunted place, a grid of highly sensitised earth that is ghosted by urgent treble voices and lost energy and small, fierce dreams. John's dreams had flickered for years most intensely in such places. He could never stand for long watching Gary and these other boys without a lost, wandering pang from those times finding a brief home in him. On countless winter mornings he had stood beside parks like this and remembered his own childhood commitment and wondered what had made so many Scottish boys so desperate to play this game. He could understand the physical joy of children playing football in a country like Brazil. But on a Saturday morning after a Friday night with too much to drink (and since the separation, every Friday night seemed to end that way), he had turned up to watch Gary and stood, peeled with cold, feeling as if the wind was playing his bones like a xylophone, and seen children struggle across a pitch churned to a treacle of mud. In five minutes they wore claylike leggings, the ball had become as heavy as a cannonball and the wind purpled their thighs. He remembered one touching moment when a goalkeeper had kicked the ball out and then, as the wind blew it back without anyone else touching it, had to dive dramatically to save his own goalkick.

'Four-two-four! Four-two-four!' Gary's Company Leader shouted, as if he was communicating.

It was part of the current professional jargon relating to the formation in which a football team should play. Even applied to the professional game, it was, in John's opinion, the imposition of sterile theory upon the most creatively fluid ball-game in the world. Hurled peremptorily at a group of dazed and innocent ten-year-olds, it was as rational as hitting an infant who is dreaming over the head with a copy of *The Interpretation of Dreams*. The words depressed John.

They struck another plangent and familiar chord in his experience of these games. Everything was changing. Week by week, he had been learning the extent of his own failed dreams. Gary had run about so many wintry fields like the vanishing will o' the wisp of John's former expectations, moving remorselessly further and further away from him. He had already virtually lost

Carole. She was her mother's daughter, had chosen which side she was on. She would tolerate the times he took them out but, even so young, she had evolved her own discreet code for making their relationship quite formal, like invariably turning her head fractionally when he bent to kiss her, so that her hair on his lips was for him the taste of rejection. Lying in his bed at night, he used to wonder what her mother was telling her about him.

Gary was more supportive. He didn't take sides but when he was with his father he came to him openly, interested in what was happening in his life and concerned to share as much of his own as he could. Yet, in spite of himself, even Gary made John feel excluded – not just because there was so much time when he couldn't be with him but also because, during the times that they were together, it was as if they were speaking in subtly different dialects. Like a parent who has sent his child to elocution lessons, John felt slightly alienated by the gifts he had tried to give Gary.

The football games had come to encapsulate the feeling for John. They were where he had been as a boy and they were a significantly different place. He had acquired his close-dribbling skills and the sudden, killing acceleration in street kickabouts and scratch games under Peeweep Hill where as many as thirty might be playing in one game. He had practised for hours in the house with a ball made of rolled up newspapers tied with string. He had owned his first pair of football boots when he was fifteen.

'Put a pea in yer bloody whistle, ref,' one of the works' team players bellowed.

'Pull your stocking up, Freddie,' the jodhpurs sang.

And John's past and his son's future met in his head and failed to mate. The game wasn't for Gary what it had been for John, a fierce and secret romanticism that fed itself on found scraps – an amazing goal scored and kept pressed in the mind like a perfect rose – a passionate refusal to believe in the boring pragmatism of the conventional authority his teachers represented, a tunnel that ran beneath the crowds of the commonplace and would one day open into a bowl of sunlight and bright grass and the roar of adulation.

For Gary it was something you did for the time being, an orderly business of accepted rules and laundered strips and football boots renewed yearly. He could take it or leave it. In a year or two, he would probably leave it. He was starting to play tennis.

Farewell to the
Ultimate Football Man

from McIlvanney on Football

HUGH McILVANNEY

★ ★ ★

In the introductory chapter to this book, mention was made of the congruence of sports journalism and literature about sport that occurs when real quality of writing is present. In a way, this is symbolically realised in the case of the two brothers McIlvanney. One of them, Hugh, was the best football and boxing writer of his generation, and the other, William, was, as we have seen, a top-notch novelist with both social realism and crime fiction in his armoury, together with an ability to capture sporting action with equivalent skill.

This obituary of Manchester United's Sir Matt Busby, written by Hugh in January 1994, is a masterpiece, an essay worthy of Hazlitt or Lamb. He crafts his writing in a way that far outstrips the text messaging of most sports journalism. This piece marks the passing, not just of the great Matt Busby, but of an era. An era which had seen the flourishing of a triumvirate of Scottish managers, Shankly and Stein being the others, who had, he writes, 'seams of rich humanity, of working-class pride and wit and energy and character'.

★ ★ ★

In the language of the sports pages, greatness is plentiful. The reality of sport, like that of every other area of life, shows that it is desperately rare. Greatness does not gad about, reaching for people in handfuls. It settles deliberately on a blessed few, and Matt Busby was one of them.

If Busby had stood dressed for the pit, and somebody alongside him in the room had worn ermine, there would have been no difficulty about deciding who was special. Granting him a knighthood did not elevate him. It raised, however briefly, the whole dubious phenomenon of the honours system.

Busby emanated presence, substance, the quality of strength without arrogance. No man in my experience ever exemplified better the ability to treat you as an equal while leaving you with the sure knowledge that you were less than he was. Such men do not have to be appointed leaders. Some democracy of the instincts and the blood elects them to be in charge.

That innate distinction was the source of his effect on footballers. He never had to bully. One glance from under the eloquent eyebrows was worth 10 bellows from more limited natures. Players did not fear his wrath. They dreaded his disapproval. His judgment of the priorities of football was so sound, his authority so effortless, that a shake of his head inflicted an embarrassment from which the only rescue was recovery of his respect.

When Sir Matt died peacefully on Thursday at the age of 84, allowed to exit with the quiet dignity that was a central theme of his life, few beyond his immediate family of son Sandy and daughter Sheena would mourn more genuinely than Pat Crerand. And the Gorbals man's emotions represent a particularly relevant testimony to the influence of the manager he will never stop calling The Boss. Crerand in his playing days was street-hard to a degree that most of the notorious figures in the modern game can only imagine. He was a passer, a shaper of matches, a player of many attributes, but speed was not among them. Combativeness was. 'Where I was brought up, you had to be able to run or fight and you know about my running,' he once told me. Yet if Busby so much as looked at him the wrong way, Crerand felt like running.

There was an occasion in Europe long ago when Crerand came scrambling on to the team bus after all the other travellers were seated. 'You must be a very important person,' the manager said. 'You have kept the directors of Manchester United waiting, you have kept your team-mates waiting, you've kept the press waiting and you've kept me waiting. It must be wonderful to be as important as you are.'

'The man didn't miss you and hit the wall,' a friend said to the Glaswegian as he sank disconsolately into the nearest vacant seat. 'Don't worry about it,' Crerand said with undisguised concern. 'There's more where that came from.' But he knew Busby would forgive him the minor misdemeanour, just as he would find tolerance to cope with more serious offences born of the Gorbals temper. The reason was his appreciation of his wing-half's honesty. 'Do you notice that when Pat is having a rank bad day, when his touch is hopelessly off, he won't hide, he'll keep trying to pass the ball beyond people?' he would say with a smile of approval that precluded an answer.

The story of one footballer's relationship with his manager is worth dwelling upon because it reflects the integrity of the romantic dream that underpinned the practicality inseparable from Busby's monumental success at Old Trafford. He could be as hard as bell metal, in his dealings with other clubs or the legislators of the game as well as his own staff. If a little bit of worldliness, being a smart move ahead of the opposition in the transfer market or anywhere else, would help United, he was seldom slow. But for all his players – from the greatest, like Duncan Edwards or Bobby Charlton, Denis Law or George Best, to the most obscure – the essence of his inspiring impact was his humanity, the small miracle of a personality that embraced soaring ideals with a modesty and warmth bred in the bone.

His was a life lived with brilliance and style and more than a touch of nobility, a forceful reminder that sport, no matter how miserably it may be disfigured by the intrusion of cheap and distorted values, is still capable of providing a context in which a really big spirit can express itself. He did not have to be told that when compared with the suffering associated with the loss in the 1958 Munich air crash of Edwards and seven other members of a gloriously promising squad already immortalised as the Busby Babes, or the death of his cherished wife, Jean, anything that happens on a football field is fairly trivial.

But he knew, too, that the action out there can be magnificent, at once a wonderful respite from real life and an acceptable metaphor for it. As a player far more distinguished than the statistics indicate (his maturity coincided with the Second World War) and a manager of incomparable stature in the most truly global of games, he could be passionate about football without losing his perspective about its place in relation to the deeper concerns of the heart. His origins equipped him with such a perspective. Like his strong Catholic faith, it was merely reinforced by a narrow escape from death at Munich.

On the matter of origins, it is one of the most remarkable facts in football that the small coalfield which once spread across part of Lanarkshire and southern Ayrshire produced three of the greatest managers and most formidable individuals the game has ever known: Busby himself; Bill Shankly, the warrior-poet who created the modern Liverpool; and Jock Stein, the Big Man who made Celtic so vibrantly aggressive that they obliterated all competition in Scotland for a decade or so and became the first British club to win the European Cup, a year before United realised Busby's dream of lifting that trophy. Plainly, there were more than coal seams running through that bleak landscape in the West of Scotland. There were seams of rich humanity, of working-class pride and wit and energy and character.

The influence on Busby of his upbringing amid a loving family in the miners' rows of Old Orbiston near Bellshill was indelible. Commitment to a warm sense of family, both in his private life and at the club he made as renowned as any institution in sport, was one of the legacies. Another was the natural respect for other people's feelings that the harshness and dangers of life in a mining community encouraged. He had a gift, bordering on the magical, of making all who came in touch with him feel that they mattered.

Many have been recalling his almost eerie capacity to summon up, long after the most fleeting encounter, not only a name but a clear awareness of the person that went with it. Having the privilege of his friendship for more than three decades never diminished the awe that was stirred by the ease and depth of his courtesy. Asked to speak at a dinner in his honour a couple of years ago, I found myself expressing much of what is written here and telling of how, in the days when I regularly covered matches at Old Trafford, Matt would often take time to inquire around various groups in the tearoom afterwards until he had found me a lift to Piccadilly Station.

In the company of a Manchester audience, it had to be admitted that, yes, maybe he just wanted to make sure at least one pest got out of town. But, in fact, it was simply another manifestation of his spontaneous kindness.

Would-be sceptics used to smile and say he was a master of PR. They had it wrong. HR, human relations, were his speciality. It could be said that he conquered millions of hearts one at a time, moving out from his family through his club, and the adopted city he loved, into the world of football and the wider world beyond that. The way the huge power of his personality worked was the benign equivalent of house-to-house fighting.

All of his outstanding teams made statements about his values. United qualified as a war casualty when he took over in 1945 but the rebuilding began almost immediately and by 1952 he had taken them to the League championship for the first time since 1911. Four more titles and two FA Cup triumphs were to be added before that European Cup victory of 1968 climaxed nearly a quarter of a century of management (the knighthood came in June of that year) but the record book can never convey the significance of his achievement. Whether we think of the first Manchester United he built in those austere post-war years, or the wonderful blending of youthful verve and talent whose horizons seemed limitless until the sky fell in at Munich, or the subsequent dazzling era of Law, Best and Charlton, always there is in the mind a vision of football with the unmistakable stamp of Busby upon it. He maintained an unshakable allegiance to perhaps the most powerful basic truth about the game: that football greatness cannot be measured or recorded in statistics alone, not in the number of goals scored or matches won or trophies carried home. All these are vital, of course, but the game's extraordinary grip on the imagination of countless millions is exerted not through scorelines but through the images of grace and skill, of courage and inventiveness it leaves to shimmer in the memory.

The late Danny Blanchflower was not foolishly romantic when he said the game is not about winning, it is about glory. Danny was too much of a pro to deny that there must be sweat and grit and pragmatism in the midst of all the romance. But he knew equally that football offers an opportunity to produce something beautiful and that gifted players who do not answer the challenge are betraying themselves and the game. And if players of authentic talent apply themselves with sufficient heart and honesty and resolution to playing beautifully, they will win plenty along the way. They will not be short of prizes to go with the glory. If they ever doubt that, they need only look at Busby's career for reassurance.

Nothing could have done more to warm the late twilight of this ultimate football man's life than the resurgence of Manchester United under Alex Ferguson. The winning of the European Cup Winners' Cup in 1991 gave him immense satisfaction but there was immeasurably more in recapturing the League title last season for the first time since a team under his own guidance had taken it in 1967. And the real joy of these accomplishments lay in the knowledge that they were gained with the kind of creative and adventurous football he had always seen as the one true currency. For a long time his attempts to find a successor seemed doomed to bring pain and disappointment to himself and others. But at the end the view from the presidential chair was made cheerful by the happy conviction that in Ferguson, another working-class man from the West of Scotland, he had a genuine disciple and a worthy heir.

Using Shakespeare's words to praise somebody we know is bound to be a rather wild risk, but at that dinner in Manchester I took the chance, invoking Mark Antony's lines about Brutus: 'His life was gentle, and the elements so mixed in him that nature might stand up and say to all the world "This was a man".'

It did not seem over the top at the time. It still doesn't.

Wife of a Hero
from Doctor Finlay Stories

A.J. CRONIN

★ ★ ★

Levenford is A.J. Cronin's fictional equivalent of his own town, Dumbarton. This, one of Cronin's famous Doctor Finlay stories, tells a tragic tale of a Levenford F.C. player, Ned Sutherland, and his ailing wife. Levenford are described as formerly enjoying 'Homeric triumphs'; true, because Dumbarton was one of the great teams of the 1870s and 1880s, Scottish Cup winners and Scottish champions in the first two league championships. The story tells of a time when 'Levenford' had slipped sadly to lower levels, and when a game against 'Glasgow Rovers' (clearly Rangers) was a case of minnows versus giants. Ned Sutherland's career, as described by Cronin, followed a familiar pattern for gifted Scottish footballers of the day – he had played for a big Glasgow team (unspecified) and then, like one of George Blake's 'mercenaries', had plied his trade in the mighty English League, before returning to Levenford, his home town team. Dumbarton's ground, 'Fatal Boghead', is not named but Cronin describes it (inaccurately) as 'a small pitch'.

The plot of the story has strong elements of melodrama and Ned is a typical Cronin villain, not unlike Brodie in Hatter's Castle, *the Levenford novel made into a successful Hollywood film, an outcome shared by several other Cronin books, like* The Citadel *and* The Keys of the Kingdom.

★ ★ ★

For days Levenford had talked of nothing but the match. Of course they were always 'daft on football' in these parts. They had the tradition, you see. In the good old days, when centre-forwards wore side whiskers and the goalie's knickers buttoned below the knee, Levenford had been a team of champions.

That they had languished since those Homeric triumphs – languished to a low place in the Second League – was as nothing. Levenford was still Levenford. And now, in the first round of the Scottish Cup, they had drawn the Glasgow Rovers at home.

The Glasgow Rovers – top of the First Division – crack team of the country – and at home!

In the shipyards, the streets, the shops, in every howff from the Philosophical right down to the Fitter's Bar, the thrill of it worked like madness.

Total strangers stopped each other at the Cross.

'Can we do it?' the one would gasp. And the other, with real emotion, would reply: 'Well! Anyhow we've got Ned!'

Ned Sutherland was the man they meant – Sutherland, the idol, the prodigy, the paragon! Sutherland, subject of Bailie Paxton's solemn aphorism – 'He has mair fitba' in his pinkie than the hale team has in their heids.'

Good old Sutherland! Hurray for Ned!

Ned was not young; his age, guarded like a woman's, was uncertain. But those in the know put Ned down at forty, for Ned, they wisely argued, had been playing professional football for no less than twenty years. Not in Levenford, dear, dear, no!

Ned's dazzling career had carried him far from his native town – to Glasgow first, where his debut had sent sixty thousand delirious with delight, and then to Newcastle, from there to Leeds, then down to Birmingham – oh, Ned had been everywhere, never staying long, mark you, but always the centre of attraction, always the idol of the crowd.

And then, the year before, after a short interval when all the big clubs – with unbelievable stupidity – ignored his 'free transfer', he had returned magnificently to Levenford while still, as he said, in his prime, to put the club back upon the map.

It cannot be denied that there were rumours about Ned, base rumours that are the penalty of greatness.

It was whispered, for instance, that Ned loved the drink, that Newcastle had been glad to see the last of him, and Leeds not sorry to watch him go.

It was a shame, a scandal, an iniquity – the lies that followed him about.

What matter if Ned liked his glass? He could play the better for it, and very often did.

What matter if an occasional drink gaily marked the progress of his greatness? If his wanderings had been prodigal, was he not Levenford's famous son?

Away with the slanderers! So said Levenford, for when Ned returned she took him to her heart.

He was a biggish man, was Ned, rather bald on the top, with a smooth pale face, and a moist convivial eye.

He had the look, not of a footballer, but rather of a toastmaster at a city banquet.

In his appearance he was something of the dandy; his suit was invariably of blue serge – neat, well brushed; on his little finger he wore a heavy ring with a coloured stone; his watch chain, stretched between the top pockets of his waist, carried a row of medals he had won; and his shoes – his shoes in particular were polished till they shone.

Naturally Ned did not brush his shoes himself. Though most of the Levenford team held jobs in the shipyard and the foundry, Ned, as befitting his superior art, did not work at all. The shoes were brushed by Ned's wife.

And here, with the mention of Mrs. Sutherland, is reached the point on which everyone agreed.

It was a pity, an awful pity, that Ned's wife should be such a drag, such a burden on him – not only the wife but those five children of his as well. God! It was sickening that Ned should have tied himself up so young – that he had been forced to cart round the wife, and this increasing regiment of children upon his famous travels.

There, if you like, was the reason of his decline, and it all came back to the woman who was his wife.

As Bailie Paxton put it knowingly – with a significant gesture of distaste – 'Could she not have watched herself better?'

The plain fact is that Levenford held a pretty poor opinion of Mrs. Sutherland, a poor dowdy creature with downcast eyes. If she had been bonny once, and some would have it so, Lord! she wasn't bonny now.

Little wonder if Ned was ashamed of her, and most of all on Saturday afternoons, when, emerging from obscurity, she actually appeared outside the football ground to wait for Ned.

Mind you, she never came to see the match, but simply to wait outside till Ned got his pay. To wait on the man for the wages in his pocket. Lord, wasn't it deplorable?

It must be admitted that some stood up for her. Once in the Philosophical, when this matter was discussed, Dr. Cameron, who, strangely enough, seemed to like the woman, had sourly said:

'With five bairns to feed, she's got to steer him past the pubs – at least as many as she can!'

But then Cameron always was a heretic who held the queerest notions of things and folk. And Ned's popularity, as has been said, was far beyond the cranky notions of the few.

Indeed, as the day of the match gradually drew near, that popularity drew pretty near to glory.

Ned became a sort of god. When he walked down the High Street of Levenford, thumbs in his armholes, medals dancing, his smooth, genial smile acknowledging here, there, everywhere, they almost cheered him. At the Cross, he had a crowd about him – a crowd that hung on every word that passed those smooth convivial lips.

It was at the Cross too, that the memorable meeting took place with Provost Weir.

'Well, Ned, boy,' said the Provost, advancing his hand, affable as you like. 'Can we do it, think ye?'

Ned's eyes glistened. In no way discomposed, he shook the

Provost's hand and solemnly delivered himself of that:

'If the Rovers win, Provost, it'll be over my dead body.'

One night, a week before the match, Mrs. Sutherland came to the doctor's home.

It was late. The evening surgery was over. And, very humbly, Mrs. Sutherland came into Finlay, whose duty it was to see cases after hours.

'I'm terribly sorry to trouble you, doctor,' she began, and stood still, a neat, poorly-dressed figure, holding her mended gloves in her work-worn hands.

She was a pretty woman, or rather once she had been a pretty girl. For now there was about her a faded air; a queer transparency in her cheek and in her look, something so strained and shrinking, it cut Finlay to the quick.

'It's foolish of me to have come,' she said again, then stopped.

Finlay, placing a chair beside his desk, asked her to sit down.

She thanked him with a faint smile.

'It's not like me to be stupid about myself, doctor. I really should never have come. In fact, I've been that bothered making up my mind I nearly didn't come at all.'

A hesitating smile; he had never seen anything so self-effacing as that smile.

'But the plain truth is I don't seem to be seeing out of one of my eyes.'

Finlay laid down his pen.

'You mean you're blind in one eye?'

She nodded, then added: 'My left eye.'

A short silence fell.

'Any headache?' he asked.

'Well – whiles they come pretty bad," she admitted.

He continued to question her, as kindly and informally as he could. Then, rising, he took his opthalmoscope, and darkened the surgery to examine her eyes.

He had some difficulty in getting the retina. But at last he had a perfect view. And, in spite of himself, he stiffened.

He was horrified. He had expected trouble – certainly he had expected trouble – but not this.

The left retina was loaded with pigment which could only be melanin. He went over it again, slowly, carefully – there was no doubt about it.

He turned up the light again, trying to mask his face.

'Did you have a blow in the eye lately?' he inquired, not looking at her, but watching her reflection in the overmantel.

He saw her colour painfully, violently.

And she said too quickly: 'I might have knocked it on the dresser – I slipped, last month, I think it was.'

He said nothing, but he tried to compose his features into something reassuring.

'I'd like Dr. Cameron to see you,' he declared at length. 'You don't mind?'

She fixed her quiet gaze on him.

'It's something bad, then,' she said.

'Well,' he broke off helplessly – 'we'll see what Dr. Cameron says.' Wishing to add something but unable to find the words, very lamely he left the room.

Cameron was in his study, smoothing the back of a fiddle with fine sandpaper, humming his internal little tune.

'Mrs. Sutherland is in the surgery,' Finlay said.

'Ay,' Cameron answered, without looking up. 'She's a nice body. I knew her when she was a lass, before she threw herself away on that boozy footballer. What's brought her in?'

'I think she's got a melanotic sarcoma,' Finlay said slowly.

Cameron stopped humming, then very exactly he laid down his fiddle. His gaze fastened upon Finlay's face, and stayed there for a long time.

'I'll come ben,' he said, rising.

They went into the surgery together.

'Weel, Jenny, lass, what's all this we hear about you?' Cameron's voice was gentle as though she were a child.

His examination was longer, even more searching than Finlay's.

At the end of it a swift look passed between the two doctors, a look confirming the diagnosis, a look that meant the death of Jenny Sutherland.

When she had finished dressing, Cameron took her arm.

'Well, now, Jenny, would that husband of yours look in and see Finlay and me the morn?'

She faced him squarely, with the singular precognition of women who have known a life of trouble.

'There's something serious the matter with me, doctor.'

Silence.

All the fineness of humanity was in Cameron's face and in his voice as he answered:

'Something gey serious, Jenny.'

Now, strangely, she was more composed than he.

'What does it mean, then, doctor?'

But Cameron, for all his courage, could not speak the full, brutal truth.

How could he tell her that she stood there with her doom upon her, stricken by the most dreadful disease of any known to man, an unbelievably malignant growth which, striking into the eye, spreads through the body like flame – destroying, corrupting, choking! No hope, no treatment, nothing to do but face certain and immediate death!

Six days the least, six weeks the utmost, that now was the span of Jenny Sutherland's life.

'Ye'll have to go into hospital lass,' he temporised.

But she answered quickly

'I couldn't leave the bairns. And Ned – with the big match coming off – it would upset him too, oh, it would upset him frightful – it would never do at all, at all.' She broke off, paused.

'Could I wait, maybe, till after the match?'

'Well, yes, Jenny – I suppose if you wanted you could wait.'

Searching his compassionate face, something of the full significance of his meaning broke upon her. She bit her lip hard. She was silent. Then, very slowly, she said:

'I see, doctor, I see now. Ye mean it doesna make much difference either way?'

His eyes fell, and at that she knew.

The morning of the great match dawned misty, but before the forenoon had advanced the sun broke through magnificently. The town was quiet, tense with a terrific excitement.

As early as eleven o'clock, in the fear that they might not be able to secure a place, folks actually started to make their way to the ground. Not Ned, of course! Ned was in bed, resting, as he always did before each match. He had a most particular routine, had Ned, and this day more particular than any.

At ten Jenny brought him breakfast, a big tray loaded with porridge, two boiled eggs, a fine oatcake specially baked by herself. Then she went into the kitchen to prepare the special hough tea which, with two slices of toast, made up his light luncheon on playing days.

As she stood at the stove, Ned's voice came through complainingly:

'Fetch me another egg when ye bring in my soup. I'm thinkin' I'll need it before I'm finished.'

She heard, and made a little movement of distress; then she went into him apologetically.

'I'm sorry, Ned! I gave ye the last egg in the house this morning."

He glared at her.

'Then send out for one.'

'If ye would give me the money, Ned.'

'Money! God! It's always money! Can't ye get credit?'

She shook her head slowly.

'Ye know that's finished long enough ago.'

'My God!' he exploded. 'But ye're a bonny manager. It's a fine state of affairs when I'm sent on to the field starvin'.

'Bring in my soup quick then, and plenty of toast. Hurry up now or ye'll not have time to rub me. And for Heaven's sake keep those brats of yours quiet. They've near rung the lugs off me this morning.'

She went silently back to the kitchen and, with a warning gesture, stilled the two young children there – the others had been dressed quite early and sent, out of their father's way, to play on the green.

Then she brought him his soup, and stood by the bed while he supped it noisily. Between the mouthfuls he looked up at her and surlily demanded:

'What are ye glowerin' at – with a face that would frighten the French? God knows, I havena had a smile out of ye for the last four days.'

She found a smile – the vague, uncertain travesty of a smile.

'Lately I haven't been feeling too well, Ned, to tell you the truth.'

'That's right! Start your complaining and me on the edge of a cup-tie. Damnation, it's enough to drive a man stupid the way ye keep moanin' and groanin'.'

'I'm not complaining, Ned,' she said hurriedly.

'Then away and get the embrocation, and give us a rub.'

She brought the embrocation, and while he lay back, thrusting out a muscular leg, she began the customary rubbing.

'Harder! Harder!' he urged. 'Use yourself a bit. Get it below the skin.'

It cost her a frightful effort to complete the massage. Long before she had finished a sweat of weakness broke over her whole body. But at last he grunted:

'That'll do, that'll do. Though little good it's done me. Now bring in my shaving water, and see that it's boiling.'

He got up, shaved, dressed carefully. A ring came to the door bell.

'It's Bailie Paxton,' she announced. 'Come with his gig to drive you to the match.'

A slow smile of appreciation stole over Ned's face.

'All right,' he said. 'Tell him I'll be down.'

As he took his cap from the peg she watched him, supporting herself against the mantel-piece of the room. Sadness was in her face, and a queer wistfulness.

'I hope ye play well, Ned,' she murmured. How many times had she said these words, and in how many places? But never, never as she said them now!

He nodded briefly and went out.

The match began at half-past two, and long before the hour the park was packed to suffocation. Hundreds were refused admission, and hundreds more broke through the barrier and sat upon the touch-line.

The town band blared in the centre of the pitch, the flag snapped merrily in the breeze, the crowd was seething with suppressed excitement.

Then the Rovers took the field, very natty in their bright blue jerseys.

A roar went up, for two train loads of supporters had followed them from Glasgow. But nothing to the roar that split the air when Ned led his men from the pavilion. It was heard, they said, at Overton, a good two miles away.

The coin was spun; Ned won the toss.

Another roar; then dead silence as the Rovers kicked off. It was on at last – the great, the glorious game.

Right from the start the Rovers attacked.

They were clever, clever, playing a class of football which chilled the home supporters' hearts. They were fast, they worked the ball, they swung it with deadly accuracy from wing to wing.

And, as that were not enough, Levenford were nervous and scrappy, playing far below their best, shoving the ball anywhere in a flurry. All but Ned!

Oh, Ned was superb! His position was centre-half, but today he was everywhere, the mainstay, the very backbone of the team.

Ned was not fast, he never had been fast, but his anticipation quite made up for that – and more.

Time after time he saved the situation, relieving the pressure on the Levenford goal by some astute movement, a side step, a short pass, or a hefty kick over the halfway line.

Ned was the best man on the field, a grand, a born footballer. He towered – this bald-headed gladiator in shorts – over the other twenty-one.

It had to come, of course – one man alone could not stem that devilish attack.

Before the half-time whistle blew, the Rovers scored. Not Ned's fault. A slip by the Levenford right-back, and quick as thought the Rovers' outside-left pounced on the spinning ball and steered it into the net.

Gloom fell upon the Levenford supporters. Had the score-sheet remained blank their team might have entered on the second half with some much-needed confidence. But now, alas, a goal down, and the wind against them – even the optimists admitted the outlook to be poor.

There was only one chance, one hope – Ned – and the memory of his emphatic words: 'If the Rovers win it'll be over my dead body.'

The second half began; and with it the precious moments started to run out. Levenford were more together, they gained two corners in quick succession; when attacked they rallied, and rushed the ball forward in the teeth of the wind. But the Rovers held them tight.

True, they lost a little of their aggression. Playing on a small pitch away from home, they faded somewhat as the game went on, and it almost seemed as if they were content to hold their one-goal lead.

Quick to sense this attitude of defence, the crowd roared encouragement to their favourites.

A fine frenzy filled the air, and spread from the spectators to the Levenford players. They hurled themselves into the game. They pressed furiously, swarming round the Rovers' goal. But still they could not score.

Another corner, and Ned, taking the ball beautifully, headed against the crossbar. A groan went up of mingled ecstasy and despair.

The light was fading now, the time going fast, twenty, ten, only five minutes to go.

Upon the yelling crowd a bitter misery was hovering, settling slowly. Defeat was in the air, the hopeless wretchedness of defeat.

And then, on the halfway line, Ned Sutherland got the ball. He held it, made ground, weaving his way with indescribable dexterity through a mass of players.

'Pass, Ned, pass!' shouted the crowd, hoping to see him make an opening for the wings.

But Ned did not pass. With the ball at his feet and his head down, he bored on, like a charging bull.

Then the crowd really roared – they saw that Ned was going in on his own.

The Rovers' left-back saw it too. With Ned inside the penalty area and ready to shoot, he flung himself at Ned in a flying tackle. Down went Ned with a sickening thud, and from ten thousand throats rose the frantic yell:

'Penalty! Penalty! Penalty!'

Without hesitation the referee pointed to the spot.

Despite the protestations of the Rovers' player, he was giving it – he was giving Levenford a penalty!

Ned got up. He was not hurt. That perfect simulation of frightful injury was part and parcel of his art. And now he was going to take the penalty himself.

A deathly stillness fell upon the multitude as Ned placed the ball upon the spot. He did it coolly, impersonally, as though he knew nothing of the agony of suspense around him. Not a person breathed as he tapped the toe of his boot against the ground, took a long look at the goal, and ran three quick steps forward.

Then bang! The ball was in the net.

'Goal!' shouted the crowd in ecstasy, and at the same instant the whistle blew for time.

Levenford had drawn. Ned had saved the match.

Pandemonium broke loose. Hats, sticks, umbrellas were tossed wildly into the air. Yelling, roaring, shrieking deliriously, the crowd rushed upon the field.

Ned was swept from his feet, lifted shoulder high and borne in triumph to the pavilion.

At that moment Mrs. Sutherland was sitting in the kitchen of the silent house. She had wanted badly to go to the park for Ned; but the mere effort of putting on her coat had shown how useless it was for her to try.

With her cheek on her hand, she stared away into the distance. Surely Ned would come straight home today, surely he must have seen something of the mortal sadness in her face.

She longed desperately to ease the burden in her breast by telling him. She had sworn to herself not to tell him until after the match. But she must tell him now.

It was a thing too terrible to bear alone!

She knew she was dying; even the few days that had passed since her visit to Finlay had produced a rapid failure in her strength – her side hurt her, and her sight was worse.

An hour passed, and there was no sign of Ned. She stirred herself, got up, and put the two youngest children to bed. She sat down again. Still he did not come. The other children came in from playing, and from them she learned the result of the match.

Eight o'clock came and nine. Now even the eldest boy was in bed. She felt terribly ill; she thought, in fact, that she was dying.

The supper which she had prepared for him was wasted, the fire was out for lack of coal. In desperation she got up and dragged herself to bed.

It was nearly twelve when he came in.

She was not asleep – the pain in her side was too bad for that – and she heard the slow, erratic steps, followed by the loud bang of the door.

He was drunk, as usual; no, it was worse than usual, for tonight, treated to the limit, he had reached a point far beyond his usual intoxication.

He came into the bedroom and turned up the gas.

Flushed with whisky, praise, triumph, and the sense of his own ineffable skill, he gazed at her as she lay upon the bed; then, still watching her, he leant against the wall, took off his boots, and flung them upon the floor.

He wanted to tell her how wonderful he was, how marvellous was the goal he had scored.

He tried to repeat the noble, the historic phrase he had coined – that the Rovers would only win over his dead body.

He tried sottishly to articulate the words. But, of course, he got it mixed. What he said was:

'I'm going – I'm going – to win over your dead body.'

Then he laughed hilariously.

Jimmy's Sins Find Him Out

NEIL MUNRO

★ ★ ★

Jimmy Swan was the third of the comic characters brought to life by Neil Munro in the pages of the Glasgow Evening News. *Jimmy, the commercial traveller, made his first appearance in May 1911 and appeared occasionally until 1926. Perhaps not so popular as Erchie or Para Handy, the kindly, somewhat enigmatic character of Mr Swan, as he is generally known to his customers, is the medium of a subtle humour and vivid evocation of a long-lost world of small towns and draper's shops, and has great enthusiasms like choral singing and soiree concerts. Munro developed a rich vein of story and sentiment in the commercial traveller or travelling salesman – a kind of gentle knight-errant figure. However, this particular story is set in Glasgow, which is Jimmy's home and also his business base – it is the location of the company he represents, Campbell and Macdonald's drapery warehouse. On this occasion one of his country customers has come to town in search of a ticket for a football match – an international to be played at the home of football, Hampden Park. It turns out that Jimmy has convinced the client in the course of his sales-patter that he is an expert on football. The truth is that, despite living in Ibrox near the home of Rangers FC, Jimmy knows next to nothing about football and has a poetic strain to his nature which makes him prefer an hour or so in Camphill listening to the birdsong. As often in the case of Munro's newspaper stories, the story had a strong element of topicality when written. It appeared in The Looker-On's regular Monday spot on 6 of April 1914, two days after the international between Scotland and England. This was characteristic of Munro's method: to take a contemporary event or fashion and build an amusing tale around it. Incidentally, the match ended in a 3-1 victory for Scotland and the crowd, which did not include Jimmy Swan, numbered 105,000.*

Mr James Swan picked up a bunch of violets, which he had been refreshing in a tumbler while he wrote out his expenses for the week, and placed it in his buttonhole. From a pocket he took a small case-comb, and, borrowing from Pratt, the office 'knut', the little mirror which Pratt kept always on his desk to consult as often as the Ready Reckoner, he went to the window and combed his hair.

'What side are sheds worn this season?' he asked Pratt, whom it was the joke of the office to treat with mock deference as arbiter of fashion, expert, and authority upon every giddy new twirl of the world of elegance.

'To the left,' said Pratt, without a moment's hesitation, and with the utmost solemnity; the parting of his own hair was notoriously a matter of prayerful consideration. He was a lank lad with a long neck; it looked as if his Adam's apple was a green one and was shining through – a verdant phenomenon due to the fact that he used the same brass stud for three years.

'Can't be done on the left,' said Mr Swan. 'That's the side I do my thinkin' on, and it's worn quite thin. I envy ye your head o' hair, Pratt; it'll last ye a life-time, no' like mine.'

Pratt, with the mirror restored to him, put it back in his desk with final glance at it to see that his necktie was as perfectly knotted as it was three minutes ago; put on his hat and bolted from the office.

'They're a' in a great hurry to be off the day,' said Mr Swan to himself. 'I wonder what they're up to?'

He was to find out in two minutes, to his own discomfiture.

At the foot of the stair which led to the upper warehouse he ran against Peter Grant of Aberdeen, who was in search of him.

'My jove!' said Grant, panting; 'I'm in luck! I was sure ye would be awa' to't, and I ran doon the street like to break my legs.'

'De-lighted to see ye, Mr Grant!' said Jimmy with a radiant visage. 'This is indeed a pleasant surprise! But ye don't mean to tell me ye came from Aberdeen this mornin'?'

'Left at a quarter to seven,' said Grant. 'I made up my mind last night to come and see it. And I says to myself, "If I can just catch

Mr Swan before he goes to the field, the thing's velvet!"'

'De-lighted!' said Jimmy, and shook his hand again. But the feeling of icy despair in his breast was enough to wilt his violets.

His sin had found him out! There was only one inference to be drawn from Peter Grant's excited appearance; he had carried out the threat of a dozen years to come and see a Glasgow football match, and expected the expert company and guidance of C. & M.'s commercial traveller.

And Jimmy Swan had, so far as Grant was concerned, a reputation for football knowledge and enthusiasm it was impossible to justify in Glasgow, however plausible they seemed in a shop in Aberdeen. Grant, who had never seen a football match in his life, was a fanatic in his devotion to a game which for twenty years he followed in the newspapers. Jimmy in his first journeys to Aberdeen had discovered this fancy of his customer, and played up to it craftily with the aid of the *Scottish Referee*, which he bought on each journey North for no other purpose, since he himself had never seen a football match since the last of Harry M'Neill of the 'Queen's,' in 1881.

The appalling ignorance of Jimmy regarding modern football, and his blank indifference to the same, were never suspected by his customer, who from the traveller's breezy and familiar comments upon matches scrappily read about an hour before, credited him with knowing all there was to know about the national pastime.

When Jimmy was in doubt about the next move in a conversation with Grant, he always mentioned Quinn, and called him 'good old Jimmy'. He let it be understood that the Saturday afternoons when he couldn't get to Ibrox were unhappy – which was perfectly true, since he lived in Ibrox, though the Rangers' park was a place he never went near.

'I'll go and see a match some day!' Grant always said; he had said it for many years, and Jimmy always said, 'Mind and let me know when ye're comin', and I'll show ye fitba.'

And now he was taken at his word!

What particular match could Grant have come for? Jimmy had

lost sight of football, even in the papers, for the past three months.

With an inward sigh for a dinner spoiled at home, he took his customer to a restaurant for lunch.

'I want to see M'Menemy,' said Grant; 'it was that that brought me; he's a clinker!'

'And he never was in better form,' said Jimmy. 'Playin' like a book! He says to me last Monday, 'We'll walk over them the same's we had a brass band in front of us, Mr. Swan!'

'Will they win, do ye think?' Grant asked with great anxiety; he was so keen, the lunch was thrown away on him.

'Win!' said Jimmy. 'Hands down! The – the – the other chaps is shakin' in their shoes.

So far he moved in darkness. Who M'Menemy was, and what match he was playing in that day, he had not the faintest ideas, and he played for safety. It was probably some important match. The state of the streets as they had walked along to the restaurant suggested a great influx of young men visitors; it might be something at Celtic Park.

He looked at Grant's square-topped hat and had an inspiration.

'If ye'll take my advice, Mr Grant,' said he, 'ye'll go and buy a kep. A hat like that's no use at a Gleska fitba' match; ye need a hooker. If ye wear a square-topped hat it jist provokes them. I'm gaun round to the warehouse to change my ain hat for a bunnet; I'll leave ye in a hat shop on the road and then I'll jine ye.'

'What fitba' match is on the day?' Jimmy asked a porter in the warehouse.

'Good Goad!' said the porter with amazement at him. 'It's the International against England.'

'Where is it played?' asked Jimmy.

'Hampden, of course!'

'What way do ye get to't, and when does it start?'

'Red car to Mount Florida; game starts at three; I wish to goodness I could get to't,' said the porter.

Jimmy looked his watch. It was half-past one.

He found Grant with a headgear appropriate to the occasion, and wasted twenty minutes in depositing his hat at Buchanan Street left-luggage office. Another twenty minutes passed at the station bar, where Jimmy now discoursed with confidence on Scotland's chances, having bought an evening paper.

'Will ye no' need to hurry oot to the park?' Grant asked with anxiety. 'There'll be an awfu' crood; twenty chaps wi bunnets came on at Steenhive.'

'Lot's of time!' said Jimmy with assurance. 'Well tak' a car. Come awa', and I'll show ye a picture-palace.'

It was fifteen minutes to three when they got to Hampden. A boiling mass of frantic people clamoured round the gates, which were shut against all further entrance, to the inner joy of Mr Swan, who lost his friend in the crowd and failed to find him.

'Where on earth were you till this time?' asked his wife when he got home to Ibrox two hours later.

'Out in the Queen's Park,' said Jimmy truthfully.

'Wi' luck I lost a man outside a fitba' match, and spent an hour in Camphill – no' a soul in't but mysel' – listenin' to the birds whistlin'.'

The Final

from The Thistle and the Grail

ROBIN JENKINS

★ ★ ★

Published in 1954, The Thistle and the Grail, *by Robin Jenkins, is one of the cleverest comic novels to come from Scotland. The 'Thistle' in question is Drumsagart Thistle, a junior football team from a small Lanarkshire town; the Grail that they are seeking is the Scottish Junior Cup. In this extract we follow the Thistle to Hampden Park for the cup final against Allanbank Rangers from Ayrshire, and learn whether or not they are destined to win the 'Holy Grail'. It is difficult to say if Jenkins is using the pursuit of football success as a working out of the Arthurian legend in the manner of Bernard Malamud's baseball story* The Natural. *Perhaps Andrew Rutherford, the club chairman, is Arthur; perhaps one of the heroic knights Galahad and Percival is young Alec Elrigmuir, the team's centre forward? It is difficult to say. What is certain is that Jenkins' notion of a comic novel, written around a small mining community and the gradually building suspense of a knock-out competition, is a great one. And the Thistle's striving to find the Grail must have a flaw, in the way that all the Arthurian tales have flaws; and this one is that Drumsagart Thistle only reached the Final by bending the rules. They appealed against being knocked out and on dubious grounds won the appeal. As the author of more than twenty novels, such as the acclaimed* Guests of War *and* The Cone-Gatherers, *Jenkins brings all the elements of humour, vigour and rounded presentation of character to bear, most of all as the crowds make their way to the great 'cathedral' of Hampden. A few readers may feel there is something lacking in the actual physical description of the action in the Final. It may not be totally recognisable as a football match as we know it, but perhaps that is because nowadays we have all been desensitised by the school of football journalism which gave the language 'a game of two halves' and 'shots nestling in the onion bag'.*

★ ★ ★

To shrieks, bellows, and buglings of acclamation the teams trotted out side by side. They did not at once sprint towards their respective goals, but lined up leaving a lane between them, down which in a minute or so came walking the Lord Provost wearing his chain of office and accompanied by the Allanbank president, who presented his players, and by Andrew Rutherford, who presented his. The Provost had an amiable smile and a handclasp for each player; but for one he had an involuntary laugh. Turk McCabe had not shaved; his hair was cut close to the scalp; his shorts were so long as to be misnomers; and he wore an expression of simian melancholy. At the Provost's laughter he showed his two or three teeth in what was really reciprocal mirth, but which looked rather like resentment in the tree-tops. The Provost was a man of humour; outwardly impartial as his position demanded, he became at heart Turk's man and in the ensuing game applauded his every valiant rescue; which meant he was applauding often.

Presentations over, the teams made for the goals for some preliminary practice. Photographers waylaid one or two to snap them. Alec Elrigmuir had three snapping him like crocodiles at the same moment. It was noticed that when one approached Turk to confer on him this accolade of being photographed on the field of play, in the presence of forty thousand roaring devotees, he was repulsed either by word or glower, or by both, so precipitately did he run backwards in his retreat. The crowd roared appreciation of Turk's modesty. Without having so far kicked a ball, he was already a favourite. A thousand witticisms were launched as he set out on his usual circular canter. Many guessed this was his way of praying.

To the Allanbank's goalkeeper ran a boy in a yellow-and-gold jersey with a horseshoe of yellow-and-gold ribbons; to Sam Teem in the Drumsagart goal scooted the nephew of Ned Nicholson wearing a bright tall hat and carrying a thistle of the same colour almost as large as himself. Other worshippers leapt over the barriers to rush out on to the field and shake their champions' hands. Nathaniel Stewart was one of them. Despite the remonstrations of a policeman who followed him about, he insisted on shaking the hand of every Drumsagart player. To Alec Elrigmuir he said, 'Alec, son, I'll be dying soon. Win for me today, win for me today, and I'll die happy.' Alec politely said he would do his best. To Turk he merely said, 'Turk, for God's sake'; and Turk answered by winking.

Then the field was cleared of these interlopers, the coin was tossed up, Lachie Houston guessed wrongly, causing tremors in the hearts of his Drumsagart followers, the players took up positions, Alec Elrigmuir kicked off, and the great game, the Cup Final, was on at last.

Had one team, Drumsagart say, scored several goals early and prevented their opponents from retaliating, many souls that afternoon would have been spared the vertigo of suspense. Drumsagart souls would have kept on soaring, Allanbank souls plunging: there would have been no soarings, hoverings, and plungings in sick succession, time after time, while hands covered terrified eyes or teeth bit into scarves or eyes glistened or mouths watered or hands were clasped or legs stiffened or bottoms sprang off seats or seats were sprinkled with the tin-tacks of mortification.

It would have been known in advance that the dancing that evening on the wide pavements of Drumsagart would be natural and joyous, while the jigging in Allanbank's school playground would be half-hearted or hysterical. It would have been known, too, that the Drumsagart feast of ham and egg in the Town Hall would have the mustard of success, whereas the Allanbank boiled ham and tomato and lettuce would have lurking amidst it the maggot of disappointment. Above all, it would have been known that Drumsagart beer would be an elixir, preserving that time of bliss for ever; whereas in Allanbank pubs at the bottom of every glass would be found the frog of disenchantment, with its eyes wide open.

All that could have been known and prepared for had Drumsagart – or Allanbank, of course – scored those early goals.

But for a long time neither side could score, though one or other came very close to it almost every minute. Excitement ran among the players, teasing them into blunders that had the spectators shrieking, leaping to their feet, hammering their heads, moaning, laughing, and utterly silent. Alec Elrigmuir three times struck the cross bar with the ball, and once, from four yards, with the Allanbank goalkeeper flat on his face as if chewing daisies and the other Allanbank defenders reeling in horror at the anticipated blow, he hit the ball with all his juvenescent might and high over the bar it flew. Drumsagart howled, Allanbank smiled, Mysie Dougary turned like a wounded vixen on John Watson, who had, in company with thousands of Drumsagart well-wishers, cried: 'Oh you mug!' He was not a mug, she screamed, he was excited – that was all; he was worried too, but he would win the game in the end even if she had go to the pavilion at half-time to tell him there was no need to worry any more. Young Watson scowled, for he was not so simple as Alec.

Among the Allanbank players excitement that hampered them had an ally, as grotesque as Puck and as supernatural in his endeavours. Turk McCabe, though his feet were still tender, played as though a goal scored against the Thistle would be his own death warrant, would be the signal for him to go back to the weird underworld from which he'd obviously come. Immortal though he was, he sweated, suffered, slaved, and bled more than any human. Not even the dragon guarding the Fleece in woods of Colchis showed more devotion.

Half-time came without scoring; but three minutes after the restart Allanbank scored. While their followers were trying to express their glee, with voices, hands, eyes and lungs all inadequate, and while Drumsagart players and spectators alike were shivering at this first touch of the icy finger, Turk McCabe snatched the ball from an Allanbank foot, and instead of kicking it upfield as he'd done so often he began to charge towards the Allanbank goal as if he knew his immortality was fading and could be revived only by a goal nullifying that other. Allanbank players drew back, expecting him to pass the ball to one of his colleagues; they could not believe this freak had any virtue outside its own penalty area. But when he was within their own penalty area, and when at least three of them were hurtling themselves at him, he slipped the ball aside to Elrigmuir, who, football genius, was in the right place to kick it with wonderful élan past the Allanbank goalkeeper.

It was Drumsagart's turn now to find their rejoicing limited only by the coarseness of flesh. Mysie Dougary was on her feet, shrieking like any harridan and waving her tammy. Her rival, Margot Malarkin, shrieked too and dug her nails into her escort's knee in a way to bring tears of anguish to his mildly lewd eyes. Mrs Lockhart bounced up and down on her seat, so that her husband, remembering her fragility, was forced to chide her gently.

In the directors' box Hannah Rutherford was astonished and moved to see on her husband's face and hear in his voice a joy so spontaneous and innocent she knew, as deep in her heart she had suspected, there had been something a little false in his new delight in her company. Yet strangely she was not offended; rather did she feel an unprecedented pity for him and a fresh flow of affection. Perhaps it helped her to see on her other side that their son, too, was transformed by joy.

On the terracing, in Drumsagart corner, men who for years had disliked and distrusted one another were shaking hands. Even Rab Nuneaton, for whom friendly contacts had been so long loathsome, was taking any hand presented to him, and he was listening to yells of happiness in an unfamiliar voice that emerged from his own mouth.

On the field Turk and Alec were being pummelled by their teammates. A congratulatory thumb poked into Turk's eye, a fist struck his scalp like a hammer; but brushing these off as if they were confetti, he shouted hoarsely 'The Cup! The Cup!' as if it was a mystical slogan.

Excitement that had made them clumsy in the beginning now made the players swift and fiery. The ball flew like hawk, skimmed the grass like hare, bounced like kangaroo; it had in it not mere air but the hopes, fears, frenzies, and ecstasies of that great crowd. It went everywhere – up on to terracing even, into the grandstand, into this, that, and every section of the field – everywhere except into one or other of the goals.

Watches were in hands now; minutes, half-minutes, seconds were being counted. People anxious to be away early to avoid the homeward crush lingered, throwing backward glances, walking a step or two away, turning again, waiting, watching, groaning, sighing, and gasping. It would be a draw, everybody said; it would have to be refought next Saturday. Look, the referee was staring at his watch for the sixth or seventh time; his whistle was going to his mouth to blow for time-up. But look again. Look at young Alec Elrigmuir. He was on the ball, he was sidestepping the centre-half, dribbling past the right-back, swerving round that other player, and banging the ball well and truly past the goalkeeper.

Allanbank was stricken. Yellow-and-golden women wailed; children wept; and men whined: 'No. Offside. Time was up. Foul.' But there was no remedy. The referee was blowing his whistle for the end, no god descended, and all Drumsagart was abandoned to ecstasy and cacophony. On the field the players were being punched and kissed by hordes of fanatically grateful followers; among these was Nat Stewart, so overwrought he found himself shaking the hand of an Allanbank player. On the terracing, when other more restrained Drumsagart rejoicers wished to shake hands with their Allanbank rivals the latter declined with shudders, saying never in sobriety could they be magnanimous enough.

In the grandstand the committee-men, captains in victory, were loving one another. Angus Tennant even, with devilment in his love, kissed Sam Malarkin's cheek, which tasted, he said afterwards, like a jujube. It was the kind of daft thing expected of Angus, but nobody could have anticipated it would put Sam into such a towering pet. Indeed, Sam's wan peevishness all that evening was to be attributed wrongly to the loss of whisky, as enervating to a publican as the loss of blood.

In the directors' box Rutherford showed no restraint. He kissed his wife, lifted up his son above his head as he'd done when the boy was an infant, shook hands rapturously with Harry, and slapped Mabel's bottom.

'We've done it, Hannah,' he cried. 'We've won the Cup.'

She smiled and nodded: her thought was, What money is it putting in your purse? But she did not, as formerly, sharpen that thought and wield it; she kept it blunted and sheathed; and she found, to her surprise, she had acted not so much virtuously as happily.

'I could greet,' he cried. 'I feel so pleased I could greet.'

It was Harry's turn to smile: his meant, So you're a wean yet, Andrew, in many ways? Well, weans are amenable, especially happy weans.

'If only old Tinto could hae been spared to see this,' cried Andrew.

Hannah noted that it was the old drunkard rather than his father he wished still alive.

Then the players, still in their shorts and jerseys, and with the grime and sweat of battle, came up the steps in single file. Lachie Houston led them. From the Lord Provost he received the Cup, which he immediately held on high, the silver grail at long last achieved, so that the Drumsagart people roared their homage. Then every player got handshakes of congratulation, first from the Provost, and immediately after from their president, who had words as well for them. 'Well done, boy. Champion work, Jim. Tom, you played like a hero,' and so on. He did not, as most did, praise Turk McCabe and Alec Elrigmuir above the rest; and the rest noticed it and were grateful.

He insisted on shaking the hands of the Allanbank players, too, though they seemed to think it was an act of supreme supererogation. To the Allanbank officials he was generous in his commiserations. They had to accept them, but one incontinently muttered: 'We should never have been playing you anyway: a poor Cup that's won by a protest.' Rutherford overheard and for a moment experienced his old dismay. 'That's true,' he said, to the person nearest him.

It was Hannah. She hadn't been attending. 'What's true, Andrew?'

He began to laugh and laid his hand on her shoulder. 'Never mind, Hannah. Whoever rejoices, there are bound to be some with sore hearts. We're just not built that we can all be happy together.'

She understood now, for all round were mourning Allanbank faces. 'No, but we that can manage to be happy, Andrew, are not to be expected to give it up till everyone joins us.'

'No, Hannah. That's right.'

It was at last, she thought, the formula they had been searching for for years, reconciling their different points of view. Hampden grandstand was a queer place to find it.

'Would you mind very much,' he asked, 'if I didn't go straight back home with you? I'd like to be in Drumsagart tonight and see the celebrations. Maybe you would like to come yourself? Maybe you would all like to come?'

'Not me,' Andrew,' she said, smiling. 'But I've no objections if you want to go.'

'Thanks all the same, Andrew,' said Harry, 'but I think I'd be out of place in the celebrations. I've enjoyed myself here this afternoon, I've met some interesting and useful people, and the Thistle won. I think I can call it a day.'

'What about you, Gerald?' asked his father.

The boy gazed at his mother.

'It's up to you,' she said. 'It'll be a bit of a rabble there tonight, but surely your father can look after you.'

He saw she was no longer on his side against his father; and he felt sorry for himself.

'I don't know,' he muttered.

'It'll be great fun, Gerald,' said his father. 'There's to be dancing to the pipe band, and fireworks, and –'

'No. I want to go home.'

His father was disappointed. 'All right, son.' He looked at them all and laughed. 'Am I being thrawn?' he asked. 'Should I just go home too? Mind you, I'm the president.'

'You go to Drumsagart,' said Hannah. 'Likely it'll be your last visit there for a long time.'

So he went to Drumsagart, in the bus carrying the conquerors. Part of the roof had been slid back, and by standing on a seat a man could display the Cup to the passing world. That was a duty as much as a pleasure, but it was also less convenient than sitting comfortably in a seat; therefore it was honourably shared among the players. Only Turk refused: on the ground that it was a damned stupid way of travelling in a bus, one might as well be on a motorbike. He had to be excused; his determined, surly common sense in the midst of the exultation was a pity, but it couldn't be helped: Turk was a force of nature, like a volcano, say, and if he chose to erupt that night after consuming gallons of whisky, so that Elvan and at least three bobbies dragged him to jail – why, then, it would all be part of the saga of the winning of the Cup.

The other hero, Alec Elrigmuir, was drunk already. He had to be restrained from climbing out on to the roof of the bus. Going through villages on the road home, he threw pennies to children, some of whom cheered and some of whom searched for clods to throw back. Everybody knew it was not just because he'd scored the winning goal, nor because six Senior clubs had begged him to play for them, but because Mysie Dougary had come shouting for him at the dressing-room door, had kissed him though he was naked from the waist up, and had called him her Sandy.

Rutherford sat amidst that busload of familiar men, noticing how happiness had purged them, as it had purged him, of all characteristic meanness and selfishness. This really was how men were, how they would wish to be always if circumstances allowed them. He had been wrong to think they had begun to respect and even like him because he had thrown away all his scruples about accepting their own standards of conduct and belief, which were the standards of pigs round a trough, every man for himself and to hell with the hindmost. Surely that respect and liking had been granted simply because he had given them a chance to respect and like him. Hitherto he had been too stiff, too remote, too entangled in prejudice and illusion. Here was the proof, his hand being shaken every minute, his back slapped, his part in the general victory loudly acknowledged.

When the bus, with dozens of vehicles following it, like coaches a great hearse, came into the main street there was Bob McKelvie ready with his swollen-cheeked men. To the shrill braggadocio of 'Scotland For Ever' that vast procession crawled along to the Town Hall, where from the lofty flagpole was flying a blue flag with a crimson thistle in the centre. Along each kerb were hundreds of townspeople waving, cheering, and laughing. Boys went wild, fencing each other with stolen tulips, or hooting at the team from the tops of trees. It was not thought likely even Sergeant Elvan would be at his normal work that evening.

It seemed to Rutherford from inside the bus, with tears almost in his eyes, that his native town, evergreen, deep-rooted, but sombre, had suddenly burst forth with bright flowers.

When the bus stopped at the Town Hall entrance the crowd began to roar for speeches; but for quite ten minutes more everybody had to wait in an explosive, sentimental, derisive, hilarious patience while Bob McKelvie and his pipers exhausted lungs and repertoire. When the last ululation had died away into the sunshine the speeches were made from the top of the bus. First was Lachie Houston, who let the Cup speak for him.

'Here it is, folks,' he shouted, and held it up.

The applause was excessive; at least so Mr Lockhart thought, now back at the manse, soothing the baby in his arms.

Alec Elrigmuir was called on. 'I'll tell you this,' he cried. 'I'm glad we won. And I'll tell you something else: me and Mysie are going to get married soon.'

Again the response was loud enough to waken all babies within half a mile and to make impossible the hushing of those not asleep. Mr Lockhart had to come away from the window, and found himself uttering the ungracious wish that Nan had stayed at home to attend to her fundamental duty instead of going out to see the fun, as she called it. It seemed she was fond of pipe music.

Wattie Cleugh spoke. 'This is a proud, proud day for Drumsagart,' he said, and went on saying it in a dozen different ways until at last even pride wearied.

Other players were shouted for: some refused; those who obliged were very brief. Turk at first was a refuser. The crowd kept roaring for him. At last he sprang up through the hole in the roof of the bus. When he was seen they cheered him so mightily that what he was roaring at them was not at first heard, although he kept repeating it, more and more vehemently. Then suddenly there was a hush. They were ready to listen to the blue-chinned scowling oracle.

'You're a shower of mugs,' he roared.

The Kirkwall Ba' Game

from The Folklore of Orkney and Shetland

ERNEST MARWICK

The Christmas Bawing of Monimusk *was discussed in the introduction to this chapter, as being an example of the kind of mass football game that was once common throughout Scotland on festive occasions once or twice a year. In Kirkwall on Orkney the Ba' Game, between the 'Uppies' and 'Doonies', still flourishes and is held on Christmas Day and on New Year's Day. Photographs show the heaving mass of humanity at the harbour goal end plunging into the water. The beautifully handstitched ba' occupies a prominent position in the homes of those fortunate enough to be awarded it. Ernest Marwick was a native Orcadian from a farming family and this piece comes from a fine collection* The Folklore of Orkney and Shetland *edited by him. He was a broadcaster, journalist and poet.*

★ ★ ★

Until early this century, the favourite New Year's Day sport in Orkney was football playing. 'In the various fields of play', comments John Robertson, 'there were no sides, touchlines or goals as we understand them, and an inflated bladder of a cow, sheep or pig, encased in leather and usually fashioned by the local cobbler, was lustily kicked about in a rough and tumble on the parish Ba' Green.' Out of such a game, played in and around Kirkwall, there gradually developed in the late eighteenth century and the first half of the nineteenth, the Kirkwall Ba' Game as it is known today. So energetic is this game that, in the old part of the town through which it is played, houses and shops have their windows and doors stoutly barricaded. The contest takes place on each Christmas Day and New Year's Day, but the New Year's game is the prototypal one. From the mercat cross in front of St Magnus Cathedral, a cork-filled ball is thrown, on the stroke of 1 o'clock, to the expectant group of men waiting in the Broad Street. Before the game is over, more than a hundred players may take part, representing the opposing halves of the original town. Those born to the south of the cathedral are Up-the-Gates and those born to the north of it Doon-the-Gates, but, with the rapid growth of Kirkwall, family loyalty sometimes seems more important than geography.

The aim of both Uppies and Doonies – as the sides are popularly called – is to carry the ball against all opposition to their own end of the town, the waters of the harbour being the recognised goal of the Doonies, and the crossroads at the opposite side of Kirkwall the goal of the Uppies. Their object is attained by pushing, so that the players almost immediately form a tight scrum, bracing themselves against the walls of the houses. In their midst, locked in determined arms, is the ball. On either side of it (speaking theoretically) the players face each other and push. Although it is so hot in the centre of the scrum that steam rises in a thin cloud on the winter air, and although forceful tactics are required, tempers are usually held in check and foul play is not tolerated.

There are no rules, but skilful co-ordination may give one of the sides an advantage, and players conserve their strength for violent surges by periods of apparent inaction. The hundreds of spectators who follow the progress of the game often have to scatter quickly, for the scrum is always liable to erupt, and there is swirling disorder until it forms again a little way along the street. A good game may last for several hours, even after the short winter daylight has disappeared. Weight of numbers tells in the end, and the last few yards to the goal may be covered at a cracking pace. When Kirkwall Harbour is the goal attained, it is obligatory to throw the ball into the sea. Several players invariably plunge in after it. The leather ba', handmade for the contest, is a coveted trophy. It is always awarded by popular acclamation to some player who has been a notable participant over a period of years, and who has made his presence felt in the game just ended.

While there is no evidence that the game, played as described, existed before the nineteenth century, tales of the traditional rivalry which existed between the two sections of the town are persistent – some of them having the indubitable authority of print. A favourite tale is of a local tyrant called Tusker, who was pursued and killed near Perth by an enterprising Orcadian. As the victor brought the severed head of Tusker home to Kirkwall, swinging from the pommel of his saddle, the tyrant's protruding teeth broke the skin of his leg. Poisoning set in, and the young champion had no sooner reached the mercat cross, and flung the head to the crowd who had gathered to acclaim him, than he died. With mingled grief and anger the townsfolk kicked the head of the odious Tusker around the street, thus initiating, the legend says, Kirkwall's Ba' Game.

The Emergence of the
Rugby Code

★ ★ ★

By 1871, when Scotland first met England in a Rugby international at Raeburn Place in Edinburgh, there was still considerable confusion between different interpretations of the rules of what was generally called 'Football', although the Association or non-handling variation was beginning to take a firm hold in a wide area of society. An international match played under Association rules had taken place at the Oval cricket ground in 1870. Now the advocates of a handling game were about to propose a match with representatives drawn from English clubs who were members of the Rugby Union. The letter of invitation was signed by representatives of Edinburgh Academical Football Club, Merchistonian FC, Glasgow Academical FC, West Of Scotland FC and St Salvator FC, St Andrews. Even within the handling code there were considerable arguments about the precise rules, for example, as to whether sides should number 15 (XV) or 20 (XX); 'run-ins' or 'tries' carried no points, but merely gave the side who had crossed their opponents' line an opportunity to 'try' (or 'kick-off') and make an attempt to score a goal. Here is a newspaper report of the match.

★ ★ ★

FOOTBALL MATCH
Scotland v England

This great football match was played yesterday on the Academy Cricket Ground, Edinburgh, with a result most gratifying for Scotland. The weather was fine and there was a very large turn-out of spectators. The competitors were dressed in appropriate costume, the English wearing a white jersey, ornamented by a red rose, and the Scotch a brown jersey with a thistle. Although the good wishes of the spectators went with the Scotch team yet it was considered that their chance was poor. The difference between the two teams was very marked, the English being of a much heavier and stronger build compared to their opponents. The game commenced shortly after three o'clock, the Scotch getting the kick off, and for some time neither side had any advantage. The Scotch, however, succeeded in driving the ball down to the English goal, and pushing splendidly forward, eventually put it into the opponents' quarters, who, however, prevented any harm accruing by smartly 'touching down'. This result warmed the Englishmen up to their work, and in spite of tremendous opposition they got near the Scotch goal, and kicked the ball past it, but as it was cleverly 'touched down' they got no advantage. This finished the first 50 minutes and the teams changed sides. For a considerable time after the change the ball was sent from side to side, and the 'backs' got more work to do. By some lucky runs, however, the Scotch got on to the borders of the English land and tried to force the ball past the goal. The English strenuously opposed this attempt, and for a time the struggle was terrible, ending in the Scotch 'touching down' in their opponents' ground, and becoming entitled to a 'try'. This result was received with cheers which were more heartily renewed when Cross, to whom the 'kick off' was entrusted, made a beautiful goal. This defeat only stirred up the English to fresh efforts, and driving the ball across the field, they managed also to secure a 'try', but unfortunately the man who got the 'kick off' did not allow sufficient windage, and the ball fell short. After this the Scotch became more cautious and playing well together secured after several attempts a second 'try', but good luck did not attend the 'kick off', and the goal was lost. Time being then declared up the game ceased, the Scotch winning by a goal and a 'try'.

Glasgow Herald, Tuesday 28 March 1871

Tales of a Rugby Three-quarter

from Castle Gay

JOHN BUCHAN

★ ★ ★

In this, the opening chapter from John Buchan's 1930 sequel to Huntingtower, *we meet again several of the characters from that good-humoured comedy, including of course Dickson McCunn, the retired grocer who befriends the 'Gorbals Die-hards', young boys from the slums of Glasgow's Gorbals. The leading figure in the opening chapter is Jaikie Galt, miraculously transformed from the guttersnipe of* Huntingtower *into a Cambridge undergraduate and Scottish internationalist wing three-quarter, hero of the game against the 'Kangaroos', an antipodean touring fifteen. Buchan gives us a gripping account of the game between the Scots team and the previously all-conquering Aussies (nothing new there then). The touring team are finally edged out by the resolute play of Jaikie who is now a very model of a gentleman, as is Dougal Crombie, formerly chief of the Die-hards and now a journalist and budding politician. We learn Dougal is a follower of the Labour Party and writes a column for a leftish journal called* Outward, *seemingly modelled on Kirkintilloch-born Labour politician Tom Johnston's socialist organ* Forward. *Buchan attended Hutcheson's Grammar School in Glasgow, a rugby-playing school, and also lived for a considerable time in the Borders, Scotland's Rugby stronghold – presumably these experiences informed this piece. Writing about sport is not the same as sports writing and Buchan's prose bears many of the hallmarks of his adventure novels. In a way he treats all of his scenes of action as sport – Maurice Lindsay describes Buchan's heroes (like Richard Hannay and Edward Leithen) as being 'regularly involved in adventure for adventure's sake, as if life were a protracted affair of dangerous sport'. (Remember how the Anglo-*

Russian dispute over the north-west frontier was called 'The Great Game'.) However, the game in this extract is a pretty light-hearted affair, interesting because of the contrasts and similarities between rugby football as played in the Thirties and today: 'scrimmages' and 'halves' and so on. The traditional strength of the Scottish game, right up to the Sixties, was that demanded of the players by the crowd: 'Feet, Scotland, feet!' Or as Buchan describes it:

The Scottish forwards seemed to have got a new lease of life. They carried the game well into the enemy territory, dribbling irresistibly in their loose rushes, and hooking and heeling in the grand manner from the scrums . . .

★ ★ ★

Mr. Dickson McCunn laid down the newspaper, took his spectacles from his nose, and polished them with a blue-and-white spotted handkerchief.

'It will be a great match,' he observed to his wife. 'I wish I was there to see. These Kangaroos must be a fearsome lot.' Then he smiled reflectively. 'Our laddies are not turning out so bad, Mamma. Here's Jaikie, and him not yet twenty, and he has his name blazing in the papers as if he was a Cabinet Minister.'

Mrs. McCunn, a placid lady of a comfortable figure, knitted steadily. She did not share her husband's enthusiasms.

'I know fine,' she said, 'that Jaikie will be coming back with a bandaged head and his arm in a sling. Rugby in my opinion is not a game for Christians. It's fair savagery.'

'Hoots, toots! It's a grand ploy for young folk. You must pay a price for fame, you know. Besides, Jaikie hasn't got hurt this long time back. He's learning caution as he grows older, or maybe he's getting better at the job. You mind when he was at the school we used to have the doctor to him every second Saturday night . . . He was always a terrible bold laddie, and when he was getting dangerous his eyes used to run with tears. He's quit of that habit now, but they tell me that when he's real excited he turns as white as paper. Well, well! we've all got our queer ways. Here's a biography of him and the other players. What's this it says?'

Mr. McCunn resumed his spectacles.

'Here it is. "J. Galt, born in Glasgow. Educated at the Western Academy and St. Mark's College, Cambridge . . . played last year against Oxford in the victorious Cambridge fifteen, when he scored three tries . . . This is his first International . . . equally distinguished in defence and attack . . . Perhaps the most unpredictable of wing three-quarters now playing . . ." Oh, and here's another bit in "Gossip about the Teams."' He removed his spectacles and laughed heartily. 'That's good. It calls him a "scholar and a gentleman." That's what they always say about University players. Well, I'll warrant he's as good a gentleman as any, though he comes out of a back street in the Gorbals. I'm not so sure about the scholar. But he can always do anything he sets his mind to, and he's a worse glutton for books than me. No man can tell what may happen to Jaikie yet . . . We can take credit for these laddies of ours, for they're all in the way of doing well for themselves, but there's just the two of them that I feel are like our own bairns. Just Jaikie and Dougal – and goodness knows what will be the end of that red-headed Dougal. Jaikie's a douce body, but there's a determined daftness about Dougal. I wish he wasn't so taken up with his misguided politics.'

'I hope they'll not miss their train,' said the lady. 'Supper's at eight, and they should be here by seven-thirty, unless Jaikie's in the hospital.'

'No fear,' was the cheerful answer. 'More likely some of the Kangaroos will be there. We should get a telegram about the match by six o'clock.'

So after tea, while his wife departed on some domestic task, Mr. McCunn took his ease with a pipe in a wicker chair on the little terrace which looked seaward. He had found the hermitage for which he had long sought, and was well content with it. The six years which had passed since he forsook the city of Glasgow and became a countryman had done little to alter his appearance. The hair had indeed gone completely from the top of his head, and what was left was greying, but there were few lines on his smooth, ruddy face, and the pale eyes had still the innocence and ardour of youth. His figure had improved, for country exercise and a sparer diet had checked the movement towards rotundity. When not engaged in some active enterprise, it was his habit to wear a tailed coat and trousers of tweed, a garb which from his boyish recollection he thought proper for a country laird, but which to the ordinary observer suggested a bookmaker. Gradually, a little self-consciously, he had acquired what he considered to be the habits of the class. He walked in his garden with a spud; his capacious pockets contained a pruning knife and twine; he could talk quite learnedly of crops and stock, and, though he never shouldered a gun, of the prospects of game; and a fat spaniel was rarely absent from his heels.

The home he had chosen was on the spur of a Carrick moor, with the sea to the west, and to south and east a distant prospect of the blue Galloway hills. After much thought he had rejected the various country houses which were open to his purchase; he felt it necessary to erect his own sanctuary, conformable to his modest but peculiar tastes. A farm of some five hundred acres had been bought, most of it pasture-fields fenced by dry-stone dykes, but with an considerable stretch of broom and heather, and one big plantation of larch. Much of this he let off, but he retained a hundred acres where he and his grieve could make disastrous essays in agriculture. The old farmhouse had been a whitewashed edifice of eight rooms, with ample outbuildings, and this he had converted into a commodious dwelling, with half a dozen spare bedrooms, and a large chamber which was at once library, smoking-room, and business-room. I do not defend Mr. McCunn's taste, for he had a memory stored with bad precedents. He hankered after little pepper-box turrets, which he thought the badge of ancientry, and in internal decoration he had an unhallowed longing for mahogany panelling, like a ship's saloon. Also he doted on his vast sweep of gravel. Yet he had on the whole made a pleasing thing of Blaweary (it was the name which had first taken his fancy), for he stuck to harled and whitewashed walls, and he had a passion for green turf, so that, beyond the odious gravel, the lawns swept to the meadows unbroken by formal flower-beds. These lawns were his special hobby. 'There's not a yard of turf about the place,' he would say, 'that's not as well kept as a putting-green.'

The owner from his wicker chair looked over the said lawns to a rough pasture where his cows were at graze, and then beyond a patch of yellowing bracken to the tops of a fir plantation. After that the ground fell more steeply, so that the treetops were silhouetted against the distant blue of the sea. It was mid-October, but the air was as balmy as June, and only the earlier dusk told of the declining year. Mr. McCunn was under strict domestic orders not to sit out of doors after sunset, but he had dropped asleep and the twilight was falling when he was roused by a maid with a telegram.

In his excitement he could not find his spectacles. He tore open the envelope and thrust the pink form into the maid's face. 'Read it, lassie – read it,' he cried, forgetting the decorum of the master of a household.

'Coming seven-thirty,' the girl read primly. 'Match won by single point.' Mr. McCunn upset his chair, and ran, whooping, in search of his wife.

The historian must return upon his tracks in order to tell of the great event thus baldly announced. That year the Antipodes had dispatched to Britain such a constellation of Rugby stars that the hearts of the home enthusiasts became as water and their joints were loosened. For years they had known and suffered from the quality of those tall young men from the South, whom the sun had toughened and tautened – their superb physique, their resourcefulness, their uncanny combination. Hitherto, while the fame of one or two players had reached these shores, the teams had been in the main a batch of dark horses, and there had been no exact knowledge to set a bar to hope. But now Australia had gathered herself together for a mighty effort, and had sent to the field a fifteen most of whose members were known only too well. She had collected her sons wherever they were to be found. Four had already played for British Universities; three had won a formidable repute in international matches in which their country of ultimate origin had entitled them to play. What club, county, or nation could resist so well equipped an enemy? And, as luck decided, it fell to Scotland, which had been having a series of disastrous seasons, to take the first shock.

That ancient land seemed for the moment to have forgotten her prowess. She could produce a strong, hard-working and effective pack, but her great three-quarter line had gone, and she had lost the scrum-half who the year before had been her chief support. Most of her fifteen were new to an international game, and had never played together. The danger lay in the enemy halves and three-quarters. The Kangaroos had two halves possessed of miraculous hands and a perfect knowledge of the game. They might be trusted to get the ball to their three-quarters, who were reputed the most formidable combination that ever played on turf. On the left wing was the mighty Charvill, an Oxford Blue and an English International; on the right Martineau, who had won fame on the cinder-track as well as on the football-field. The centres were two cunning brothers, Clauson by name, who played in a unison like Siamese twins. Against such a four Scotland could scrape up only a quartet of possibles, men of promise but not yet of performance. The hosts of Tuscany seemed strong out of all proportion to the puny defenders of Rome. And as the Scottish right-wing three-quarter, to frustrate the terrible Charvill, stood the tiny figure of J. Galt, Cambridge University, five foot six inches in height and slim as a wagtail.

To the crowd of sixty thousand and more that waited for the teams to enter the field there was vouchsafed one slender comfort. The weather, which at Blaweary was clear and sunny, was abominable in the Scottish midlands. It had rained all the preceding night, and it was hoped that the ground might be soft, inclining to mud – mud dear to the hearts of our islanders but hateful to men accustomed to the firm soil of the South.

The game began in a light drizzle, and for Scotland it began disastrously. The first scrimmage was in the centre of the ground, and the ball came out to the Kangaroo scrum-half, who sent it to his stand-off. From him it went to Clauson, and then to Martineau, who ran round his opposing wing, dodged the Scottish full-back, and scored a try, which was converted. After five minutes the Kangaroos led by five points.

Presently the Scottish forwards woke up, and there was a spell of stubborn defence. The Scottish full-back had a long shot at goal from a free kick, and missed, but for the rest most of the play was in the Scottish twenty-five. The Scottish pack strove their hardest, but they did no more than hold their opponents. Then once more came a quick heel out, which went to one of the Clausons, a smart cut-through, a try secured between the posts and easily converted. The score was now ten points to nil.

Depression settled upon the crowd as dark as the weather, which had stopped raining but had developed into a sour *haar*. Followed a period of constant kicking into touch, a dull game which the Kangaroos were supposed to eschew. Just before half-time there was a thin ray of comfort. The Scottish left-wing three-quarter, one Smail, a Borderer, intercepted a Kangaroo pass and reached the enemy twenty-five before he was brought down from behind by Martineau's marvellous sprinting. He had been within sight of success, and half-time came with a faint hope that there was still a chance of averting a runaway defeat.

The second half began with three points to Scotland, secured from a penalty kick. Also the Scottish forwards seemed to have got a new lease of life. They carried the game well into the enemy territory, dribbling irresistibly in their loose rushes, and hooking and heeling in the grand manner from the scrums. The white uniforms of the Kangaroos were now plentifully soiled, and the dark blue of the Scots made them look the less bedraggled side. All but J. Galt. His duty had been that of desperate defence conducted with a resolute ferocity, and he had suffered in it. His jersey was half torn off his back, and his shorts were in ribbons: he limped heavily, and his small face looked as if it had been ground into the mud of his native land. He felt dull and stupid, as if he had been slightly concussed. His gift had hitherto been for invisibility; his fame had been made as a will-o'-the-wisp; now he seemed to be cast for the part of that Arnold von Winkelried who drew all the spears to his bosom.

The ball was now coming out to the Scottish halves, but they mishandled it. It seemed impossible to get their three-quarters going. The ball either went loose, or was intercepted, or the holder was promptly tackled, and whenever there seemed a chance of a run there was always either a forward pass or a knock-on. At this period of the game the Scottish forwards were carrying everything on their shoulders, and their backs seemed hopeless. Any moment, too, might see the deadly echelon of the Kangaroo three-quarters ripple down the field.

And then came one of those sudden gifts of fortune which make Rugby an image of life. The ball came out from a heel in a scrum not far from the Kangaroo twenty-five, and went to the Kangaroo stand-off half. He dropped it, and, before he could recover, it was gathered by the Scottish stand-off. He sent it to Smail, who passed back to the Scottish left-centre, one Morrison, an Academical from Oxford who had hitherto been pretty much of a passenger. Morrison had the good luck to have a clear avenue before him, and he had a gift of pace. Dodging the Kangaroo full-back with a neat swerve, he scored in the corner of the goal-line amid a pandemonium of cheers. The try was miraculously converted, and the score stood at ten points to eight, with fifteen minutes to play.

Now began an epic struggle, not the least dramatic in the history of the game since a century ago the Rugby schoolboy William Webb Ellis first 'took the ball in his arms and ran with it.' The Kangaroos had no mind to let victory slip from their grasp, and, working like one man, they set themselves to assure it. For a little their magnificent three-quarter line seemed to have dropped out of the picture, but now most theatrically it returned to it. From a scrimmage in the Kangaroo half of the field, the ball went to their stand-off and from him to Martineau. At the moment the Scottish players were badly placed, for their three-quarters were standing wide in order to overlap the faster enemy line. It was a perfect occasion for one of Martineau's deadly runs. He was, however, well tackled by Morrison and passed back to his scrum-half, who kicked ahead towards the left wing to Charvill. The latter gathered the ball at top-speed, and went racing down the touch-line with nothing before him but the Scottish right-wing three-quarter. It seemed a certain score, and there fell on the spectators a sudden hush. That small figure, not hitherto renowned for pace, could never match the Australian's long, loping, deadly stride.

Had Jaikie had six more inches of height he would have failed. But a resolute small man who tackles low is the hardest defence to get round. Jaikie hurled himself at Charvill, and was handed off by a mighty palm. But he staggered back in the direction of his own goal, and there was just one fraction of a second for him to make another attempt. This time he succeeded. Charvill's great figure seemed to dive forward on the top of his tiny assailant, and the ball rolled into touch. For a minute, while the heavens echoed with the shouting, Jaikie lay on the ground bruised and winded. Then he got up, shook himself, like a heroic, bedraggled sparrow, and hobbled back to his place.

There were still five minutes before the whistle, and these minutes were that electric testing time, when one side is intent to consolidate a victory and the other resolute to avert too crushing a defeat. Scotland had never hoped to win; she had already done far better than her expectations, and she gathered herself together for a mighty effort to hold what she had gained. Her hopes lay still in her forwards. Her backs had far surpassed their form, but they were now almost at their last gasp.

But in one of them there was a touch of that genius which can triumph over fatigue. Jaikie had never in his life played so gruelling a game. He was accustomed to being maltreated, but now he seemed to have been pounded and smothered and kicked and flung about till he doubted whether he had a single bone undamaged. His whole body was one huge ache. Only the brain under his thatch of hair was still working well . . . The Kangaroo pack had gone down field with a mighty rush, and there was a scrum close to the Scottish twenty-five. The ball went out cleanly to one of the Clausons, but it was now very greasy, and the light was bad, and he missed his catch. More, he stumbled after it and fell, for he had had a punishing game. Jaikie on the wing suddenly saw his chance. He darted in and gathered the ball, dodging Clauson's weary tackle. There was no other man of his side at hand to take a pass, but there seemed just a slender chance for a cut-through. He himself of course would be downed by Charvill, but there was a fraction of a hope, if he could gain a dozen yards, that he might be able to pass to Smail, who was not so closely marked.

His first obstacle was the Kangaroo scrum-half, who had come across the field. To him he adroitly sold the dummy, and ran towards the right touchline, since there was no sign of Smail. He had little hope of success, for it must be only a question of seconds before he was brought down. He did not hear the roar from the spectators as he appeared in the open, for he was thinking of Charvill waiting for his revenge, and he was conscious that his heart was behaving violently quite outside its proper place. But he was also conscious that in some mysterious way he had got a second wind, and that his body seemed a trifle less leaden.

He was now past the half-way line, a little distance ahead of one of the Clausons, with no colleague near him, and with Charvill racing to intercept him. For one of Jaikie's inches there could be no hand-off, but he had learned in his extreme youth certain arts not commonly familiar to Rugby players. He was a most cunning dodger. To the yelling crowd he appeared to be aiming at a direct collision with the Kangaroo left-wing. But just as it looked as if a two-seater must meet a Rolls-Royce head-on at full speed, the two-seater swerved and Jaikie wriggled somehow below Charvill's arm. Then sixty thousand people stood up, waving caps and umbrellas and shouting like lunatics, for Charvill was prone on the ground, and Jaikie was stolidly cantering on.

He was now at the twenty-five line, and the Kangaroo full-back awaited him. This was a small man, very little taller than Jaikie, but immensely broad and solid, and a superlative place-kick. A different physique would have easily stopped the runner, now at the very limits of his strength, but the Kangaroo was too slow in his tackle to meet Jaikie's swerve. He retained indeed in his massive fist a considerable part of Jaikie's jersey, but the half-naked wearer managed to stumble on just ahead of him, and secured a try in the extreme corner. There he lay with his nose in the mud, utterly breathless, but obscurely happy. He was still dazed and panting when a minute later the whistle blew, and a noise like the Last Trump told him that by a single point he had won the match for his country.

There was a long table below the Grand Stand, a table reserved for the Press. On it might have been observed a wild figure with red hair dancing a war dance of triumph. Presently the table collapsed under him, and the rending of timber and the recriminations of journalists were added to the apocalyptic din.

At eight o'clock sharp a party of four sat down to supper at Blaweary. The McCunns did not dine in the evening, for Dickson declared that dinner was a stiff, unfriendly repast, associated in his mind with the genteel in cities. He clung to the fashions of his youth – ate a large meal at one o'clock, and a heavy tea about half-past four, and had supper at eight from October to May, and in the long summer days whenever he chose to come indoors. Mrs. McCunn had grumbled at first, having dim social aspirations, but it was useless to resist her husband's stout conservatism. For the evening meal she was in the habit of arraying herself in black silk and many ornaments, and Dickson on occasions of ceremony was persuaded to put on a dinner jacket; but to-night he had declined to change, on the ground that the guests were only Dougal and Jaikie.

There were candles on the table in the pleasant dining-room, and one large lamp on the sideboard. Dickson had been stubborn about electric light, holding that a faint odour of paraffin was part of the amenities of a country house. A bright fire crackled on the hearth, for the October evenings at Blaweary were chilly.

The host was in the best of humours. 'Here's the kind of food for hungry folk. Ham and eggs – and a bit of the salmon I catched yesterday! Did you hear that I fell in, and Adam had to gaff me before he gaffed the fish? Everything except the loaf is our own providing – the eggs are our hens', the ham's my own rearing and curing, the salmon is my catching, and the scones are Mamma's baking. There's a bottle of champagne to drink Jaikie's health. Man, Jaikie, it's an extraordinary thing you've taken so little hurt. We were expecting to see you a complete lameter, with your head in bandages.'

Jaikie laughed. 'I was in more danger from the crowd at the end than from the Kangaroos. It's Dougal that's lame. He fell through the reporters' table.'

The Missing Wing Three-quarter

ARTHUR CONAN DOYLE

★ ★ ★

The title of this story sounds a bit like a newspaper headline of a report of a poor Scottish international performance, when the backs have been caught out in defence and blame is being handed out. However, it is a Sherlock Holmes story and nothing so trivial. It is a Cambridge and England three-quarter who has disappeared – no mere forward but a winger and a 'flyer' at that.

Holmes is surely the archetypal English detective, whether seated in his rooms at 221B Baker Street puffing away at a three-pipe problem, or rushing in a hansom cab through the fog-shrouded streets of London on his way to the scene of yet another mystery that has baffled Inspector Lestrade of Scotland Yard. Yet Holmes' essential Scottishness is all too often overlooked. While certainly not Scottish in ancestry – 'my ancestors were country squires', he tells his chronicler Dr Watson – he is undoubtedly Scots in inspiration and genesis, and the London setting owes a surprising amount to Edinburgh, the city of his creator's birth.

Arthur Conan Doyle was born in Edinburgh of Irish parentage and studied medicine at the university where Dr Joseph Bell was one of his lecturers in surgery. Bell, something of a showman, made a practice of demonstrating deduction based on close observation and acute reasoning. The rigorous training and the testing of each stage of a hypothesis before reaching a diagnosis helped create the detective who observed 'It is a capital mistake to theorise before one has data.' Here are the story's opening passages.

★ ★ ★

We were fairly accustomed to receive weird telegrams at Baker Street, but I have a particular recollection of one which reached us on a gloomy February morning some seven or eight years ago, and gave Mr. Sherlock Holmes a puzzled quarter of an hour. It was addressed to him, and ran thus:

'Please await me. Terrible misfortune. Right wing three-quarter missing; indispensable tomorrow. – OVERTON.'

'Strand postmark, and despatched ten thirty-six,' said Holmes, reading it over and over. 'Mr. Overton was evidently considerably excited when he sent it, and somewhat incoherent in consequence. Well, well, he will be here, I dare say, by the time I have looked through *The Times*, and then we shall know all about it. Even the most insignificant problem would be welcome in these stagnant days.'

Things had indeed been very slow with us, and I had learned to dread such periods of inaction, for I knew by experience that my companion's brain was so abnormally active that it was dangerous to leave it without material upon which to work. For years I had gradually weaned him from that drug mania which had threatened once to check his remarkable career. Now I knew that under ordinary conditions he no longer craved for this artificial stimulus; but I was well aware that the fiend was not dead, but sleeping; and I have known that the sleep was a light one and the waking near when in periods of idleness I have seen the drawn look upon Holmes' ascetic face, and the brooding of his deep-set and inscrutable eyes. Therefore I blessed this Mr. Overton, whoever he might be, since he had come with his enigmatic message to break that dangerous calm which brought more peril to my friend than all the storms of his tempestuous life.

As we expected, the telegram was soon followed by its sender, and the card of Mr. Cyril Overton, of Trinity College, Cambridge, announced the arrival of an enormous young man, sixteen stone of solid bone and muscle, who spanned the doorway with his broad shoulders and looked from one of us to the other with a comely face which was haggard with anxiety.

'Mr. Sherlock Holmes?'

My companion bowed.

'I've been down to Scotland Yard, Mr. Holmes. I saw Inspector Stanley Hopkins. He advised me to come to you. He said the case, so far as he could see, was more in your line than in that of the regular police.'

'Pray sit down and tell me what is the matter.'

'It's awful, Mr. Holmes, simply awful! I wonder my hair isn't grey. Godfrey Staunton – you've heard of him, of course? He's simply the hinge that the whole team turns on. I'd rather spare two from the pack and have Godfrey for my three-quarter line. Whether it's passing, or tackling, or dribbling, there's no one to touch him; and then, he's got the head and can hold us all together. What am I to do? That's what I ask you, Mr. Holmes. There's Moorhouse, first reserve, but he is trained as a half, and he always edges right in on to the scrum instead of keeping out on the touch-line. He's a fine place-kick, it's true, but, then, he has no judgment, and he can't sprint for nuts. Why, Morton or Johnson, the Oxford fliers, could romp round him. Stevenson is fast enough, but he couldn't drop from the twenty-five line, and a three-quarter who can't either punt or drop isn't worth a place for pace alone. No, Mr. Holmes, we are done unless you can help me to find Godfrey Staunton.'

My friend had listened with amused surprise to this long speech, which was poured forth with extraordinary vigour and earnestness, every point being driven home by the slapping of a brawny hand upon the speaker's knee. When our visitor was silent Holmes stretched out his hand and took down letter 'S' of his commonplace book. For once he dug in vain into that mine of varied information.

'There is Arthur H. Staunton, the rising young forger,' said he, 'and there was Henry Staunton, whom I helped to hang, but Godfrey Staunton is a new name to me.'

It was our visitor's turn to look surprised.

'Why, Mr. Holmes, I thought you knew things,' said he. 'I suppose, then, if you have never heard of Godfrey Staunton you don't know Cyril Overton either?'

Holmes shook his head good-humouredly.

'Great Scott!' cried the athlete. 'Why, I was first reserve for England against Wales, and I've skippered the 'Varsity all this year. But that's nothing. I didn't think there was a soul in England who didn't know Godfrey Staunton, the crack three-quarter, Cambridge, Blackheath, and five Internationals. Good Lord! Mr Holmes, where *have* you lived?'

Holmes laughed at the young giant's naïve astonishment.

'You live in a different world to me, Mr. Overton, a sweeter and healthier one. My ramifications stretch out into many sections of society, but never, I am happy to say, into amateur sport, which is the best and soundest thing in England. However, your unexpected visit this morning shows me that even in that world of fresh air and fair play there may be work for me to do; so now, my good sir, I beg you to sit down and to tell me slowly and quietly exactly what it is that has occurred, and how you desire that I should help you.'

Young Overton's face assumed the bothered look of the man who is more accustomed to using his muscles than his wits; but by degrees, with many repetitions and obscurities which I may omit from his narrative, he laid his strange story before us.

'It's this way, Mr. Holmes. As I have said, I am the skipper of the Rugger team of Cambridge 'Varsity, and Godfrey Staunton is my best man. To-morrow we play Oxford. Yesterday we all came up and we settled at Bentley's private hotel. At ten o'clock I went round and saw that all the fellows had gone to roost, for I believe in strict training and plenty of sleep to keep a team fit. I had a word or two with Godfrey before he turned in. He seemed to me to be pale and bothered. I asked him what was the matter. He said he was all right – just a touch of headache. I bade him good night and left him. Half an hour later the porter tells me that a rough-looking man with a beard called with a note for Godfrey. He had not gone to bed, and the note was taken to his room. Godfrey read it and fell back in a chair as if he had been pole-axed. The porter was so scared that he was going to fetch me, but Godfrey stopped him, had a drink of water, and pulled himself together. Then he went downstairs, said a few words to the man who was waiting in the hall, and the two of them went off together. The last that the porter saw of them, they were almost runing down the street in the direction of the Strand. This morning Godfrey's room was empty, his bed had never been slept in, and his things were all just as I had seen them the night before. He had gone off at a moment's notice with this stranger, and no word has come from him since. I don't believe he will ever come back. He was a sportsman, was Godfrey, down to his marrow, and he wouldn't have stopped his training and let in his skipper if it were not for some cause that was too strong for him. No; I feel as if he were gone for good and we should never see him again.'

4

HIGHLAND GAMES

Introduction

★ ★ ★

Possibly the earliest evidence of sport in Scotland is the Pictish carving in St Andrews Cathedral showing hunters in pursuit of their quarry. The exuberance of the carving, it could be argued, reflects the thrill and joy of the chase, reminiscent of the wonderful flowing movement of animals in the cave paintings of Southern France. Sport, according to the *Concise Oxford Dictionary*, is firstly described as amusement and yet there has been from earliest beginnings an ambiguity about it, between sporting activity with a purpose, for food, prestige and so on, and activity for enjoyment. (In our day the equivalent difference has been, arguably, between amateurism and professionalism.)

No one loved the earliest form of sport, the hunt or 'chase', more than the Stewart kings, and here, as imagined by Walter Scott in *The Fortunes of Nigel*, is James VI (and I) hunting in the vicinity of London, some time after the Union of the Crowns of 1603:

> A single horseman followed the chase, upon a steed so thoroughly subjected to the rein, that it obeyed the touch of the bridle as if it had been a mechanical impulse operating on the nicest piece of machinery . . . The security with which he chose to prosecute even this favourite, and in ordinary case, somewhat dangerous amusement, as well as the rest of his equipage, marked King James.

In their origins sport and games in Scotland probably had partly a utilitarian function. Competing at wrestling, foot races and Scottish specialities like hurling the stone and tossing the caber – 'caber' being a Celtic word meaning a beam and a perversely difficult activity which is surely due for discovery as a televised spectacle – were good for developing warriors' qualities of skill, strength and endurance. Celtic tales speak of chieftains keeping a large rock or two handy for trying the mettle of their followers or of challengers from abroad. There follows an extract from a newspaper account of a nineteenth-century attempt to revive these traditions among those of Highland parentage by Alasdair Macdonell of Glengarry, the so-called 'Last of the Chiefs'. The means he adopted was the formation of a 'Society of True Highlanders' and in a wide and sweeping programme printed in the *Inverness Journal* of 23 June 1815 we read:

> To preserve pure and uncontaminated the genuine charac-
> teristics and national distinctions of the SONS OF THE
> GAEL must be one of the dearest wishes of every patriotic
> Highlander. To him the nervous, energetic and harmonious
> LANGUAGE of his ancestors of unrivalled antiquity – the
> simplicity and sublimity of Gaelic POETRY – the martial,
> exhilirating, and melodious Music which charmed his youth –
> the graceful GARB in which the Roman Legions overcame all
> but the Sons of Caledonia – the fraternal affection of
> KINDRED, and reverence for patriarchal CHIEFS and
> hereditary Leaders – and the venerable, ancient, and becom-
> ing CUSTOMS and MANNERS of his forefathers, are
> subjects of veneration – stimuli to exertion – his boast in
> prosperity – his solace in adversity, and at all times the object
> of his solicitude and regard . . .

The other Inverness paper, the *Courier*, later chose to print a waspish piece about the Society's Highland Gathering of 10 October 1822, held at Duncanroy near Inverness:

At these sports Glengarry (Macdonell) presided in all his glory, and had the field almost to himself, the other judges probably conceiving themselves ill qualified to decide in matters which lay altogether between the Chief and the gentlemen of his tail . . . The tail, we regret to state, rather failed in 'lifting the stone', a Garry pebble of some 18 stones' weight, to be lifted and thrown over a bar more than five feet from the ground . . . The feat was . . . accomplished by a mere stone-mason, after having foiled all the 'pretty men' of Glengarry . . . another of our ancient sports, namely falling upon a cow, in the 'deadthraw', and manfully tearing the still reeking animal limb from limb, by dint of muscular strength. Some people were, we saw, squeamish enough to be shocked by this exhibition, and did not scruple to use the epithets, 'brutal', 'disgusting' and so forth . . . Even the most expert of the operators took from four to five hours in rugging and riving, tooth and nail, before they brought off the limbs of one cow.

The titanic wrenching apart of a beast in this way makes sumo wrestling or a modern rugby maul seem tame in comparison, and 'competitive butchery', as it might be dubbed, has not retained its popularity. However, Glengarry's nineteenth-century dream of reviving other ancient sports like 'lifting the stone' has been realised to an extent by the institution, mostly dating from the Victorian era, of the Highland Games or Gathering. Events such as tossing the caber and the hammer still make an annual appearance at Games held in many towns and villages, and most of such gatherings are patronised by local gentry or even royalty. Just as Wilson (whom we met in the first chapter) was a kind of superhero of fiction, Scotland's real-life superheroes were the strong man Donald Dinnie, who mopped up the prizes at many Gatherings, and, an early entry in Scotland's new 'hall of fame', Captain Robert Barclay Allardice. Allardice was the laird of Ury near Stonehaven. As Ian Mitchell wrote in *The Scots Magazine*:

He was enormously strong and could lift an 18-stone person with one hand, had a huge appetite, consuming an 8lb leg of mutton to the bone in 10 minutes, and was also addicted to gambling on sport . . . In 1809 Barclay wagered that he would walk 1,000 miles in 1,000 hours for 1,000 guineas. He went into a very modern form of preparation for this event, dieting and exercising under the guidance of expert trainers, and tens of thousands gathered to see him complete the challenge on 12th July on Newmarket Heath. So important was this event that the course was lit by gas light at a time when this was a rare novelty on streets.

So, right from the outset, there were clear indications that sports and games could be seen as a badge of class, rank or privilege. In particular, as we have seen, there was one field sport that was largely reserved for the few, perhaps the warrior class or perhaps for the leader's immediate coterie – the chase, the royal hunt of the king. Those splendid hunting scenes carved on Pictish and neo-Pictish stones show only the few in pursuit of the quarry, with the many doubtless employed in beating and flushing out activities and, at least in the later medieval period, savagely punished for spoiling the king's sport. The chase, or pursuit of animals, first on foot, and then on horseback, was the most prized form of hunting, with other forms, like falconry, also flourishing in the Scottish countryside.

> The stag at eve had drunk his fill,
> Where danced the moon on Monan's rill . . .
> The deep-mouthed blood-hound's heavy bay
> Resounded up the rocky way,
> And faint, from farther distance borne,
> Were heard the clanging hoof and horn.
>
> *The Lady of the Lake*

The modern era has seen the decline in popularity of this kind of hunting with hounds – although see below for fox-hunting. The once aristocratic sport of stalking is now more plutocratic, with a strong German representation. Fishing is still the most popular of all sports, and it and other field sports' disreputable successor and alter ego, poaching, have also survived. Most of these are represented in our selection.

Poaching of course is not confined to the capture of fish, but also to the illegal killing of deer and other game. The thrill of the chase, of which the huntsman speaks, can even be compared to the excitement of the contest between poacher and keeper or gillie. John Buchan brings all these simmering ingredients to the boil in the splendidly anarchic novel *John Macnab,* where the sportsmen turn poacher and form unholy alliances against landowners, and the highest and the lowest combine against the unspeakable *nouveaux riches.*

There are two other specifically Scottish sports that find a place in this chapter. These are shinty and the sport known as 'the Roaring Game', curling. Among the extracts included in the chapter is a piece with that title, written by the celebrated Scots novelist, Neil Gunn. In it Gunn shows an affection for the old country sports, because the curling he describes is conducted in the open air, on a winter's day when a body of water has frozen hard enough to bear the participants, their curling stones and refreshments and all. The bonspiel is quite a contrast with the indoor curling rinks of the modern era, where male and female curlers of the highest class still learn their game – the Olympic and world champion ladies' rinks currently hailing from Scotland. Players have always recognised the uniqueness of curling and its special relationship with Scotland, even though it is now played in more than a handful of countries. It is still as true now as it was in 1715 when Alexander Pennicuik wrote:

> To Curle on the Ice, does greatly please,
> Being a Manly Scottish Exercise;
> It Clears the Brains, stirs up the Native Heat,
> And gives a gallant Appetite for Meat.

The magnificent pan-Celtic (being closely related to Irish hurling) sport of shinty has yet to taste the same kind of success as curling, being confined to a small number of first-class teams in the north and west of the country, together with pockets of enthusiasm in Canada. It has nevertheless a long and distinguished cultural heritage and literary history, as the *Inverness Courier* indicated in June 1841:

> Highlanders in London were greatly interested in a shinty match organised by the committee of a body which called itself 'The Society of True Highlanders'. The match took place in Copenhagen Fields, an extent of rich meadow land lying on the outskirts of Islington. There was much enthusiasm and keenly contested games. It is said that before the gathering half the glens of Lochaber had been ransacked for shinty clubs (sticks or caman).

Returning to the exportation of shinty to North America – there is a considerable body of opinion that ice-hockey (and possibly lacrosse) has its roots in *Camanachd*. An early organiser of Canadian ice-hockey in a memoir of his childhood recalled it being known as 'shinny' and recalled:

> As a small boy I played 'shinny' on the ice opposite the city of Montreal from November to early January. After that time the snows made it impossible to skate on the river. To play 'shinny' one had to have a good stick – no umbrella handle, or any stick that was cross-grained, would do. So early in the Fall, the boys who contemplated playing later on, would go to the mountains and hunt for small maple trees which had roots which, when trimmed and dried, made ideal sticks with which to play the game

– just as the men of North and South Uist used 'the tangle of the Isles' for the same purpose, in the days before the game of shinty was driven out of the Long Island by the football bladder.

Finally, we have a modern manifestation of what was perhaps the earliest form of sport, namely hunting. After including various literary descriptions of traditional Scottish fishing and deer-hunting, this chapter ends with two looks at the classic British version of hunting, dressed up in 'hunting pink'. At the time of publication of this book, fox-hunting, the most controversial of 'blood-sports', has been more or less outlawed by the Scottish Parliament. This has not yet occurred in the legislature south of the Border, and, as opponents of the 'sport' would say, it remains a hangover from a cruel past. Two relatively mild Scots responses to this issue therefore seem in order: a newspaper article by Neil Munro and a third extract from A.G. Macdonell's brilliant 1933 satire *England, their England*. The extract is titled 'The Unspeakable' – a reference to Oscar Wilde's description of fox-hunting as 'The unspeakable in full pursuit of the uneatable.'

Tam Samson's Elegy

ROBERT BURNS

Burns, farmer and countryman, evidently knew the sport of curling very well, as can be gleaned from this mock elegy for Thomas Samson, 'a seedsman of good credit, a zealous sportsman, and a good fellow', according to the poet's notes. When out moor-fowling one day Samson announced that this might be his last hunting trip, and expressed a wish to be buried 'in the muirs'. Burns often met Samson at a tavern called the 'Bowling-green house' – a reminder of the close connection between curling and bowls – and it was there that Burns read out the following hurriedly-penned humorous verses, produced in response to Samson's wish. Verses 4 and 5 of the poem give a lovely glimpse of the winter game and terms such as 'guard' and 'draw' recognisable today were evidently in use in the 1780s. Finally, it is interesting to note that the playing area of the frozen 'lough' is called the rink and the poem also includes fine references to the country sports of fishing and shooting.

★ ★ ★

Has auld Kilmarnock see the Deil?
Or great M'Kinlay thrawn his heel?
Or Robertson again grown weel,
     To preach an' read?
'Na, waur than a'!' cries ilka chiel,
     '*Tam Samson's* dead!'

Kilmarnock lang may grunt an' grane,
An' sigh an' sob, an' greet her lane,
An' cleed her bairns, man, wife, an' wean,
                    In mourning weed;
To Death she's dearly pay'd the kane,
                    Tam Samson's dead!

The Brethren o' the mystic *level*
May hing their head in wofu' bevel,
While by their nose the tears will revel,
                    Like ony bead;
Death's gien the Lodge an unco devel,
                    Tam Samson's dead!

When Winter muffles up his cloak,
And binds the mire like a rock;
When to the loughs the curlers flock,
                    Wi' gleesome speed,
Wha will they station at the *cock*,
                    Tam Samson's dead?

He was the king of a' the core,
To guard, or draw, or wick a bore,
Or up the rink like *Jehu* roar
                    In time o' need;
But now he lags on Death's *hog-score*,
                    Tam Samson's dead!

Now safe the stately Sawmont sail,
And Trouts bedropp'd wi' crimson hail,
And Eels weel kend for souple tail,
                    And Geds for greed,
Since dark in Death's *fish-creel* we wail
                    Tam Samson dead!

Rejoice, ye birring Paitricks a';
Ye cootie Moorcocks, crousely craw;
Ye Maukins, cock your fuds fu' braw,
                              Withoutten dread;
Your mortal Fae is now awa',
                              Tam Samson's dead!

That woefu' morn be ever mourn'd
Saw him in shootin graith adorn'd,
While pointers round impatient burn'd,
                              Frae couples freed;
But, Och! he gaed and ne'er return'd!
                              Tam Samson's dead!

In vain Auld-age his body batters;
In vain the Gout his ankles fetters;
In vain the burns cam down like waters,
                              An acre-braid!
Now ev'ry auld wife, greetin, clatters,
                              'Tam Samson's dead!'

Owre monie a weary hag he limpit,
An' ay the tither shot he thumpit,
Till coward Death behind him jumpit,
                              Wi' deadly feide;
Now he proclaims, wi' tout o' trumpet,
                              Tam Samson's dead!

When at his heart he felt the dagger,
He reel'd his wonted bottle-swagger,
But yet he drew the mortal trigger
                              Wi' wee-aim'd heed;
'L—d, five!' he cry'd, an' owre did stagger;
                              Tam Samson's dead!

Ilk hoary Hunter mourn'd a brither;
Ilk Sportsman-youth bemoan'd a father;
Yon auld gray stane, amang the heather,
    Marks out his head,
Whare *Burns* has wrote, in rhyming blether,
    Tam Samson's dead!

There, low he lies in lasting rest;
Perhaps upon his mould'ring breast
Some spitefu' moorfowl bigs her nest,
    To hatch and breed:
Alas! nae mair he'll them molest –
    Tam Samson's dead!

When August winds the heather wave,
And Sportsmen wander by yon grave,
Three volleys let his mem'ry crave
    O'pouthor an'lead,
Till Echo answer frae her cave,
    Tam Samson's dead!

Heav'n rest his saul, where'er he be!
Is th' wish o' mony mae than me:
He had twa fauts, or maybe three,
    Yet what remead?
Ae social, honest man want we:
    Tam Samson's dead!

THE EPITAPH.

Tam Samson's weel-worn clay here lies,
Ye canting Zealots, spare him!
If Honest Worth in heaven rise,
Ye'll mend or ye win near him.

PER CONTRA.

Go, Fame, and canter like a filly
Thro' a' the streets an' neuks o' *Killie,*
Tell ev'ry social, honest billie
                  To cease his grievin,
For yet, unskaith'd by Death's gleg gullie,
                  Tam Samson's livin!

The Roaring Game
from Highland Pack

NEIL GUNN

In this evocative little essay published during World War II, Neil Gunn paints a picture of a rural idyll that sits nicely alongside Burns' poem. Gunn was then earning enough to be writing full time – two of the great novels, The Silver Darlings *and* Green Isle of the Great Deep *were issued in wartime, as was the fine* Highland Pack *collection. Gunn was once again living in the Inverness area, and it is in a Highland rural setting that we meet a small group of local curlers (older men and girls mostly) enjoying a game. The mood of sociability and conviviality on the ice is immediately captured and in the inn parlour afterwards (again like Burns, showing the everlasting appeal of the social side of curling). Mention is made of the fact that too many men are away at (Hitler's) war for there to be a grand match or bonspiel. The story ends with a most evocative description of Gunn's walk home in the late winter afternoon.*

★ ★ ★

Not for many years has the small loch been frozen so deeply or for so long as it has this February. Odd afternoons were smuggled from business to 'draw the bottle' or 'crack an egg' with round heavy lumps of polished grey or black granite in the 'roaring game' of curling. 'Can you see that?' shouts the skip to the member of his team about to play the next shot. 'No.' 'Ah well, just try and draw. That's our own and if you promote it a foot you'll do no harm . . . Ay, take him with you! *Take him with you!* . . . Brooms up! Gr-r-reat shot!' It's a pleasant moment in an anxious match when the skip's broom salutes one's prowess.

Afterwards in the convivial inn parlour, with hot water in the jug ('Hot, not warm,' said the ancient skip to the young lassie) Hitler is directly accused of having bust what would have been a certain and great bonspiel at Carsebreck. An international bonspiel to settle all our troubles (says the skip, for it's a good dram) and, faith, we would crack eggs and fill a few pot-lids to some purpose! 'The same again, and see that it's *hot* this time.'

The skip grows warm with reminiscence. In the old days it wasn't a case of snatching a couple of hours with a feeling of guilt. He shook his head. From morning till night the roaring game went on, with that glorious interval for hot stew, real stew, in the middle of it. Business was left to look after itself. The gamekeeper forsook his game, the shopkeeper his shop, the farmer his farm, ay, and the very sheriff his court, so that Justice herself had to wait until this more serious communal matter had first been dealt with.

'Sweep him up!' shouted old Jock the poacher to the sheriff, and the sheriff swept for dear life. 'You for a player!' roared the town clerk to the provost, who had just laid the perfect guard, and the provost looked modest as he turned for his next stone. What a tame little affair, pursued the skip, had been our last autumn 'annual meeting'! Compared with what he could remember! . . . It was enough to make one wonder, right enough, what the world was coming to. It did, honestly. For he could remember five skips closeted in this very sanctum 'like the Cabinet itself', for hours, choosing their teams, while outside, crowding the bar and everywhere else, men waited anxiously on their decisions. Sometimes and in devious fashion drams would find their way to the inner sanctum from those who were, as one might say, a little over-anxious; not of course that anything in the way of influencing decisions was intended. No, no, far from it! But you know how, in the press of great decisions, a good man's name may be clean forgotten. Ay, ay! It was something to be chosen a member of a rink in those days . . .

But such as we are to-day, we did contrive a few friendly matches with neighbouring teams during this remarkable spell of ice. And I think, perhaps, I caught at least one glimpse of the ancient spirit. The loch we visited was in a pine wood and the sunlight streamed across the tree-tops from a pale blue sky, moderating the frosty air to a degree that remained invigorating yet mild.

'Man,' said Uilleam to me, 'it's not that I want us to beat them – but they're that keen. They must win at all costs. They're like that. They always have been here. They can't help it.'

'You think I should button my jacket?'

'To the very last button,' said Uilleam.

During a recent game, some specially good shots were played after an air-raid warning had sounded, and as I cast my eye around I knew that some veteran brooms would have sloped quite smartly had the need arisen.

Later, as I walked home from the bus-stop through the frost haze, with a red horizon portending a continuation of the hard weather, there was little doing in the countryside. Here a farm hand was forking turnips out of a field-pit into his cart, and there some sheep were grouping together on a strip of turnip ground that had been fenced off for their use. It was a very quiet world, and the thin covering of snow caught and reflected the fading light in a spectral beauty. Trees and bushes were dark and motionless.

Two blackbirds began scolding in some undergrowth and I know of no sounds more characteristic of a late winter afternoon in the country. I seem to have heard these sounds at such moments all through my life, and for some mysterious reason there is youth in them and vigour and promise, and they always raise a friendly smile. One seems to know why they are scolding without quite knowing it, as if the whole performance were an earnest yet wanton excess, not far removed from certain moods which have a wanton way of assailing ourselves. A sheep coughed, with a regular old man's cough, a hoast, chesty and pretty rheumy, poor fellow. His face looked very grey – though for that matter all the sheep-faces looked grey, ghost-grey. But two or three of them, pressing up against a low hedge, suddenly began to box playfully and make little leaps. They had youth on their side, however, and their elders were clearly not impressed. And then from down by the edge of the turnip field, there all at once came a handful of clear singing bird-notes, as if a few thrushes or larks were laughing together. I have rarely heard anything so unexpected, so spontaneous, so happy. It was a singing from the ground, not from trees or the air. I listened for some time but did not hear it repeated, and it was almost as though a trick had been played on me. But I knew I had got an insight into the bird-mind and found it, in a certain respect, not so vastly different from the mind of a boy I had known long ago. As I pursued my way happily tired along the hard-rutted cart road, a new sound, like the drone of an aeroplane, came down through the frosted evening. I remembered the 'warning'. I looked at the vacant sky. But once more it was the blessed drone of the threshing-mill.

The Game of Shinty

REV. DR NORMAN MACLEOD

★ ★ ★

Shinty is yet another game that has an exclusively Scottish origin, although this one has not gone round the world in the same way as curling has. Nor has shinty enjoyed anything like the recent expansion of the phenomenon that is golf. Shinty was once played throughout Scotland, but the last hundred years has seen its area of influence shrink to the present modest extent. Newtonmore and Kingussie, Inveraray, Oban and Kyles Athletic, have all enjoyed periods of hegemony, and with others have hopes of revival; but the game has almost totally vanished from places like the Outer Hebrides. This massive change came about for a number of reasons but the technological innovation of the inflatable football was probably the biggest single factor in shinty's collapse in islands like the Uists. Back in 1908, Alexander Morrison from Uist could write:

> *Shinty is a favourite game. Equal sides are picked, the object of the game being to score as many goals as possible. Stones are used for goals – the ball may be of wood, hard wound worsted, or of hair, peat, or other available material, while the caman is a bent stick of wood or a large tangle. In these islands people have to be ingenious and to make the best of the materials they have . . . The Uist boys used to be, and in some places still are, very proficient at the game, the main qualities necessary for an ideal 'iomain' player being speed and dexterity.*

The famous Reverend Doctor Norman MacLeod, churchman, theologian and writer, who came from Fiunary in Morvern, wrote this charming part-memoir, part-fictional account of a grand New Year's Day match.

Like football, shinty was for a long time a communal event occurring only on high days and holidays.

★ ★ ★

The time of parting came. The gentry gave us the welcome of the New Year with cordiality and kindliness, and we set off to our homes.

'My lads,' says he himself, 'be valiant on the field tomorrow. The seaboard men boast that they are to meet us glen men at the shinty match this year.'

On this New Year's morn, the sun was late of showing his countenance, and when later he came in sight his countenance was pale and drowsy. The mist was resting lazily on the hill-side; the crane was rising slowly from the meadow; the belling of the stag was heard on the mountain; the black cock was in the birch wood, dressing his feathers, while his sonsie mate, the grey hen, was slowly walking before him.

After I had saluted my family and implored the blessing of the Highest on their heads, I prepared the Christmas sheep (Caora Nollaig), gave a sheaf of corn to the cattle, as was customary, and was getting myself in order when in walked Pàra Mòr and my gossip, Angus Og. They gave me the welcome of the New Year. I returned it with equal heartiness. Then Pàra Mòr produced a bottle from his pocket.

'A black cock,' says he, 'whose gurgling is more musical than any *ràn* that ever came out of the chanter of thy pipe.'

We toasted to one another, and then Mary, my wife, set before us a small drop of the genuine Ferintosh, which she had stored up long ago in the big chest for grand occasions.

It was my duty to gather the people together this morning with the sound of the pipe. So we set off, going from farm to farm up the glen, making the son of the cave of the rock (the echo) answer to my music. I played *A Mhnathan a' Glinne So* (the Women of the Glen), and if the pipe had been dry that day it had ample means of quenching its thirst!

The company continually increased in numbers until we came down by the other side to the ground-officer's house, where it was appointed for us to get our morning meal. The lady had sent a three-year-old wether to his house. We had a roe-buck from the corrie of yew trees; fish from the pool of whiting; and such quantities of cheese, butter and solid oatcake, sent by the neighbours round about, as would suffice for as many more – though we were fifty men in number, besides women and children. Grace was said by Lachlan Ceistear, the Bible-reader. We had an ample and a cheerful breakfast.

Breakfast over, I set off and played the tune of the *Glasmheur* while Red Ewen, the old soldier, was marshalling the men. We reached Guala-nam-Càrn where the gentry were to meet us; and before we knew where we were, who placed himself at our head but our own young Donald, the heir of the family! Dear heart, he was the graceful sapling!

The people of the seaboard then came into view, Alastair Roy of the Bay at their head. When the two companies observed each other, they raised a loud shout of mutual rejoicing. We reached the field, and many were the salutations between friends and acquaintances exchanged there.

The sun at length shone out brightly. On the eminences around the field were the matrons, the maidens and the children of the district, high and low, all assembled to watch the camanachd. The goal at each end of the large field was pointed out, and the two leaders began to divide and choose each his men.

'Buailidh mi ort,' says young Donald.

'Leigidh mi leat,' says Alastair Roy of the Bay.

'If so,' says young Donald, 'then Donald Bàn of Culloden is mine.'

This was by far the oldest man present, and you would think that his two eyes would start from his head with delight as he stepped proudly forward, at being the first chosen.

When the men were divided into two companies – forty on each side – Alastair Roy flung his caman high up into the air.

'*Bas no Cas*, Donald of the Glen?' said he.

'Handle, which will defy your handling until nightfall!' replies Donald.

Alistair won the throw, and was about to strike the ball immediately when the other exclaimed: 'A truce! Let the rules of the game be first proclaimed, so that there may be fairness, good fellowship and friendship observed among us, as was wont among our forefathers.'

On this, Evan Bàn stepped forth and proclaimed the laws, which forbade all quarrelling, swearing, drunkenness and coarseness; all striking, tripping or unfairness of any kind; and charged them to contend in a manful but friendly spirit, without malice or grudge, as those from whom they were descended were wont to do.

Alastair Roy gave the first stroke to the ball, and the contest began in earnest; but I have no language to describe it. The seaboard men gained the first game. But it was their only game. Young Donald and his men stripped to their work, and you would think the day of *Blàr na Léine* (the Battle of the Shirt) had come again.

Broad John gave a tremendous blow, and we raised the shout of victory; but all was kindliness and good feeling among us. In the midst of our congratulations, Pàra Mor shouted out, 'Shame on ye, young men! Don't you see those nice girls shivering with cold? Where are the dancers? Play up the reel of Tullochgorum, Finlay!'

The dancing began, and the sun was bending low towards the western ocean before we parted. We returned to the house of nobleness, as on the preceding evening. Many a torch was beaming brightly in the hall of hospitality. We passed the night amid music and enjoyment, and parted not until the breaking of the dawn guided us to our homes.

Many good results followed from this friendly mingling of gentles and commons. Our superiors were at that time acquainted with our language and our ways. There were kindness, friendship, and fosterage between us; and whilst they were apples at the topmost bough, we were all the fruit of the same tree.

. . . Now our superiors dwell not among us; they know not our language, and cannot converse with us . . . All this has passed as a dream.

Fishing the Shore of the Loch

JOHN WILSON

By one definition angling ought to be a world sport and therefore placed in the opening chapter – however this sport is so intimately connected with the land it is carried on in, that it finds its place here, in Scotland and its rivers and lochs. John Wilson ('Christopher North'), reviewer and essayist, was born in Paisley in 1785. Wilson's best known association was with Blackwood's Edinburgh Magazine, *and in its pages he developed his controversial reputation, under the literary disguise of 'Christopher North'. He was an athletic figure with considerable prowess in several sports, and he had considerable merit as a journalist as well as producing a series of rural short stories,* Lights and Shadows of Scottish Life.

* * *

If you have no boat, you had better fish from the shore. Some people (Professor Wilson, for example) prefer doing so, whether they have a boat or not; and if you don't desire to keep your feet particularly dry (in which case you had better also keep your room for a few days), you must wade – sometimes to a considerable actual depth, if you are a tall bold man, or to a proportional apparent depth, if you are a short shy one. A young bachelor may, of course, wade deeper than a married man, of the same dimensions, who has a wife and family.

In fishing from shore, try to get the wind behind you, and – at least if you have that object in view, – don't fish on the lee-side of the loch. When you have waded in as far as you feel inclined, and supposing the wind to blow either directly or diagonally from the shore, say into your right ear when your face is lake-ward, then take a few casts before you, and rather to the right hand, bringing your flies across and somewhat down the wind, then stretch out with a more lengthened throw directly forward, then sweep away, cast after cast, to the left, taking always two or three throws in every radius in a straight line with each other, beginning with the shorter and ending with the more extended stretch. Always complete your semicircle by casting quite in shore, almost in a line, though slightly in advance, from where you entered; for, if the place is good, the very ground on which you stand, may be a favourite haunt for food or play. Then take a step or two onwards, and recommence again from right to left, or *vice versa*, as your case may be – for if the wind, that fickle element, chops about, you must also act the weathercock, and change your tactics.

With Rod and Line

from Looking Back

NORMAN DOUGLAS

Norman Douglas was born in 1868 in the village of Tilquhillie on Deeside. He worked for the Foreign Office in St Petersburg before taking to writing full-time. Douglas settled on Capri, where Compton Mackenzie was among his circle. A novelist and essayist, he also wrote some highly regarded travel books. His autobiography, Looking Back *(1933) was highly unorthodox – as* Chambers Scottish Biographical Dictionary *puts it: '[It] is an unusual autobiography, in which he recalls his life and his friends by taking up their calling cards and describing them one by one, at length or tersely, depending on his mood.'*

★ ★ ★

The stones of Banchory were not worth talking about; shooting and fishing made up for them. Those hours devoted to fly-fishing during the evenings under the beeches, with the brown stream rippling at my feet – they were sacred; how glad one was to escape after dinner to the Feugh! During a spate we generally fished in the pool below the bridge with a worm or minnow and watched the salmon leaping up; the maximum I remember counting was sixty-three in one minute. And the strangest fish I ever drew out of that pool was a flounder. 'That's nothing,' said a friend to whom I once related the fact. 'I've caught a swordfish on the Bosphorous with a fly – I'll take my Bible oath on it. Can you beat that?' . . .

My thoughts often wander in the direction of Banchory. There are moments when I feel the need of that landscape, when I wonder whether I shall ever return to savour the charm of those long-drawn twilights and the perfume of its woodlands.

Ballade of the Tweed

ANDREW LANG

Andrew Lang again, this time using the Scots tongue in his verses to convey the delights of angling and in particular of the great River Tweed (Lang was born at Selkirk in 1844). Quite clearly Lang was an accomplished angler, as he compares his beloved Tweed to other famous Scottish fishing rivers and lochs like the Spey and Loch Awe. Ashiesteel is the name of a house on the south bank of the Tweed where Walter Scott lived before he built Abbotsford and while he was Sheriff of Selkirk from 1804–12. The pollution ('dyes and poisons') alluded to in the 'Envoy' was a by-product of the new textile mills further upstream.

★ ★ ★

The ferox rins in rough Loch Awe,
A weary cry frae ony toun;
The Spey, that loups o'er linn and fa',
They praise a' ither streams aboon;
They boast their braes o' bonny Doon:
Gie *me* to hear the ringing reel,
Where shilfas sing and cushats croon
By fair Tweed-side, at Ashiesteel!

There's Ettrick, Meggat, Ail, and a',
Where trout swim thick in May and June;
Ye'll see them take in showers o' snaw:
Some blinking, cauldrife April noon:
Rax ower the palmer and march-broun,

278

And syne we'll show' a bonny creel,
In spring or simmer, late or soon,
By fair Tweed-side, at Ashiesteel!

There's mony a water, great or sma',
Gaes singing in his siller tune,
Through glen and heugh, and hope and shaw,
Beneath the sun-licht or the moon:
But set us in our fishing-shoon
Between the Caddon-burn and Peel,
And syne we'll cross the heather broun
By fair Tweed-side at Ashiesteel!

Envoy
Deil take the dirty, trading loon
Wad gar the water ca' his wheel,
And drift his dyes and poisons doun
By fair Tweed-side at Ashiesteel!

paitricks, partridges	*cootie*, leg-feathered
maukin's, hares	*fud*, tail
graith, attire	*couples*, leashes
loups, leaps	*shilfas*, chaffinches
cushats, wood-doves	

The Fortunes of Nigel
Chapter XXVII

WALTER SCOTT

★ ★ ★

The Fortunes of Nigel, *from which this scene of a hunt in Greenwich Park is taken, was published in 1822 and is largely set in London in the years immediately following the Union of the Crowns. Many of the characters are Scots and speak Scots, including the pedantic King James VI and I, the 'wisest fool in Christendom'. James was famous for his love of the chase and other sports, including golf, which he commended to his son and heir in* Basilikon Doron *(The Royal Gift), a manual 'of kingship' written by James himself, and containing precepts for the proper education of the young Prince Henry. An extremely literate monarch, James put forward notions not dissimilar to modern coaching manuals, with allusions to the ancient Greek philosophy of moderation in all things and the Roman ideal of 'mens sana in corpore sano'. James preferred riding and hunting in the ancient manner, 'with running hounds', instead of the newer 'thievish form' with guns.*

Several other real historical personages including Prince Charles and 'Jinglin' Geordie' Heriot (founder of Heriot's School in Edinburgh) make an appearance in the novel. The young Nigel Olifaunt, Lord Glenvarloch, who is threatened with the loss of his estate if he is unable to redeem a mortgage, comes to London to try to recover a large sum previously lent to 'Jamie the Saxt' by Nigel's father. Others, including the king's current favourite, Buckingham, oppose this and Nigel has to contrive an interview with James, as described in this scene.

James adored hunting, like many of the Stewart kings, and would often spend hours in the saddle. Scott adds an amusing note to the passage (referring to his over indulgence): Whether it was from drinking these wines, or from some other cause, the King became so lazy and unwieldy, that he was trussed on horseback, and as he was set, so would he ride, without stirring himself in the saddle; nay when his hat was set upon his head he would not take the trouble to alter it, but it sate as it was put on.

★ ★ ★

He was in one of those long walks by which the Park was traversed, when he heard first a distant rustling, then the rapid approach of hoofs shaking the firm earth on which he stood; then a distant halloo, warned by which he stood up by the side of the avenue, leaving free room for the passage of the chase. The stag, reeling, covered with foam, and blackened with sweat, his nostrils expanded as he gasped for breath, made a shift to come up as far as where Nigel stood, and, without turning to bay, was there pulled down by two tall greyhounds of the breed still used by the hardy deer-stalkers of the Scottish Highlands, but which has been long unknown in England. One dog struck at the buck's throat, another dashed his sharp nose and fangs, I might almost say, into the animal's bowels. It would have been natural for Lord Glenvarloch, himself persecuted as if by hunters, to have thought upon the occasion like the melancholy Jacques; but habit is a strange matter, and I fear that his feelings on the occasion were rather those of the practised huntsman than of the moralist. He had no time, however, to indulge them, for mark what befell.

A single horseman followed the chase, upon a steed so thoroughly subjected to the rein, that it obeyed the touch of the bridle, as if it had been a mechanical impulse operating on the nicest piece of machinery; so that, seated deep in his demi-pique saddle, and so trussed up there as to make falling almost impossible, the rider, without either fear or hesitation, might increase or diminish the speed at which he rode, which, even on the most animating occasions of the chase, seldom exceeded three-fourths of a gallop, the horse keeping his haunches under him, and never stretching forward beyond the managed pace of the academy. The security with which he chose to prosecute even this favourite, and, in ordinary case, somewhat dangerous amusement, as well as the rest of his equipage, marked King James. No attendant was within sight; indeed, it was often a nice strain of flattery to permit the Sovereign to suppose he had outridden and distanced all the rest of the chase.

'Weel dune, Bash – weel dune, Battie!' he exclaimed, as he came up. 'By the honour of a King, ye are a credit to the Braes of Balwhither! – Haud my horse, man,' he called out to Nigel, without stopping to see to whom he had addressed himself – 'Haud my naig, and help me doun out o' the saddle – deil ding your saul, sirra, canna ye mak haste before these lazy smaiks come up? – haud the rein easy – dinna let him swerve – now, haud the stirrup – that will do, man, and now we are on terra firma.' So saying, without casting an eye on his assistant, gentle King Jamie, unsheathing the short, sharp hanger (*couteau de chasse*), which was the only thing approaching to a sword that he could willingly endure the sight of, drew the blade with great satisfaction across the throat of the buck, and put an end at once to its struggles and its agonies.

Lord Glenvarloch, who knew well the silvan duty which the occasion demanded, hung the bridle of the King's palfrey on the branch of a tree, and, kneeling duteously down, turned the slaughtered deer upon its back, and kept the *quarrée* in that position, while the King, too intent upon his sport to observe anything else, drew his *couteau* down the breast of the animal, *secundum artem*; and, having made a cross cut, so as to ascertain the depth of the fat upon the chest, exclaimed, in a sort of rapture, 'Three inches of white fat on the brisket! – prime – prime, as I am a crowned sinner – and deil ane o' the lazy loons is by mysell! Seven – aught – aught tines on the antlers. By G—d, a hart of aught tines, and the first of the season! Bash and Battie, blessings on the heart's-root of ye! Buss me, my bairns, buss me.' The dogs accordingly fawned upon him, licked him with bloody jaws, and soon put him in such a state that it might have seemed treason had been doing its full work upon his anointed body. 'Bide doun, with a mischief to ye – bide doun, with a wanton,' cried the King, almost overturned by the obstreperous caresses of the large stag-hounds. 'But ye are just like ither folks, gie ye an inch and ye take an ell. – And wha may ye be, friend?' he said, now finding leisure to take a nearer view of Nigel, and observing what in his first emotion of silvan delight had escaped him, – 'Ye are nane of our train, man. In the name of God, what the devil are ye?'

'An unfortunate man, sire,' replied Nigel.

'I dare say that,' answered the King, snappishly, 'or I wad have seen naething of you. My lieges keep a' their happiness to themselves; but let bowls row wrang wi' them, and I am sure to hear of it.'

'And to whom else can we carry our complaints but to your Majesty, who is Heaven's viceregent over us?' answered Nigel.

'Right, man, right – very weel spoken,' said the King: 'but you should leave Heaven's viceregent some quiet on earth, too.'

'If your Majesty will look on me' (for hitherto the King had been so busy, first with the dogs, and then with the mystic operation of *breaking*, in vulgar phrase cutting up the deer, that he had scarce given his assistant above a transient glance), 'you will see whom necessity makes bold to avail himself of an opportunity which may never again occur.'

King James looked; his blood left his cheek, though it continued stained with that of the animal which lay at his feet, he dropped the knife from his hand, cast behind him a faltering eye, as if he either meditated flight or looked out for assistance, and then exclaimed, – 'Glenvarloch! as sure as I was christened James Stewart. Here is a bonny spot of work, and me alone, and on foot too!' he added, bustling to get upon his horse.

'Forgive me that I interrupt you, my liege,' said Nigel, placing himself between the King and the steed; 'hear me but a moment!'

'I'll hear ye best on horseback,' said the King. 'I canna hear a word on foot, man, not a word; and it is not seemly to stand cheek-for-chowl confronting us that gate. Bide out of our gate, sir, we charge you, on your allegiance. – The deil's in them a', what can they be doing?'

'By the crown which you wear, my liege,' said Nigel, 'and for which my ancestors have worthily fought, I conjure you to be composed and to hear me but a moment.'

That which he asked was entirely out of the monarch's power to grant. The timidity which he showed was not the plain downright cowardice, which, like a natural impulse, compels a man to flight, and which can excite little but pity or contempt, but a much more ludicrous, as well as more mingled sensation. The poor King was frightened at once and angry, desirous of securing his safety, and at the same time ashamed to compromise his dignity; so that, without attending to what Lord Glenvarloch endeavoured to explain, he kept making at his horse, and repeating, 'We are a free King, man – we are a free King – we will not be controlled by a subject. – In the name of God, what keeps Steenie? And, praised be his name, they are coming – Hillo, ho – here, here – Steenie, Steenie!'

The Duke of Buckingham galloped up, followed by several courtiers and attendants of the royal chase, and commenced with his usual familiarity, – 'I see Fortune has graced our dear dad, as usual – but what's this?'

'What is it? It is treason, for what I ken,' said the King; 'and a' your wyte, Steenie. Your dear dad and gossip might have been murdered, for what you care.'

'Murdered? Secure the villain!' exclaimed the Duke. 'By Heaven, it is Olifaunt himself!' A dozen of the hunters dismounted at once, letting their horses run wild through the Park. Some seized roughly on Lord Glenvarloch, who thought it folly to offer resistance, while others busied themselves with the King. 'Are you wounded, my liege – are you wounded?'

'Not that I ken of,' said the King, in the paroxysm of his apprehension (which, by the way, might be pardoned in one of so timorous a temper, and who, in his time, had been exposed to so many strange attempts) –| 'Not that I ken of – but search him – search him. I am sure I saw firearms under his cloak. I am sure I smelled powder – I am dooms sure of that.'

Lord Glenvarloch's cloak being stripped off, and his pistols discovered, a shout of wonder and of execration on the supposed criminal purpose, arose from the crowd, now thickening every moment. Not that celebrated pistol, which, though resting on a bosom as gallant and as loyal as Nigel's, spread such causeless alarm among knights and dames at a late high solemnity – not that very pistol caused more temporary consternation than was so groundlessly excited by the arms which were from Lord Glenvarloch's person, and not Mhic-Allastar-More himself could repel with greater scorn and indignation, insinuations that they were worn for any sinister purposes.

'Away with the wretch – the parricide – the bloody-minded villain!' was echoed on all hands; and the King, who naturally enough set the same value on his own life at which it was, or seemed to be, rated by others, cried out, louder than all the rest, 'Ay, ay – away with him. I have had enough of him, and so has the country. But do him no bodily harm – and, for God's sake, sirs, if ye are sure that ye have thoroughly disarmed him, put up your swords, dirks, and skenes, for you will certainly do each other a mischief.'

There was a speedy sheathing of weapons at the King's commands; for those who had hitherto been brandishing them in loyal bravado, began thereby to call to mind the extreme dislike which his Majesty nourished against naked steel, a foible which seemed to be as constitutional as his timidity, and was usually ascribed to the brutal murder of Rizzio having been perpetrated in his unfortunate mother's presence before he yet saw the light.

Final Farewell to the Bens

from In Praise of Ben Doran

DUNCAN BAN MACINTYRE
(Translation by Angus MacLeod)

★ ★ ★

This is an extract translated from Macintyre's wonderful long poem in which he recalls his time spent as a keeper of the great deer forests in Argyll and Breadalbane. 'Final Farewell to the Bens' is a series of poignant and nostalgic recollections of nature, of the deer and of happy times with the people he knew as a keeper. He realises that the physical demands of the sport involved in stalking 'a wild high-headed one' have become too great for him, and consequently, 'Now, being sadly short of breath, (he) cannot go a-chasing them.' Duncan Ban Macintyre had also served as a soldier in the Argyll Militia, fighting against the Jacobites, a period when sport was replaced by the more serious business of war, even though:

> *While we were campaigning,*
> *Cheery were we then,*
> *Nor was the dram to us a novelty.*

★ ★ ★

I was on Ben Dobhrain yesterday,
no stranger in her bounds was I;
I looked upon the glens
and the bens that I had known so well;
this was a happy picture –
to be tramping on the hillsides,

at the hour the sun was rising,
and the deer would be a-bellowing.

The gallant herd is joyous,
as they moved off with noisy stir;
the hinds are by the spring,
and the speckled calves looked bonny there;
then the does and roe-bucks,
the black-cocks and the grouse cocks –
the sweetest music ever heard
was their sound when heard at dawn of day.

Blithely would I set out
for stalking on the hill passes,
away to climb rough country,
and late would I be coming home;
and clean rain and the air
on the peaks of the high mountains,
helped me to grow, and gave me
robustness and vitality.

I earned my living for a time,
at shielings that I knew full well,
with frolic, fun, flirtation,
enjoying maidens' tender fellowship;
'twere contrary to nature
that this should still obtain there;
we had perforce to leave them,
when the time arrived to separate.

Now since old age has stricken me,
I have an ailment that will cleave to me,
that has wrought havoc on my teeth,
while my vision is beclouded;
I am not fit for exploit
though I might find it needful,

and though pursuit were on my trail,
I could not step out very fast.

Although my head is hoary
and my locks have become scanty,
oft have I loosed a deer-hound
against a wild, high-headed one:
though I, who loved them always,
were to see them on the hillside,
now, being sadly short of breath,
I cannot go a-chasing them.

In their rutting season,
devotedly I followed them;
then an interlude with country folk,
while giving them new songs and verse;
another spell with comrades,
while we were campaigning:
cheery were we then,
nor was the dram to us a novelty.

John Macnab

JOHN BUCHAN

* * *

The three participants in John Macnab *(1925), this elaborate 'thriller-as-game', are of course not 'desperate' at all. Nor are they representatives of the sorts of anarchic forces who generally provide the villains in Buchan's 'shockers', as he called his novels, like* The Thirty-Nine Steps *and* Greenmantle. *They are all 'sportsmen' and firmly establishment figures in the usual Buchan mould – Lord Lamancha is a member of the Cabinet (need one enquire which party?) and a great landowner, Sir Edward Leithen is a 'great lawyer' and (plain, untitled) John Palliser-Yeates is an 'eminent banker'. Their host at the shooting lodge is another highly respectable figure, Sir Archie Roylance, flying ace and generally good egg. He and Leithen make appearances in other Buchan novels.*

Prior to the events described in the following extract, the three aforementioned, who collectively make up the fictitious gentlemanly poacher 'John Macnab', have issued their challenge to three different neighbouring landowners: 'Sir, I have the honour to inform you that I propose to kill a stag – or a salmon as the case may be – on your ground between midnight on ___ and midnight on___. The animal, of course, remains your property and will be duly delivered to you . . .' Sir Archie is the Conservative candidate for the Highland constituency where this drama is played out. And drama it is, because in John Macnab *Buchan has created a marvellously balanced tale. Each of the participants is allocated certain advantages and handicaps and each plays the game in a different environment or landscape. The separate stories fit together beautifully and by the end the reader has learned a great deal about the Highlands and the class structure of Britain in the nineteen twenties.*

So what we have in the novel are the descendants of the hunting aristocracy. They have their own code and rules. The book is ostensibly about poaching, but in the end they are not really poachers, at least not criminal poachers. When Wattie the stalker suggests that he might 'sniggle a salmon in one of the deep pots' (i.e. not on rod and line), Leithen replies, 'No, we must play the game by the rules. We're not poachers.' Note the terminology of 'game' and 'rules'. And here is one of the landowners targeted by John Macnab: 'Colonel Raden could be emphatic enough on the rights of property, but no Highlander can ever grow excited about trespass. "The fellow has made a sporting offer and is willing to risk a pretty handsome stake . . . I might have done the same thing as a young man, if I had had the wits to think of it."

In the way that the respective landowners reply to the challenge, we see how close they approach to the author's ideal of sportsmanship, or 'gentlemanliness'. And yet, one of the best speeches in a very good book comes from the same Wattie, when Lord Lamancha has shot his beast. Wattie is moved to pronounce his epitaph (and in a way to make the case for hunting, a case that will be answered elsewhere in this chapter): 'It's yoursel, ye auld hero, and ye've come by a grand end. Ye've had a braw life traivellin' the hills, and ye've been a braw beast, and the fame of ye gaed through a' the country-side; Ye micht have dwined awa' in the cauld winter and dee'd in the wame o' a snawdrift. Or ye micht have been massacred by ane o' thae Haripol sumphs wi' ten bullets in the big bag. But ye've been killed clean and straucht by John Macnab, and that is a gentleman's death whatever.'

Even the stag has unwittingly become a player in the game.

★ ★ ★

The next hour was one of the severest bodily trials which Lamancha had ever known. Wattie led him up a chimney of Sgurr Mòr, the depth of which made it safe from observation, and down another on the north face, also deep, and horribly loose and wet. This brought them to the floor of the first corrie at a point below where the deer had been observed. The next step was to cross the corrie eastwards towards Sgurr Dearg. This was a matter of high delicacy – first because of the number of deer, second because it was all within view of Macqueen's watch-tower.

Lamancha had followed in his time many stalkers, but he had never seen an artist who approached Wattie in skill. The place was littered with hinds and calves and stags, the cover was patchy at the best, and the beasts were restless. Wherever a route seemed plain the large ears and spindle shanks of a hind appeared to block it. Had he been alone Lamancha would either have sent every beast streaming before him in full sight of Macqueen, or he would have advanced at the rate of one yard an hour. But Wattie managed to move both circumspectly and swiftly. He seemed to know by instinct when a hind could be bluffed, and when her suspicions must be laboriously quieted. The two went for the most part on their bellies like serpents, but their lowliness of movement would have been of no avail had not Wattie, by his sense of the subtle eddies of air, been able to shape a course which prevented their wind from shifting deer behind them. He well knew that any movement of beasts in any quarter would bring Macqueen's vigilant glasses into use.

Their task was not hard so long as they were in hollows on the corrie floor. The danger came in crossing the low ridge to that farther corrie which was beyond Macqueen's ken, for, as they ascended, the wind was almost bound to carry their scent to the deer through which they had passed. Wattie lay long with his chin in the mire and his eyes scanning the ridge till he made up his mind on his route. Obviously it was the choice of the least among several evils, for he shook his head and frowned.

The ascent of the ridge was a slow business and a toilful. Wattie was clearly following an elaborate plan, for they zigzagged preposterously, and would wait long for no apparent reason in places where Lamancha was held precariously by half a foothold and the pressure of his nails. Anxious glances were cast over his shoulder at the post where Macqueen was presumably on duty. The stalker's ears seemed of an uncanny keenness, for he would listen hard, hear something, and then utterly change his course. To Lamancha it was all inexplicable, for there appeared to be no deer on the ridge, and the place was so much in the lee that not a breath of wind seemed to be abroad to carry their scent. Hard as his condition was, he grew furiously warm and thirsty, and perhaps a little careless, for once or twice he let earth and stones slip under his feet.

Wattie turned on him fiercely. 'Gang as if ye was growin', he whispered. 'There's beasts on a' sides.'

Sobered thereby, Lamancha mended his ways, and kept his thoughts rigidly on the job before him. He crept docilely in Wattie's prints, wondering why on a little ridge they should go through exertions that must be equivalent to the ascent of the Matterhorn. At last his guide stopped. 'Put your head between thae rashes,' he enjoined. ' Ye'll see her.'

'See what?' Lamancha gasped.

'That dour deevil o' a hind.'

There she was, a grey elderly beldame, with her wicked puck-like ears, aware and suspicious, not five yards off.

'We canna wait,' Wattie hissed. 'It's ower dangerous. Bide you here like a stone.'

He wriggled away to his right, while Lamancha, hanging on a heather root, watched the twitching ears and wrinkled nozzle . . . Presently from farther up the hill came a sharp bark, which was almost a bleat. The hind flung up her head and gazed intently . . . Five minutes later the sound was repeated, this time from a lower altitude. The beast sniffed, shook herself, and stamped with her foot. Then she laid back her ears, and trotted quietly over the crest.

Wattie was back again by Lamancha's side. 'That puzzled the auld bitch,' was his only comment. 'We can gang faster now, and God kens we've nae time to loss.'

As Lamancha lay panting at last on the top of the ridge he looked down into the highest of the lesser corries, tucked right under the black cliffs of Sgurr Dearg. It was a little corrie, very steep, and threaded by a burn which after the rain was white like a snowdrift. Vast tumbled masses of stone, ancient rock-falls from the mountain, lay thick as the cottages in a hamlet. At first sight the place seemed to be without deer. Lamancha, scanning it with his glass, could detect no living thing among the débris.

Wattie was calling fiercely on his Maker.

'God, it's the auld hero,' he muttered, his eyes glued to his telescope.

At last Lamancha got his glass adjusted, and saw what his companion saw. Far up the corrie, on a patch of herbage – the last before the desert of the rocks began – stood three stags. Two were ordinary beasts, shootable, for they must have weighed sixteen or seventeen stone, but with inconsiderable heads. The third was no heavier, but he had a head like a blasted pine – going back fast, for the beast was old, but still with thirteen clearly marked points and a most noble spread of horn.

'It's him,' Wattie crooned. 'It's the auld hero. Fine I ken him, for I seen him on Crask last back-end rivin' at the stacks. There's no a forest hereaways but they've had a try for him, but the deil's in him, for the grandest shots aye miss. What's your will, my lord? Dod, if John Macnab gets yon lad, he can cock his bonnet.'

Lamancha felt his heart beat faster.

'I don't know, Wattie. Is it fair to kill the best beast in the forest?'

'Keep your mind easy about that. Yon's no a Haripol beast. He's oftener on Crask than on Haripol. He's a traiveller, and in one season will cover the feck o' the Hielands. I've heard that oreeginally he cam oot o' Kintail. He's terrible auld – some says a hundred year – and if ye dinna kill him he'll perish next winter, belike, in a snaw-wreath, and that's a puir death to dee.'

'It's a terrible pull to the Beallach.'

'It will be that, but there's the nicht afore us. If we don't take that beast – or one o' the three – I doubt we'll no get anither chance.'

'Push on, then, Wattie. It looks like a clear coast.'

'I'm no so sure. There's that deevil o' a hind somewhere afore us.'

Down through the gaps of the Pinnacle Ridge blew fine streamers of mist. They were the precursors of a new storm, for long before the two men had wormed their way into the corrie the mountain before them was blotted out with a curtan of rain, and the wind, which seemed for a time to have died away, was sounding a thousand notes in the Pan's-pipes of the crags.

'Good,' said Lamancha. 'This will blanket the shot.'

'Ba-ad too,' growled Wattie, 'for we'll be duntin against the auld bitch.'

Lamancha believed he had located the stags well enough to go to them in black darkness. You had only to follow the stream to its head, and they were on the left bank a hundred yards or so from the rocks. But when he reached the burn he found that his memory was useless. There was not one stream but dozens, and it was hard to say which was the main channel. It was a loud world again, very different from the first corrie, but, when he would have hastened, Wattie insisted on circumspection. 'There's the hind,' he said, 'and maybe some sma' stags. It's early in the day, man, and since we're out o' Macqueen's sicht there's nae need to hurry.'

His caution was justified. As they drew themselves up the side of a small cascade the tops of a pair of antlers were seen over the next rise. Lamancha thought they were those of one of the three stags, but Wattie disillusioned him. 'We're no within six hundred yards o' yon beasts,' he said.

A long circuit was necessary, happily in good cover, and the stream was not rejoined till at a point where its channel bore to the south, so that their wind would not be carried to the beasts below the knoll. After that it seemed advisable to Wattie to keep to the water, which was flowing in a deep-cut bed. It was a job for a merman rather than for breeched human beings, since Wattie would permit of no rising to a horizontal or even to a kneeling position. The burn entered at their collars and flowed steadily through their shirts to an exit at their knees. Never had men been so comprehensively and continuously wet. Lamancha's right arm ached with pulling the rifle along the bank – he always insisted on carrying his weapon himself – while his body was submerged in the icy outflow of Sgurr Dearg's springs.

The pressure of Wattie's foot in his face halted him. Blinking through the spray, he saw his leader's head raised stiffly to the alert in the direction of a little knoll. Even in the thick weather he could detect a pair of bat-like ears, and he realized that these ears were twitching. It did not need Wattie's whisper of 'the auld bitch' to reveal the enemy.

The two lay in the current for what seemed to Lamancha at least half an hour. He had enough hill-craft to recognize that their one hope was to stick to the channel, for only thus was there a chance of their presence being unrevealed by the wind. But the channel led them very close to the hind. If the brute chose to turn her foolish head they would be within view.

With desperate slowness, an inch at a time, Wattie moved upwards. He signed to Lamancha to wait while he traversed a pool where only his cap and nose showed above the water. Then came a peat wallow, when his face seemed to be ground into the moss, and his limbs to be splayed like a frog's and to move with frog-like jerks. After that was a little cascade, and, beyond, the shelter of a big boulder which would get him out of the hind's orbit. Lamancha watched this strange progress with one eye; the other was on the twitching ears. Mercifully all went well, and Wattie's stern disappeared round a corner of rock.

He laboured to follow with the same precision. The pool was easy enough except for the trailing of the rifle. The peat was straight-forward going, though in his desire to follow his leader's example he dipped his face so deep in the black slime that his nostrils were plugged with it, and some got into his eyes which he dared not try to remove. But the waterfall was a snag. It was no light task to draw himself up against the weight of descending water, and at the top he lay panting for a second, damming up the flow with his body . . . Then he moved on; but the mischief had been done.

For the sound of the release of the pent-up stream had struck a foreign note to the hind's ear. It was an unfamiliar noise among the many familiar ones which at the moment filled the corrie. She turned her head sharply, and saw something in the burn which she did not quite understand. Lamancha, aware of her scrutiny, lay choking, with the water running into his nose; but the alarm had been given. The hind turned her head and trotted off up-wind.

The next he knew was Wattie at his elbow making wild signals to him to rise and follow. Cramped and staggering, he lumbered after him away from the stream into a moraine of great granite blocks. 'We're no twa hundred yards from the stags,' the guide whispered. 'The auld bitch will move them, but please God we'll get a shot.' As Lamancha ran he marvelled at Wattie's skill, for he himself had not a notion where in the wide world the beasts might be.

They raced to a knoll, and Wattie flung himself flat on the top.

'There,' he cried. 'Steady, man. Tak the nearest. A hundred yards. Nae mair.'

Lamancha saw through the drizzle three stags moving at a gentle trot to the south – up-wind, for in the corrie the eddies were coming oddly. They were not really startled, but the hind had stirred them. The big stag was in the centre of the three, and the proper shot was the last – a reasonable broadside.

Wattie's advice had been due to his loyalty to John Macnab, and not to his own choice, and this Lamancha knew. The desire of the great stag was on him, as it was on the hunter in Homer, and he refused to be content with the second-best. It was not an easy shot in that bad light, and it is probable that he would have missed; but suddenly Wattie gave an unearthly bark, and for a second the three beasts slowed down and turned their heads towards the sound.

In that second Lamancha fired. The great head seemed to bow itself, and then fling upwards, and all three disappeared at a gallop into the mist.

'A damned poor tailoring shot!' Lamancha groaned.

'He's deid for all that, but God kens how far he'll run afore he drops. He's hit in the neck, but a wee thing ower low . . . We can bide here a while and eat our piece. If ye wasna John Macnab I coud be wishin we had brought a dog.'

Lamancha, cold, wet, and disgusted, wolfed his sandwiches, had a stiff dram from his flask, and smoked a pipe before he started again. He cursed his marksmanship, and Wattie forbore to contradict him; doubtless Jim Tarras had accustomed him to a standard of skill from which this was a woeful declension. Nor would he hold out much hope. 'He'll gang into the first corrie, and when he finds the wund different there he'll turn back for the Reascuill. If this was our ain forest and the weather wasna that thick, we might get another chance at him there . . . Oh aye, he might gang for ten mile. The mist is a good thing, for Macqueen will no see what's happenin', but if it was to lift, and he saw a' the stags in the corrie movin', you and me wad hae to find a hidy-hole till the dark . . . Are ye ready, my lord?'

They crossed the ridge which separated them from the first corrie, close to the point where it took off from the *massif* of Sgurr Dearg. It was a shorter road than the one they had come by, and they could take it safely, for they were now moving up-wind, owing to the curious eddy from the south. Over the ridge it would be a different matter, for there the wind would be easterly as before. But it was a stiff climb and a slow business, for they had to make sure that they were on the track of the stag.

Wattie trailed the blood-marks like an Indian, noticing splashes on stones and rushes which Lamancha would have missed. 'He's sair hit,' he observed at one point. 'See! He tried that steep bit and couldna manage it. There's the mark o' his feet turnin' . . . He's stoppit here . . . Aye, here's his trail, and it'll be the best for you and me. There's nothing like a wounded beast for pickin' the easiest road.'

On the crest the air stirred freely, and, as it seemed to Lamancha, with a new chill. Wattie gave a grunt of satisfaction, and sniffed it like a pointer dog. He moistened his finger and held it up; then he plucked some light grasses and tossed them into the air.

'That's a mercifu' dispensation! Maybe that shot that ye think ye bauchled was the most providential shot ye ever fired . . . The wund is shiftin'. I looked for it afore night, but no that early in the day. It's wearin' round to the south. D'ye see what that means?'

Lamancha shook his head. Disgust had made his wits dull.

'Yon beast, as I telled ye, was a traiveller. There's nothing to keep him in Haripol forest. But he'll no leave it unless the wund will let him. Now it looks as if Providence was kind to us. The wund's blawin' from the Beallach, and he's bound to gang upwund.'

The next half-hour was a period of swift drama. Sure enough, the blood-marks turned up the first corrie in the direction from which the two had come in the morning. As the ravine narrowed the stag had evidently taken to the burn, for there were splashes on the rocks and a tinge of red in the pools.

'He's no far off,' Wattie croaked. 'See, man, he's verra near done. He's slippin' sair.'

And then, as they mounted, they came on a little pool where the water was dammed as if by a landslip. There, his body half under the cascade, lay the stag, stone dead, his great horns parting the fall like a pine swept down by a winter spate.

The two regarded him in silence, till Wattie was moved to pronounce his epitaph.

'It's yoursel, ye auld hero, and ye've come by a grand end. Ye've had a braw life traivellin' the hills and ye've been a braw beast, and the fame o' ye gaed through a' the country-side. Ye micht have dwined awa in the cauld winter and dee'd in the wame o' a snawdrift. Or ye micht have been massacred by ane o' thae Haripol sumphs wi' ten bullets in the big bag. But ye've been killed clean and straucht by John Macnab and that is a gentleman's death, whatever.'

'That's all very well,' said Lamancha, 'but you know I tailored the shot.'

'Ye're a fule,' cried the rapt Wattie. 'Ye did no siccan thing. It was a verra deeficult shot, and ye put it deid in the only place ye could see. I will not have seen many better shots at all, at all.'

'What about the gralloch?' Lamancha asked.

'No here. If the mist lifted Macqueen micht see us. It's no fifty yards to the top o' the Beallach, and we'll find a place there for the job.'

Wattie produced two ropes and bound the fore-feet and the hind-feet together. Then he rapidly climbed to the summit, and reported on his return that the mist was thick there, and that there were no tracks except their own of the morning. It was a weary business dragging the carcass up a nearly perpendicular slope. First, with difficulty they raised it out of the burn channel, and then drew it along the steep hillside. They had to go a long way up the hillside to avoid the rock curtain on the edge of the Beallach, but eventually the top was reached, and the stag was deposited behind some boulders on the left of the flat ground. Here, even if the mist lifted, they would be hid from the sight of Macqueen, and from any sentries there might be on the Crask side.

The Sport Royal

NEIL MUNRO

★ ★ ★

Neil Munro's 'Looker-On' column appeared every Monday in the Glasgow Evening News *from 1897 until 1927. A selection from over 2,000 columns of a consistent excellence and astonishing variety featured in George Blake's two collections* The Brave Days *and* The Looker-On, *and now in* That Vital Spark *by the present editors. The subject of fox-hunting, controversial in 1926 as today, is given a nicely restrained, tongue-in-cheek treatment by Munro.*

★ ★ ★

The most invigorating, picturesque, romantic and dignified outdoor sport in the West of Scotland must be Hunting. When you write of Hunting with an initial capital, it means, of course, the fox – rabbiting and wild-duck shooting do not count. Yet, how little is made of Hunting, by the Saturday evening papers, and how few take part in it compared with the crowds who go to football, or the dancing palaces, or twirl the knobs of wireless instruments!

For some reason or other, Glasgow neglects the Hunt. For many years the Eglinton hounds and the Lanark and Renfrew, have been hunting, each winter, with the utmost enthusiasm on the very confines of the city almost, yet the public attendance is hardly greater than at a village tournament in dominoes.

Something really should be done to popularise this grand old sport if foxes are not to get the upper hand of us entirely and terrorise the milkboys of Hillhead and Pollokshields in the early mornings. The Meets should be regularly advertised. Let them start from George Square, and ride over Jamaica Bridge, winding their horns and tally-hoing. More should be made of the competitive spirit. There should be handsome prizes – a cup for smartest turn-out in hats and harness: a case of fish-knives, say, for the boldest rider through the pack and the first to score a hit on Reynard.

As it is, the sport of old John Peel is pursued in the West of Scotland almost surreptitiously. The same small group of ladies and gentlemen turns out on each occasion, as it were to a Repertory Theatre or a Monday morning in the Central Police Court.

The only handicap to Hunting as a Glasgow pastime is that it involves early rising in the morning and the hire of a horse. There is, too, a prescribed uniform – a pink coat, reinforced cord breeches, Wellington boots, a silk hat and a horseshoe tie-pin.

You have to be up as early as 8 a.m. if you want to see Glasgow huntsmen start for the chase by taking a railway ticket for Houston or Carstairs. They go forth furtively, jingling their spurs as little as possible and wrapped up in trench-coats to divert suspicion.

The Meet is usually on an extensive patch of gravel in front of a stately old mansion-house standing in its own grounds. An unforgettable scene! The hounds, baying loudly, and gambolling over the recently-planted beds of wall-flower; the huntsmen cracking their whips or playing a merry roundelay on their horns; selected villagers in the avenue singing some fine old hunting-songs in four-part harmony. Through vistas in the stately trees are delightful prospects of pastoral country, arable land, and fir plantations, all swarming with foxes.

Someone comes out with a tray and passes round a spot of the famous old Madeira and a bit of ginger cake, and the ladies, having dusted a final coat of powder on their noses, the Charge is sounded and the cavalcade streams out to draw the nearest covert.

I have never seen the Hunt myself, but I love to read about it every other day just now as described with accomplished pens by 'Knockjarder' and 'Tantivy', who seem in journalism to have got the most enviable job I know. They wake in me old memories of Mr Jorrocks, read about in boyhood; I listen again to the horn in

Troutbeck; hear John Peel hallooing. Landscapes familiar to me by walking through them, or from a train or automobile, take on a fairy, wizard, old-world aspect. Georgetown becomes a place of becks and thickets, filled with canine music; the Fullwood Moss is no longer a dump for city refuse but a place enchanted.

It is, as I think then, always a tender gloaming there, with starlight and a touch of frost. Sweeter than Roland's horn 'on Fontarabian echoes borne', we have heard to-day the pack give tongue at Barochan, and now Diana and I ride home a little wearied, but bantering merrily.

Alas! I do not know the real Dianas, but always I figure them as young and brave, and beautiful – the most glorious subjects for the paintings of Mr Furze or Mr Munnings, for the poetry of Mr Masefield.

Now, the strange thing is that I have never seen a fox, except the Highland kind we shoot (with all respect to the M.F.H. of Eglinton), without compunction. I have spent years in Renfrewshire and Lanarkshire, without seeing a single 'varmint' except an occasional stuffed one in a farmer's lobby – deliberately trapped, I fear, in his poultry-yard.

Yet the whole of the country south and south-west of Glasgow seems to be infested with Reynard, who apparently never comes into the open unless he is fascinated by a red coat or a cry of 'joicks!' There are days, it is true, when the Eglinton and Lanark and Renfrew draw blank, which are the days I like best, for then 'Tantivy' and 'Knockjarder' get a chance to be picturesque and poetic. But more frequently there seems to be a fox in every covert.

There is one in Dargavel Moss five minutes after the Madeira, and with a vigorous view halloa from Dickinson, the field pelts after him by Barngary Farm and Bishopton, through Glenshinnoch to Barochan Moss and the woods of Houston, where the scent is lost.

Never mind! There's another fox on North Brae willing to enter into the spirit of the game. He gives us a run across the hill past Barochan Mill, through a poultry yard, to near Corslie Hill, and onwards to Barnmore and the Drums covert, where he 'bites the dust' in the grand old phrase of venery.

The mask and brush are cut off and ceremoniously presented to young sports who do not yet suspect what a nuisance they may be to dust in after years. Experienced grim old riders who have balked at no fences, draw apart, I fancy, and lubricate the oesophagus from cute little silver hunting-flasks.

'Hoicks!' again, and there breaks from his lair in Knockmountain Bog a third fox, who goes steaming down the valley. The pack in full cry go chiming after him in a dappled wave over stubble pasture, plough and moorland. Intrepidity leaps its fences like a lifting plane; Caution trots along the road and looks for a gate to bunch at; the sheer poltroon dismounts and conceals himself in a spinney, hoping the scent will soon be lost.

In well-organised Meets, the last fox of the day, I gather, is usually permitted to escape into a culvert or unsuspected earth, having given the company a pleasant run as savoury to the menu.

And how magnificently the whole thing ends! I have almost the style of it – 'By this time the shades of evening were descending on the uplands. Lights began to twinkle in the farms. Hounds filled the bosky hollows round Auchentibbert with their eager cries as they quartered the woody dells, having come through the taint of wintering sheep and lost the varmint's scent near the Black Bull Inn. It was in a lovely night of stars we rode home after one of the best days of the season.'

On second thoughts, I declare it would be a pity to spoil it all by running char-a-bancs and motor-buses to the Meets. Dickinson wouldn't like it.

The Unspeakable

from England, their England

A.G. MACDONELL

★ ★ ★

*Donald Cameron, the Scots innocent abroad, follows a fox-hunt on foot
in the Vale of Aylesbury; Macdonell's verdict on the pastime appears to
closely resemble the famous one of Oscar Wilde. The full quotation from
Wilde is: 'The English country gentleman galloping after a fox – the
unspeakable in full pursuit of the uneatable.' Donald comes upon
members of the hunt incensed by a gypsy who has been cruel to his horse.
In a subtle inversion of their own position they rail against cruelty to
animals.*

*Another Scots writer who thought poorly of the fox-hunting classes was
the Gaelic poet, Dhomnall Ruadh Coruna, a contemporary of A.G.
Macdonell, and one who wrote about the ghastly experiences of World
War I. His poem 'Oran na Seilge' ('Hunting Song') is a savage rather
than subtle or ironic attack on what he might have called the same class
enemy. In English translation it runs:*

> *The hunting and fishing which we were defending for them*
> *In the blood and clay of the soil of France,*
> *We shall never taste a morsel of that –*
> *The laws decree that our rights are worthless.*
> *But the gentry will – they who sleep on pillows,*
> *With their despicable blankets over their heads,*
> *While we faced frightful odds,*
> *The whine of bullets constantly around our ears.*

★ ★ ★

Breakfast at 'The Golden Hind' was at 8.30, and at 9 o'clock sharp a maid came into the breakfast-room and announced in an almost unintelligible Buckinghamshire accent:

'Thatcher come, sir.'

Mr Fielding threw down his *Times* and bustled out, and Donald strolled after him unobtrusively. The thatcher was a tall, thin man of an indeterminate age – perhaps forty, perhaps seventy. His cheeks, of course, were a healthy red, like all Buckinghamshire cheeks, and a long brown moustache drooped down past each corner of his mouth almost to the edges of his chin. His eyes were pale blue. He wore corduroys and an old army leather jerkin without sleeves, and a tie without a collar, and he held his old tweed cap in both hands in front of him.

Mr Fielding plunged at once into a complicated conversation, full of technical terms of carpentering and thatching, full of joists and trusses and ties and overhang and twists and pins. Each appeared to understand the other perfectly. Donald could make head or tail of neither.

'There's a fine old trade dying out,' said Mr Fielding, after the man had gone. 'Old Mells is the only thatcher for many miles round and there's not a better craftsman in the land. And yet he can't get enough work to keep him busy all the week. He has to do hedging and ditching and odd-job gardening, and he's the village sexton too. Sad, isn't it? When he's dead there won't be a thatcher at all.'

'Hasn't he got any sons?' inquired Donald. 'A lot of these trades are hereditary, aren't they?'

'They were hereditary,' replied Mr Fielding, 'but this is the last generation of it. There has been a thatcher called Mells in this village for centuries, I expect, but the old man you saw just now – he's got two sons and both of them are motor mechanics in Aylesbury. That's the rule nowadays. The stupid sons become farm labourers and the clever ones become mechanics. In the old days both clever sons and stupid sons followed their father's trade, except the occasional enterprising one who joined the army. But garages have spoilt all that.'

Mrs Fielding, a bundle of tradesmen's books under each arm,

letters and bills and receipts and circulars and bulb catalogues and newspapers in her hands, and a cheque-book in her mouth, came out of the dining-room. Her husband relieved her of the impediment to speech, and she asked Donald what he would like to do.

Donald said that he had thought of walking over to Tainton Green to see the Meet, and he fancied that a fleeting glimmer of relief was visible on the faces of both host and hostess. A guest in the country who cannot amuse himself is a nuisance to busy people.

'Would you like the car? Or a bicycle?' asked Mr Fielding promptly.

'I think I'd sooner walk,' replied Donald, and again he thought they looked relieved.

'It's about two miles,' said Mrs Fielding. 'If you start a little after 10 you'll be in plenty of time. The Meet's at 11 o'clock.'

It was a warm January morning, sunny and spring-like, and Donald felt that there should have been buttercups in the meadows with larks above them, and swallows fooling about, and cowslips, and great drifts of the flower which the English call bluebells but the Scots wild hyacinths. The air was very still, and far away a bell was tolling. Cows and sheep grazed in the fields, and ploughland chequered the greenness of the pasture with dark, kindly smears of earth. Somewhere near an axe was pecking at a tree, and on the edge of a copse of young oaks a band of small children were happily collecting firewood and putting it into a cart, home-made from a soap-box and a pair of ancient bicycle wheels.

Donald dived into a network of narrow lanes, un-signposted, untouched by the influence of Mr Macadam, and flanked on each side by strips of grass which were a good deal wider than the lanes themselves. No buildings were visible. There was no sign of human life. Donald was in the heart of rural England.

He was recalled from his day-dreaming about village Hampdens and plodding ploughmen, and the short and simple annals of the poor, by a terrific blast upon an electric motor-horn about two yards behind him. He sprang into the air in alarm and spun round to find himself facing the silver bonnet of a colossal pale-blue-and-silver Rolls Royce, out of the driver's seat of which was leaning a young man with a red face. It was not the pink of the gaffers' faces in the Crooked Billet, but a mottled red.

'Hey! You!' shouted the young man. 'When you've finished sleeping in the middle of the road, where the devil's Tainton Green?'

'I imagine it's straight on,' replied Donald politely, 'but I'm afraid –'

'Oh God!' interrupted the young man, 'another bloody stranger!' and he released the clutch and the great car slid away.

Tainton Green looked as if a celestial town-planner had scattered Tudor cottages out of a pepper-pot and then, as an afterthought, had flung down a handful of rather larger Queen Anne houses. The newest house in the village must have been about two hundred years old. There was in Tainton Green what house-agents call 'a wealth of old timber', and the cottages which it adorned stood at every conceivable angle to each other in an irregular ring round the Green.

But Donald had no desire at the moment to examine architecture. His whole attention was concentrated upon the most famous of all English sporting spectacles, the Meet of a pack of English foxhounds. As he had expected, there was no detail missing from the scene that has been so often described in books and pictures. Everything was there – dogs, shiny horses, admiring villagers, huntsmen in velvet caps, a horseman with a long whip and a brass horn, sharp-looking grooms in neat leggings and black-and-white check breeches, rows of motor-cars of immense brilliance and beauty (even the pale-blue-and-silver Rolls-Royce which had passed Donald in the lane was not particularly conspicuous), motor horse-boxes, liveried chauffeurs, liveried footmen, each carrying a fur rug over his left arm and looking bored and contemptuous, and here and there an occasional pony-trap. The pony-traps – there were not more than half a dozen of them – roused the chauffeurs a little from their massive stolidity into lofty smiles.

And, of course, there were the ladies and gentlemen who were going to risk their bones, perhaps even their necks, for the sake of sport. The first thing that struck Donald was the drabness of the feminine hunting-kit and the gorgeousness of the masculine. The women mostly wore queer-shaped bowler hats and black habits, with here and there a touch of white. But the men wore shiny toppers and scarlet coats and white or pale-yellow breeches and huge orange-topped boots and high stocks, and they strode about the Green like captains of Spanish galleons, or colonels of Napoleon's light cavalry, seeing no one except each other, but allowing themselves to be seen by everyone, chins out, heads high, superbly disdainful, like the camels of Bactria who alone know the hundredth name of God.

One of them stepped heavily into a puddle beside Donald and splashed him with mud and went on, his eyes fixed on eternal space, as if neither Donald nor the puddle had ever existed. Another, seated upon his charger like Bellerophon upon Pegasus, halted a yard or two away, and addressed a beautiful girl who was curveting round and round upon a mettlesome steed. 'These bloody yokels who clutter up the place ought to be shot,' he said. 'Don't you agree, Pud.'

The beautiful girl persuaded her horse to stand still for a moment and looked at Donald as if he was some kind of slug. 'Bloody bastards,' she agreed, and then was curveted away again.

A colonel of Napoleonic light cavalry came past, perhaps a Hussar of Conflans – Donald could almost hear the clatter of his sabre upon the streets of Vienna or Warsaw or Berlin, and see the swing of the pale-blue, silver-buttoned dolman and the nodding of the horse-hair plume – stopped, put an eyeglass in his eye, and addressed the horseman.

'Hullo, Ted!' said Lasalle.

'Hullo, Squibs,' replied Bellerophon, looking more than ever like a Bactrian camel, 'I say, these bloody yokels who clutter up the place ought to be shot.'

The *beau sabreur* looked quickly round and, seeing that at the moment no one was within ear-shot – for Donald, being only a yokel, was like a stone or a stump or a cow, and could not actually be said to be there at all – he lowered his voice and said urgently, 'Look here, Ted, don't touch Moggeridge Ordinaries till they hit half a dollar. We're doing a wrangle, see? Weinstein's coming in with us, and so's old Potts and old Finkelberg. Get me?'

He winked, and Donald thought that somehow he looked less like a swaggering hussar than before. For some ridiculous reason, Donald found himself thinking of week-ends at Brighton and peroxide.

All this time more cars and more horses and more intrepid sportswomen and sportsmen had been arriving, and punctually at 11 o'clock the whole apparatus of fox-killing, dogs, horses, women, and men moved off sedately towards a wood outside the village. Donald counted a hundred and seven riders and approximately sixty dogs. It was a formidable cavalcade. From a little rising ground he watched them enter a field and gradually spread out into a scattered semi-circle as they approached the wood which was presumed to be the lair of one of the doomed vermin. They rode slowly, in little groups, and halted while the advance guard of scarlet and velvet and horn vanished among the trees. There was a pause of ten minutes, and then came the sound of distant shouting, and the horses sprang into activity. The hunt was up. The riders streamed away along the edges of the wood and vanished over a slope and reappeared on a far-off hill-side, a spectacle of unbelievable picturesqueness and romance. Donald stood and strained his eyes until the last scarlet pin-head had vanished behind the horizon of dark woods, leaving an empty landscape of dull greys and browns and greens. The splendour had gone, and Donald walked slowly homewards.

Half-way home he found that at his rate of walking he would be back at 'The Golden Hind' before 12 o'clock, which would never do. Mr and Mrs Fielding would be busy, and they would abandon their busyness to try and entertain him and everyone would feel embarrassed. It was a warm morning; a tree-stump on the edge of a coppice was dry, and Donald had a book. He sat down in the sunshine and plunged into *The Trail of the Poisoned Carpet*, a work of fiction of which the nature and the absorbing interest can be readily judged when it is stated that Donald had just reached the point when the heroine, slim Miranda Tremayne, drugged, and bound hand and foot, was being lowered in an empty caviar barrel into a disused mineshaft by La Sapphirita, a Bolshevik spy, and Boris Fernandowski, agent of the Ogpu.

Donald was soon completely absorbed. He read the chapter which described the brilliant rescue of slim Miranda by huge, ugly Dick Trelawney, who happened to alight providentially at the mouth of the mineshaft in a racing balloon. He read the great scenes of Dick's fight with Ah Boo Wu and his gang in the Limehouse main drain, the reappearance of the secret submarine off Valparaiso, the forgery of Sir Dalhousie Canning's signature to the Bungiskhan Treaty, and the theft of the Poisoned Carpet itself from the nunnery in Hull, and he had just reached the point at which La Sapphirita has put cyanide upon the claws of a Siamese cat and, disguised in black satin trousers as a Government window-cleaner, has inserted the animal into the Far Eastern Department of the Foreign Office where huge, ugly Dick Trelawney is at work with an atlas and a manual of geography trying to discover exactly where Bungiskhan is, with which he has negotiated the Treaty. Donald had just reached this point when he became slowly aware that the stillness of the country-side was being broken by distant voices. A faint hallooing came across the fields, and then suddenly, out of the hedge on the other side of the road – tired, muddy, panting, limping, desperate – came the fox. He passed within a yard of Donald without appearing to see him and lolloped slowly into the coppice.

Donald watched him go and wished him good luck, adding aloud, 'And a fat chance you've got! All alone against sixty dogs and a hundred and seven riders and a hundred and seven horses – two hundred and seventy-four against one.'

He moved down the road to get out of the way of the pursuing angels, who were so nobly bent upon saving the countryside from vermin. The shouting and hallooing came nearer, but the human sounds were overwhelmed in the wild, excited, parrot-like, monkey-like yapping and screaming of the hounds, as they came pouring through the hedge in brave pursuit, all sixty of the intrepid heroes. Then came the first of the riders, the men in velvet caps and the men with the horns, taking the hedges with the lovely slow curve of a horse that knows it can jump and knows that its rider can be trusted. Behind them came the mob, galloping like Prince Rupert across the fields, the leaders unerringly finding the gaps and the gates, and the followers forming up into blasphemous queues behind them. Donald was astonished that so few of them made any attempt to jump the hedges. One or two deliberately set their horses at them, and five or six were obviously less keen about it than their mounts, and did their unsuccessful best to dissuade them from the perilous leap, but at least eighty per cent disdained such showy tactics and preferred the gates and gaps, where a reputation for hard riding could be more easily obtained by a lot of hard swearing.

There was a halt at the edge of the coppice, for the fox had gone to ground. He had outrun the whole two hundred and seventy-four of them, and in doing so he had provided an hour and a half of the best sport which the Hunt had seen that season. But though he had outrun them all, and though he had provided such sport, they had the laugh on him in the end. For they got a lot of spades and a couple of terrier dogs and dug him out of his hole and killed him; because, after all, the countryside must be saved from vermin even if ladies and gentlemen have to chase them on horseback for an hour and a half, and furthermore it would be an act of callous cruelty to dumb animals, which no Englishman could be guilty of, to deprive the sixty dogs of the midday meal which they had so bravely earned.

Donald resumed his homeward journey and in ten minutes came upon an animated scene. Just where his winding lane joined the main road, a caravan of gypsies had halted their motley crew of painted wagons. They could only have arrived within the last two hours, because Donald had not seen them on his way to Tainton Green.

The T-head where the lane actually joined the road was almost blocked with horses, and six or eight of the fox-hunters were standing dismounted among the riders, all with their backs to Donald and facing the main road. Beyond this facade of mud-bespattered black and scarlet and horse-flesh, furious voices were being raised, and language that would have startled Nell Gwynne, or brought a blush to the cheeks of Burke and Hare, was being freely used. Donald edged his way between the ditch and one of the horses into the front row of the stalls, and by the time he had reached his place, the flow of words had given way to a fast bout of fisticuffs. One of the antagonists was a six-foot, scarlet-coated, scarlet-faced young man; the other was a lean, dirty, dark gypsy. The muddied Adonis fought with a classical straight left; the smoky *chal* relied upon short-arm punches, low when possible. The bout only lasted a few seconds, for the fighters were dragged apart by other gentlemen in red coats, and the gypsy retired sullenly under the overwhelming force with which he was now faced.

The comments of the ring were so clear, and expressed so forcibly and so repeatedly, that Donald had no difficulty in discovering what it was all about.

'The bloody swine was kicking his horse!' said a girl of about nineteen, with lips like the petals of a rose.

'Bloody swine!' said another girl, the perfection of whose fragile face was a little marred by a diagonal stain of mud about six inches long and three inches broad.

A short, tubby man, who looked very rich, shouted out:

'Bravo, Ralph! Well done, boy!'

Two men on foot discussed the matter in grave undertones.

'Thank God it was a gypsy and not an Englishman,' the first said.

'An Englishman wouldn't do a thing like that,' said the second, rather shocked.

'If there's one thing that gets me mad,' said the first, 'it's cruelty to animals. I don't care whether it's a mouse or an elephant, it simply makes me see red.'

'Absolutely,' said the second. 'One can stand a good deal, but one can't stand that.'

'I never go abroad nowadays,' said the first, 'except to Le

Touquet and Monte Carlo and Switzerland and so on, because I simply cannot stand the way those chaps treat animals.'

'Just like this dago,' assented the other. 'Do you know the first thing I'm going to do when I get back to town tonight? I'm going to invite Ralph out to the best dinner at the Ritz that money can buy.'

'By jove!' cried the second enthusiastically. 'Let me in on that, old chap. We'll share exes.'

They drifted away.

A horseman, pale with passion, and covered with clay from silk hat to orange-topped boots, was staring wildly in front of him and repeating over and over again to the world in general, 'I'll report him to the Society for the Prevention of Cruelty to Animals, I'll report him to the Society for the Prevention of Cruelty to Animals!'

An old lady of about seventy, perched like a sparrow upon an enormous black horse, kept on saying plaintively: 'Why doesn't someone flog him? I can't understand why no one flogs him.'

Donald heard no more, for at that moment the shoulder of a horse took him neatly in the small of the back and knocked him into the hedge. The woman who was riding never even glanced in his direction. She was about fifty years of age and her mouth and jaw were resolute and her eye unwavering, and Donald recognized her at once as one of the nurses in a hospital near Hazebrouck in Flanders in which he had had measles. One pouring wet night when the hospital, which by an unfortunate mischance had been placed immediately beside a large ammunition dump, was being bombed by German aircraft, this hard-faced Diana carried out seven wounded officers from a burning ward into which the stretcher-bearers refused to go, and rigged up a shelter for them from the rain, and boiled tea for them by the light of the blazing huts, to the accompaniment of a full orchestra of machine-guns, anti-aircraft artillery, bombs, pattering splinters, and screams and groans. And on another occasion she held the icy hand of a dying subaltern for twenty-seven hours. And on another she told the Matron what she thought of her.

Donald picked himself out of the hedge and went slowly back to 'The Golden Hind'. Another fox had been found and the hunt had vanished with extraordinary swiftness, leaving nothing behind them save innumerable hoof-marks in the mud, a few gaps in fences for the farmers to repair, and the memory of a gallant panorama.

Donald had just time before lunch to reach the chapter in which Miranda, slimmer than ever, is lured by a false message into the bargain basement of an antique shop in Fez.

On Monday morning he read in *The Times* that the second fox had completely let down the North Bucks Hunt. The wretched creature had nipped off at a great rate and in five minutes had dived into a hole from which not even the valiant terriers could extract him. He was, in fact, as *The Times* said, 'a bad fox'.